to major tom
dave thompson

D1313344

Sanctuary

Introduction

My name's Gary and I write letters to pop stars.

It's funny, but that really isn't how I thought I'd be beginning my life story. Back when my entire future lay ahead of me and everything seemed possible to my barely teenaged self, it was more likely to begin, 'My name's Gary and I *am* a pop star.' Or 'My name's Gary, but you knew that already.'

But no, not only am I Gary who writes letters to pop stars, in fact I've only ever written to one pop star. And he's never even written back.

Maybe he was too busy. Looking back at the 30 years of one-way correspondence that passed between myself and David Bowie, it's difficult to believe he had much free time at all, particularly in the days when he was Ziggy and everything he touched turned to stardust.

Every time you opened a music paper, he was doing something new; every time you heard a rumour, he'd be at the thick of it; every time you switched on the television, he'd be there, in increasingly garish and otherworldly outfits, and so skilfully did he weave his spell that even his most unutterable inanities took on the substance of the Sermon on the Mount.

I hung on every word. I was constantly updating my scrapbook, then painstakingly gumming every cutting into place. When I open those books today, their very odour transports me back to that distant age of Gloy-stained glory, while long-brittled

Sellotape has left its own legacy on the fragile newsprint of period tabloids and *NMEs*.

It wasn't an obsession. There's no numbering how many hours I spent with those scrapbooks, but life went on around them regardless. Airfix models, Subbuteo tournaments and the weekly *Lion* and *Victor, Top Of The Pops* on Thursday, youth club on Friday and, every other Saturday, a mile or so walk to Dean Court in Boscombe, home of the all-not-conquering Bournemouth and Boscombe Athletic FC, and a theatre of dreams a full 20 years before dilapidated Victoriana ever took on such lofty titles. But how many of those activities are now cherished memories? And how many am I aware of because I wrote to David Bowie about them?

That is a conundrum I will never solve. Other people kept diaries. I kept copies of letters, rambling compilations of thoughts, dreams and observations that would, with a diligence my teachers never dreamed I was capable of, then be mailed to wherever I thought they had the best chance of reaching Bowie.

At first I addressed them to Haddon Hall, the Bowie home address that was, somewhat oddly, common knowledge to anyone who even glanced at his name in the papers. Later, concerned that probably every fan in the world was writing to him there, I started addressing them to Mainman, his management company of the time – which, conveniently, lay a few streets away from my family home in Chelsea. A couple I even hand-delivered, although only after office hours.

Others were sent to his record company, particularly as the years went by and Bowie himself became difficult to pin down to any single address – Los Angeles, Berlin, Switzerland, New York. And others still travelled to studios where I'd heard he was recording. No wonder he never wrote back. I sometimes wonder whether he even received them.

When I first started writing to David, I was 12, approaching the end of my first year at a boarding school in Bournemouth, and just discovering the right to decide for myself what music

I liked. At the age of 11, when everything still seems new and exciting, there's no such thing as good and bad; just songs you like and songs you don't. At 12, the first stirrings of the inner critic are felt and it suddenly becomes crucial to make others understand why one artist is worth listening to and makes meaningful music, and another is crap and farts unpalatable pap.

Now I'm 42 and the voyage of discovery ceased long ago. I still buy new music and listen to it conscientiously, but the physical thrill disappeared years ago, around the same time as a sensible waist measurement and half my hair. Now if I want to dance, sing or (as The Faces put it) anything, I return to the music I was discovering then, or even to the music that I once rejected. The 1970s might not have been a golden era for rock and pop music, but they still sound pretty good. And I was lucky – I had a bloody good guide, and I trusted him implicitly.

Lou Reed and the Velvets, Iggy And The Stooges, Mott The Hoople, Dana Gillespie, Cherry Vanilla, Wayne County – Bowie only had to mention a band and I was scouring the second-hand shops in search of further enlightenment. Now I look back and wonder how I could have been so trusting. I didn't do what my teachers told me, I rarely did what my stepfather ordered. But put some painted buffoon in *Melody Maker* and I was his faithful, obedient slave.

He talked about *Stranger In A Strange Land*; I read every book by Robert A Heinlein. He quipped Kahlil Gibran; I tried to read *The Prophet*, but got lost three pages in and pretended I'd finished it. He namechecked The Kings Of Oblivion; I found a Pink Fairies album with the same title and wore it out in search of its secrets. The strange thing is, I found them as well. But stranger still is the knowledge that, if anyone but Bowie had planted the seed, I'd not have given it a second glance. Again, how could I have been so trusting?

But trust is what sets a fan aside from a mere consumer. A lot of people buy David Bowie's records. But how many buy the records that David Bowie buys? Or read the books he reads, watch the films he sees and... Thankfully I didn't get enough pocket money or else I'd be adding 'wearing the clothes he wears'. Jump suits with '69' embroidered on the crotch really weren't appropriate apparel for Boscombe High Street in 1972.

In History, we were taught to recite the kings and queens of England by rote. Over the years, I've known a few people who could reel off the names of every FA Cup winner since 1872. But I'm the only person I've met who could recite the A- and B-side of every UK Bowie single in order. Including reissues.

There's an episode of *Doctor Who* where the aliens try to suck the Doctor's brain clean, wiping out all his memories, so that he might be reprogrammed to their own specifications. As the machinery does its dirty work, those memories flash on a monstrous television screen positioned above his head. Reading these letters, I knew exactly how he felt while the process was taking place. Finishing them, I knew what he'd have felt like if it had been successfully completed.

I could not believe how much of my modern mental furniture was installed by my devotion – musical, cultural and otherwise – nor how hard, in recent years, it's become to keep that furniture polished and dusted. Times change, people change, dreams explode and worlds collide. And, if you think it's foolish to spend your life living in the past, imagine what it's like to live in somebody else's.

Sometimes, I wish Ziggy had played the flugelhorn instead.

Gary Weightman
Hammersmith, London W6
Saturday 8 June 2002

To Major Tom

Bournemouth, Hants
Monday 10 July 1972

Dear David Bowie

My name's Gary Weightman. I'm 12, and I'm at boarding school in Boscombe, near Bournemouth, although I live in Chatham, Kent.

I'm writing to tell you that 'STARMAN' is the <u>BEST RECORD OF THE YEAR!</u> I saw you on *Lift Off With Ayshea* a couple of weeks ago, and then again on *Top Of The Pops* on Thursday, and I couldn't believe what a fab song it was, and how brilliant you and your band, THE SPIDERS FROM MARS, looked. I loved the bass player's silver sideburns. Are they real? They must have taken him years to grow!

Is your hair really that red? Some of the boys in my school think it's dyed because it's so bright, but my aunt is Scottish and her hair is almost that colour. Are you Scottish?[1] I'd love to have a hairstyle like yours, but I can't because my hair is a straggly blond mess that looks a bit like a rat's nest. In fact, for a while, that's what some of the other kids called me, but then I had it cut really short, sort of skinhead but not quite, so they had to stop. Now they call me Fat Boy because of my surname, 'Weight-Man', and because I'm so skinny,

---

1   Strangely, he isn't.

but I don't mind that. At least it's better than what some of the other kids here are called. One boy with braces is named Tin Teeth and once, when a teacher told him to shut his mouth at breakfast, half the dining room shouted out, 'Clang!' Then there's Cripple Foot, who has a limp, and one boy with asthma, whose nickname is Iron Lung. So Fat Boy really isn't that bad.

Anyway, as soon as I was given my pocket money on Saturday I ran to WH Smith's on the High Street to buy 'Starman'. I was sure they'd be sold out, because EVERYBODY agrees that it's a great record. I bought the last copy. You're going to go to No.1, because the other side, 'Suffragette City', is just as good. I used to like T Rex and Argent, and I bought 'Debora' (by Tyrannosaurus Rex) and 'Hold Your Head Up' during the last holidays. But 'Starman' is a million times better than both of them.

Is this your first record? My friend Jonathan James reckons you had another one out a few years ago, about an astronaut named Major Tom,[2] but he says it sounded very different. He said you looked very different as well, with curly blond hair. Is that your real colour or was that dyed? Either way around, I don't blame you for changing.

How do you pronounce your surname? I've heard you called 'Bow-ee', like a dog (bow-wow), 'Boo-ie', like a ghost and 'Bo-wee', like the ribbon on a Christmas present. I think it's 'Bo-wee', but I wanted to make sure.

Nobody can stop talking about what you did on *Bottom Of The Wellington Boot*,[3] when you put your arm around your guitarist's shoulders. Some of the older boys here say that means you're a queer, and that anybody who likes you has to be a queer as well, but that's a gormless thing to say. My school is all boys, and a lot of them like 'Starman', but I don't think they could all be queer, do you? Besides, the real queers here all like different sorts of music, and one of them doesn't like music at all, so he listens to jazz instead.

2 'Space Oddity' reached No.5 in 1969.
3 *Top Of The Pops*.

It's a good school. It was opened in the 1930s and there are 100 boarders here, plus 50 daykids who live around the local area. We're divided into five groups, or years – I'm in the first year (Group One), which is for 11- and 12-year-olds and there are 29 of us. It goes up to the fifth year (Group Five), who are 15 and 16, so that means I've only another four years to go. There are kids here from all over the country, but most of us are from the south and southeast.

All the boarders in each class are also in the same dormitory together – there are 20 beds in each dorm, divided into cubicles of two by curtains and walls made from our lockers. I share my cubicle with my best friend, Paul Banion, who comes from Portsmouth. He wants to join the RAF when he leaves school, and he's mad about World War II fighter planes. When you ask him who his favourite groups are, he'll say 'T Rex, Lindisfarne and No.309 Polish Squadron', which was an RAF squadron during the war. His nickname is Fly Boy.

I used to share with Alan Nantwich, who lives in Southampton. He wants to join the army when he leaves, so he and Paul have regular bundles over which is better, the air force or the army. Alan usually wins, not because he's a better fighter but because Paul's such a poxy one. I was watching him once, and he closes his eyes when he punches!

Alan's best friend is Danny Meath, who is from Farnborough and is the class freak-out. He says he wants to be a tramp when he grows up, and his favourite television show is *Catweazle*, because he's also interested in black magic. When we first came here last September, he tried to scare us all by saying he could cast spells and things. He goes up into the woods at night to sacrifice insects to the Devil and, when you really piss him off, he stares at you and chants the words 'SATOR, AREPO, TENET, OPERA, ROTAS'.

He tells us they're magical, because when you write them down, whichever way you read them, they spell the same words. Paul said later that he'd read the same thing on a box of Ricicles, but we didn't say anything to Danny, in case there is something in it.

I'll tell you about some of the other Bowie fans in our dorm. Jon (the one who remembers Major Tom) is from Barnstaple in Devon, and his family has tons of money. Every holiday he comes back to school with new clothes, and loads of records and books. What's funny is he's always completely broke, even after we've been given our pocket money, so he's always on the scrounge.

Michael Nish is from Bristol and reckons he's related to David Nish, the Leicester City footballer. We sort of believed him at first, but not any more. John Westland comes from Chatham, like me. He's nicknamed Rubber, because when his mum brought him back to school after the Christmas holidays, he wandered off without saying goodbye while she was talking to one of the teachers. She then came flying through our dormitory calling at the top of her voice, 'Johnny, where's my Johnny?' Nish shouted back, 'Under the bed with a knot in it.'

Flipflan is from Oop North somewhere. His real name is Philip Fallon, but he talks so fast that you can't understand a word he says, including his name. 'Flipflan'. Then there's Stefan, who's half-Hungarian and also likes Mungo Jerry, and Joseph Berry, who we call Coconut because his head is shaped like one. He almost went mad when The Sweet brought out the song 'Hey Poppa Joe Coconut', because we told him we'd written to the band about what a big fan of theirs he was, and suggested they should do a song about him. Now we tell him they've recorded another one – 'Little Willy'.

We have school Mondays to Fridays, and then we have weekends off. During the week, our day begins at 7:30am, when either our housemaster (Mr Crickton, the Bearded Git) or the duty master wakes us up. We have half an hour to clean our teeth and wash, and then we go down to breakfast with the whole school. When that's over, we have 30 minutes to tidy our lockers before school starts.

You always know what sort of day it's going to be by who takes assembly. When it's Warthead, the headmaster, that usually means somebody's done something wrong and he wants to freak out at us. Other times, it's taken by whichever teacher lost the daily staffroom arm-wrestling contest (that's what we reckon, anyway). It's always the skinny, weedy ones – today it was the Bearded Git.

After assembly we have classes until 10:30am, when we have first break. Dinner is from 12:45pm until 1:15pm, and then we can go outside again until 2:00pm. After that, it's more lessons until 3:10pm, when we have a 20-minute break. From 3:30pm till 4:00pm we have the last lesson, except on Fridays, when we have games. During the winter, we have football training, and in the summer it's athletics – I'm on the school 100 metres team (10.9 seconds). Do you play any sports?

On Tuesday mornings, we have swimming in the pool behind the gym. The lesson's over at 12:30 and if we're out of the water and changed fast enough, we're in time to catch the new Top 20 chart rundown on *The Johnny Walker Show* on Radio 1. This week, the Top Five was:

5 'Vincent' – Don McLean (soppy)
4 'Little Willy' – Sweet (stupid)
3 'Take Me Bak 'Ome' – Slade (sounds like all their other records)
2 'Rock And Roll Part 2' – Gary Glitter (<u>brilliant!</u>)
1 'Puppy Love' – Donny Osmond (rubbish!!!!)

'Starman' is only No.29, but I bet it goes a lot higher next week.

School's out (Alice Cooper!) at 4:00pm, and we have 45 minutes to change out of uniforms into our casual clothes before tea. Then we have prep 6:00 till 7:00pm, supper at 8:00pm and lights out at 9:00pm for Group One. Group Five stay up until 10:00pm.

Of course, we never go to sleep after lights out. We talk, and I listen to Radio Luxembourg on my tranny – I have a little earplug, so if any teachers come in they won't hear it. Sometimes I can pick up Radio North Sea International as well, which is my favourite station (especially when they do their own chart rundown on Friday nights), but the reception usually isn't very good.

At weekends, we do prep on Saturday mornings and go to church on Sunday mornings, but in the afternoons we're allowed out unless we've done something wrong, in which case you're stuck on the Restricted List (which means you are barred from leaving school grounds and can only leave the school if you're accompanied by a teacher). I go out most weekends, either to the shops or to the football, but I sometimes stay at school and listen to Alan Freeman on the radio.

I'll tell you more about the school next time I write, if you like. I hope this letter reaches you. I'm using the address for the RCA record label.

Your biggest fan, always...

Gary Weightman

Bournemouth, Hants
Monday 17 July 1972

Dear David Bowie

I haven't had a reply from you after my last letter, but I thought I'd write to you again because I heard your *Ziggy Stardust* album at the weekend and it was brilliant! I've not been able to afford to buy a copy yet, as we only get 50p a week pocket money and the LP costs £2.19. But there's a record shop in Bournemouth called Tiffany's, and they have little soundproof cubicles where you can sit and listen to one side of an LP to see if you want to buy it.

Paul Banion (who now says you're as good as No.309 squadron – he's becoming normal at last), Jonathan James and I went there on Saturday and asked them to play *Ziggy*. We had them put on side one, because that's the side with 'Starman' on it. My favourite song was 'Moonage Daydream', but Jon and Paul say they liked 'Five Years' more, because every line in the song is like a little picture and it sets a really dramatic mood for the rest of the record. People are calling *Ziggy* a concept album, like *Tommy* or ELP's *Tarkus*. Do you agree?

Tiffany's had another of your LPs, *Hunky Dory*. The man behind the counter said it was even better than *Ziggy Stardust*, and the first song, 'Changes', was played a lot on the Tony Blackburn show in January.[4] I must have heard it, because when we get up in the morning I always have my tranny on in the dorm, but I don't remember it. Hopefully I'll hear it again soon.

He said you also sing 'Oh You Pretty Thing' by Peter Noone.[5] Jonathan calls him Peter Goon, because he looks a bit goofy, but I like some of his Herman's Hermits records. I'm looking forward to hearing your version of the song. I expect it's very different. We're going to go back to hear side two of *Ziggy Stardust* next Saturday, and then *Hunky Dory*. I'm going to ask for them both for Christmas.

4   'Changes' was Blackburn's Record Of The Week from 7 January 1972.
5   In fact, Bowie wrote the song and played piano on Noone's version.

I have also heard 'Space Oddity'. It was on the radio before we went into assembly a couple of days ago. As soon as it came on, I remembered it was the music they played for the moon landing in 1969. My mum let me stay up to watch it, even though I was only 9 at the time. I've watched the others since then, but I don't think they were as interesting. Mum says once you've seen one moon you've seen them all, and that the Americans only went there to take people's minds off the Vietnam War, by giving them something to cheer about.

I tried to write down the words to 'Space Oddity' while it was playing. I didn't catch all of them, but it seems to tell the same kind of story as Elton John's 'Rocket Man'. Do you think he ripped your idea off?[6] We were talking about it and Paul said 'Space Oddity' might have been better for the Apollo 13 mission, as those astronauts very nearly were lost in space. I replied that the difference is, Major Tom wants to be lost.

Did you read the article about your concert in Dunstable in last week's *Melody Maker*? The writer[7] said it was 'the first recorded act of fellatio in the British Isles'.[8] One of the big kids told us that meant that you sucked him off, but you only pretended to do it, didn't you? I saw the picture afterwards, and his guitar was definitely in the way (unless he had a hole drilled in it!), but from a distance I bet that's exactly what it looked like. Do you play the guitar with your teeth while you're doing that? I heard that Jimi Hendrix could do that, but not while someone else was holding the guitar.

Anyway, I'd love to see you play a concert. There are several places here that you could play: the Bournemouth Winter Gardens, the Chelsea Village and Starkers. But please play after 4 September, because that's when we come back to school after the summer holidays.[9] I don't care if Warthead (our headmaster) says I can't go – I'll sneak out after lights out if I have to.

---

6 Apparently he did. In interviews around this time, Bowie made several not-so-veiled references to similarities between the songs, before adding the line 'I'm a rocket man' to a version of 'Space Oddity' recorded for the BBC on 22 May 1972.
7 Michael Watts – author, also, of Bowie's infamous 'I'm gay' revelations in the same paper's 22 January issue.
8 It was the second. Photographer Mick Rock witnessed the same display two nights earlier (17 June) in Oxford.
9 Bowie played Bournemouth on 31 August. The rotter.

I promised I'd tell you more about the school. In fact, I expect you're wondering why I'm even *at* boarding school? It's alright, I'm not MAD or anything. It's my stepfather's fault. My real dad died when I was 4, and my mum remarried two years ago. I never liked him, but I didn't tell her that. I told *him*, though, so as soon as they were married he decided I should go away to school because I'd get a better education. He's probably right, although I'd never admit that. My last school only taught us English, History, Geography and Maths, while this place adds Physics, Woodwork and our choice of Latin or French (I take French). It's enough to make your brain explode, trying to keep it all in, but the lessons themselves aren't too hard, especially English and History. I hate Maths and Physics, on the other hand, and languages are stupid because most of the foreigners you're likely to meet can already speak English. Otherwise, what would they be doing over here?

Actually, he sent me here (my stepfather, that is) because he wanted to get rid of me. I don't know why my mum agreed, but now I'm glad she did, because I only have to deal with him during school holidays. Plus it costs him a fortune in school fees keeping me here, which means he has less money to spend on stinking aftershave and squeaky white shoes. He can afford it, though, as he's a partner in a haulage company and owns a fleet of lorries that drive all over England and the Continent. I'm not really sure what they transport – I tell the other boys that he's an international arms smuggler, but it's probably nothing that exciting.

When I first came here last September, I was expecting boarding school to be a cross between the *Jennings* books by Anthony Buckeridge and the Winker Watson stories in the *Dandy,* with a supersonic tuck shop, spiffing midnight feasts, ultra-ozard prefects and so on. It wasn't – in fact, we don't have any of those things. And it wasn't like *Tom Brown's Schooldays* either, although some of the older boys wish it was. We did get picked on a bit when we first started, although more by the second years than anyone else. It's settled down now, but the only second year I talk to is Graeme Jones, who I go with to Dean Court (home of the mighty Bournemouth and Boscombe Athletic FC). He's one of the dayboys, and he smuggles sweets and cigarettes in all the time.

We call the school Colditz because, with all the rules and regulations, it really feels like we're in prison. But, according to one of the teachers, who was a pupil here himself (back when the school first opened, I should think!), we have a lot more freedom than he did. At least we can go out at weekends (so long as we tell them where we're going), we can hang posters on our dormitory walls and wear our own choice of clothes when we're not in uniform. When he was here, he said, he didn't even know the name of some of the masters, because he had to call everyone 'sir'. I said that must have been really confusing if you were having a conversation with more than one at a time, and he replied that they didn't have conversations. They just obeyed orders. Phew!

Anyway, I'd better go, so I hope you are well. Please write back if you can.

Yours sincerely

Gary Weightman

Chatham, Kent
Thursday 31 August 1972

Dear David Bowie

Gary Weightman here again. I'm at home in Chatham for a few more days, then it's back to Colditz on Monday. I read in *NME* that 'John I'm Only Dancing' will be out by then. I can't wait to hear it. Is it as good as 'Starman' and *Ziggy*?

I love the school holidays, cos I get to stay at home and I can do what I like. Boarding school is fine, but I am jealous of my old friends sometimes, as they still go to normal schools and they have a lot more freedom. We have to ask permission to do everything, like go into town, watch TV shows, play music in our common room and so on. They can do what they like, when they like.

My friend Steve is the same age as I am (he's three months younger) and he's allowed to stay up to watch *The Old Grey Whistle Test* every week, even though it's on a school night. My mum lets me when I'm at home, but I know I miss a lot of worthwhile stuff when I'm at school because everyone goes on about how much better than *Top Of The Pops* it is, but whenever I see it, they always have either really poxy groups who can't play, or singers with acoustic guitars and beards, who drone on and on about the price of posting a letter for hours on end. I don't know why anybody want to listen to records like that, you might as well save your money and ask your grandma what she thinks about decimal coinage. Then all you have to do is strum a guitar while she's talking.

The only thing I can do at school that I can't do at home is go to football matches. The local team is Gillingham, who I've supported for years, but Mum doesn't want me to go to games cos of hooliganism. I don't think they have hooligans at Gillingham, but you know what mothers are like! At school, they're happy to let us go to see Bournemouth when they're playing at home, and last season I went to eight matches. I was so sure they were going to get promoted at the end of the season, but in the end they finished third.

I'd have loved to see the FA Cup game against Margate, because Bournemouth won 11–0 and Ted MacDougall scored nine! I wasn't there cos I was still new at school and didn't know we were allowed to go to games. It was only at teatime, when everyone was talking about it, that I found out. Now I go whenever I can, and I'm collecting Bournemouth programmes. Are you a football fan? What team do you support? You live in Beckenham, so I bet it's either Charlton or Crystal Palace.

Last week I bought 'All The Young Dudes' by Mott The Hoople, which you wrote and produced. I'd never heard of them before this record, but Steve's big brother, Sparksy, is a greaser, and he has two of their old records, *Mad Shadows* and *Brain Capers*, which he played to us. They were OK. *Brain Capers* was better, but not as good as 'All The Young Dudes'.

Sparksy calls them Mott (only idiots add 'The Hoople', he reckons) and says it's nice that they are successful at last, cos they deserve it after working so hard for so long. But he's worried in case you turn them into a bunch of homos. I replied I didn't think that was very likely, but he looked at me really funnily and said, 'You *would* say that'.

People seem to think being a bender is some sort of disease that can be spread around like a cold, but I don't agree. I asked my mum about that and she said there's a lot of stupid people around, who are scared of what they don't understand. She reminded me about this man who used to live in the flat below us, and how she once told me to tell her if he ever touched me 'there' – he *wasn't* a queer, she says; just a dirty old man. Then she told me that someone else we knew was queer, but she'd never warned me about him, because that wasn't the kind of way he would behave.

The problem is, it's very difficult to explain that to anybody, particularly people older than you, like Sparksy. They immediately think that if you know so much about it you must be one, and then you'll never hear the end of it. There's one boy at school who's two years older than me and wants to join the navy when he leaves. So of course everybody calls him 'Sailor' and flaps their wrists at him. What makes it even worse for him is that advert that says, 'Join the navy and feel a man'. I know what it means, but it does have a funny double meaning if you have a dirty enough mind.

How old were you when you realised you were bisexual? Did you wake up one day and think, 'I'll give it a go', or did it just slowly dawn on you that you fancied as many boys as you did girls? I was thinking about that the other day and wondering: *if* I found out that I was queer, who at school did I fancy, and I couldn't think of anyone I'd be even remotely interested in. Which means either that I'm completely straight or I'm at school with a bunch of ugly, mutant freaks. I also wonder if some people go through life thinking they're straight – get married, have kids and all that, and then one day BONG!, and they're madly in love with their milkman. I can think of a few people I'd love to see that happen to, just to watch their reaction.

At the same time, though, I really don't understand why people are so interested in what goes on in other people's bedrooms. If it was suddenly announced that Winston Churchill was bisexual, would it make any difference at all to what he did as a politician? Or if you turned around and said that you weren't, would it change what you did with your music?

That would be a really interesting experiment. We all know Ziggy Stardust is a kind of made-up figure, and that if you'd told his story on film instead of music, you'd be called a movie star, not a pop star. Now, if you were to say that Ziggy is the queer but you're not, would people who dislike you because of what they think you are suddenly be forced to change their minds?

I have a question about 'All The Young Dudes'. What is 'the news' that they are carrying? I was thinking it might have something to do with the Ziggy Stardust story. The dudes know there's only five years left until the end of the world, so they're running around telling everyone to stop worrying and enjoy themselves instead. One of our set books in English next year (there's a dozen of them) is Evelyn Waugh's *Vile Bodies*, so I decided to get a head start on the others and read up about it. It seems to me that it's set in a similar period to *Ziggy Stardust*, on the eve of a major war. They don't know it, of course, but there's still a sense of making hay while the sun shines. Take that situation and give people a time limit, and who knows what they would do?

Some of the other books we've got this term look interesting as well – *Animal Farm*, *Kes*, *Walkabout* and *Zigger-Zagger*, which is a play about football hooligans. Have you read any of those? It's about time they gave us things with a bit of action in them: this summer, I started reading Sven Hassell's books about the Russian front in World War II. They're extremely violent, but very realistic.

What other records do you like at the moment? I love 'School's Out', although they look a bit fake on *Top Of The Flops*. Alice is trying really hard to be evil and menacing, but the band are a bunch of normal hippy types. Hawkwind's 'Silver Machine' is superb as well, and Gary Glitter's 'Rock And Roll' is amazing, even if Glitter doesn't look anything like a pop star. He reminds me of someone you'd see at the talent night at Butlin's holiday camp, who spent so long getting dressed up for the show that he forgot to learn the words to his song. So he sings 'Hey' a lot and waves his arms around – which is perfect, because sometimes a song doesn't need lyrics. It's the beat and the riffs that make it work, and the grunts are another instrument. Plus, it really shows up all those bands who come along who think they're so clever and important, and their song is the best ever.

I often wonder how they would feel if they knew we just sit and laugh at their poxy little efforts and think of new names for them and new words for their songs? They would probably be horrified. The Who doing 'Join Together' are one. They used to make such good records, but now they're boring. I also hate the Vile-listics,[10] cos they don't have any balls and their dances are dead spazzy, and Gilbert O'Suckerpan[11] is embarrassing. Remember when he used to wear that flat cap and old-fashioned suit all the time? Then he decided he wanted to be taken seriously, so he started dressing like someone's uncle.

People like Gary Glitter are important, though, because they know they look and sound like a bunch of gorms, and they play it up. Besides, if you play the other side of the single, there are lyrics after all. If he does an LP, he should put the two parts together for one really long song. I'd certainly buy it.

Have you heard Blackfoot Sue's 'Standing In The Road'? I was so shocked when I saw them on TV with beards and long hair. They look completely out of place. It's a terrific record, though, and I love the way it ends, then begins again. If I had more money, I could have spent it all on records this summer – I bought those three, and my New Year's resolution (four months early!) is to buy a new single every week. Beginning with 'John I'm Only Dancing'.

Yours sincerely

Gary Weightman

PS Next evening. On the way to the shops this morning, we stopped at a record shop in Rochester and they had 'John I'm Only Dancing'! I played it as soon as we arrived home. It's brilliant, and it was really exciting to find another song from *Ziggy Stardust* on the B-side.[12]

---

10 Philadelphia soul exponents The Stylistics, renowned for their ethereal falsettos and slick dance routines.
11 Gilbert O'Sullivan, Irish singer-songwriter once prone to wearing a flat cap and singing songs about suicide, but now (summer 1972) resting his literary laurels on 'Ooh-Wakka-Doo-Wakka-Day'.
12 'Hang Onto Yourself'.

Bournemouth, Hants
Thursday 26 October 1972

Dear David Bowie

I'm sorry 'John I'm Only Dancing' didn't do as well as 'Starman'.[13] I don't think it was as catchy the first time you heard it, and you had to play it a lot before it started to really grow on you, and a lot of people don't do that – they want to be hit on the head really hard every time they switch on the radio, because that's the only way a record will sink into their thick skulls. Try them with something a little trickier and they move on. Next time around, you should come up with something that's really commercial. Then, you watch: it'll be No.1 within days. If you hadn't wasted it as the B-side of 'Starman', 'Suffragette City' would have made a good single, but maybe you don't want to release too many songs off the same LP in case people might think they're being cheated.

I read that Roxy Music's new single, 'Virginia Plain', isn't on their LP cos Bryan Ferry, their singer, wants to give the fans value for money. That's a good idea, but I also think it's nice to have singles on LPs as well, cos that way if you missed the single you don't lose the song for ever.

Roxy Music opened for you at the London Rainbow last month, didn't they? Did you see them? 'Virginia Plain' is so strange-sounding, it reminds me of some old 1950s rock 'n' roll song, played by spacemen. Did you see them doing it on *Top Of The Pops*? One of the older kids here, Dale Hartley, comes from Aylesbury and he reckons he saw Roxy Music opening for a biker group called The Pretty Things there last year. The audience was full of greasers, so Roxy quiffed their hair up like teddy boys and played all their songs like Elvis Presley. I don't know if it's a true story, but I hope it is.

The other one I like now is 'Donna' by 10cc, which also sounds like an old 1950s song. Isn't it funny how many people

13 It reached No.12. 'Starman' got to No.11.

are going for that sound these days? That's why glam rock is so good, cos it takes the best of older forms of music and mixes them up with new ideas, so people who weren't around in the 1950s can hear what all the fuss was about back then, without it sounding so old-fashioned. I heard Bill Haley And His Comets' 'Rock Around The Clock' on the radio and I cannot believe the music made people riot and tear up cinema seats, because it sounds so tame and weedy. But something like T Rex's 'Metal Guru' is really exciting and new-sounding, even though it's the same kind of rock 'n' roll music. Maybe you should do something in that style. I know it'd be really good.

I don't have much news to give you. We've been back at Colditz for a month and I'm in Group Two now. The work isn't much harder than it was in Group One, although we do seem to get more prep. We're allowed to stay up until 9:15 every evening, and 10:00pm at weekends, but I won't bore you with the gruesome details of everyday life – you can probably imagine what it's like. I can't wait to leave school and be able to do what I want all the time. I don't know what I want to do when I leave. Is it hard to become a pop star?

I've kept to my resolution (which I told you about in my last letter) and bought loads of new singles. I now have more than 20. I'll put a list of them at the end of this letter, to give you some idea of my taste in music.

I also have some LPs but, apart from *Electric Warrior*, they're all those *Top Of The Pops* ones, which don't have the proper songs on them and are so poxy they should be outlawed. Last Christmas I asked my stepfather if he could buy me 'Coz I Luv You' by Slade, and of course I meant the single. Instead he bought me *The Best Of Top Of The Pops* cos it was the same price as a single and had other songs on it as well. I tried to explain that it wasn't the same thing, but he wouldn't listen and now he buys them all the time and keeps posting them to me at school. The other kids think it's really funny and take the piss out of me all the time cos he's such a spaz, but when I asked him not to buy any more and give me the money instead, I was given a lecture on how singles are a rip-off, and that a song's a song whoever plays it.

He's so gormless and I know my mum agrees with me, cos she then bought me 'Coz I Luv You' herself. I even stopped telling him what records I like, but it hasn't made a difference. You're lucky: I don't think they've done 'Starman' or 'John I'm Only Dancing' yet, so you've been spared.

There's a new boy in our class who is almost as big a David Bowie fan as Jonathan James and I. His name is Jeffrey Chambers, although we call him Gnome's Head. He has a hairstyle like yours (he didn't dye it, though) and he says he has all your records at home. I'm not sure whether I believe him, cos he also said he saw you playing in Leicester during the summer holidays and I know you didn't play there. I don't know why some kids tell lies like that, which can be so easily found out. There's another boy here named Steve Jaffers. He's in Group Three and is a big fat bully and everybody hates him, but he swaggers around telling us how his dad knows all these pop stars and he spent the summer with Mick Jagger and Elton John, and things like that. I'd love to ask him why people like that would hang around with a stupid fat bloater like him, but he'd only go mental, so it's best to ignore him.

The other big news, if you like football, is that Ted MacDougall, who is Bournemouth's best player by miles, has been sold to Manchester United. MacDougall owns a sports shop on Boscombe High Street – we sometimes go in there and hum the theme to the *Magic Roundabout* in Scottish accents while looking at the Subbuteo stuff, but I don't know if it comes out as funny as we think it is. It's hard to hum in Scottish – unless you are Scottish, I suppose. Anyway, we went down there before the match on Saturday to say goodbye and wish him luck; of course he wasn't there. He'll probably play his first game for United tomorrow against West Bromwich Albion. I hope he does well.[14]

Well, that's all for now. I hope this letter finds you well. Are you making a new record yet?[15]

14 Sadly, he didn't.
15 Bowie was in the US when this letter was mailed.

Yours sincerely

Gary Weightman

MY RECORD COLLECTION
Singles
Alice Cooper – 'School's Out'
Argent – 'Hold Your Head Up'
Blackfoot Sue – 'Standing In The Road'
David Bowie – 'John I'm Only Dancing'
David Bowie – 'Starman'
Gary Glitter – 'Rock And Roll Parts 1 And 2'
Hawkwind – 'Silver Machine'
Kinks – 'Supersonic Rocket Ship'
Lindisfarne – 'Lady Eleanor'
Lindisfarne – 'Meet Me On The Corner'
Mott The Hoople – 'All The Young Dudes'
Roxy Music – 'Virginia Plain'
Shag – 'Loop Di Love'
Shangri-Las – 'Leader Of The Pack'
Slade – 'Coz I Luv You'
Ringo Starr – 'Back Off Boogaloo'
Rod Stewart – 'Maggie May'
10cc – 'Donna'
T Rex – 'Jeepster'
T Rex – 'Metal Guru'

EPs
Beatles – 'All My Loving'
Tyrannosaurus Rex – 'Debora'

LPs
T Rex – *Electric Warrior*

Bournemouth, Hants
Monday 20 November 1972

Dear David Bowie

I don't think much of your timing! Every year for Christmas, Colditz asks us to make a list of three things we want, and gives us one of them as a present at the school party. The limit is 50p, and we all put down singles we want. But your new record, 'The Jean Genie', wasn't released until the week after we had to hand the lists in, so none of us was able to get it.

I ended up asking for either Family ('Burlesque' – I like the way the singer sounds like a sheep), Python Lee Jackson ('In A Broken Dream', which is Rod Stewart under a different name) or Judge Dread ('Big Six' – it's been banned by the BBC so this is the only way I'll get to hear it), but I wasn't the only person here who would have asked for 'The Jean Genie' if it had been out in time.

I hope your American tour went well. Was it your first?[16] There was quite a lot of coverage in the music press. It sounded good. It must have been exciting to travel there on the QE2. Are you really afraid of flying? I've never tried, although I did get to go on a BAC 1-11 a few weeks ago. One of my mum's cousins works at Herne Airport, which is quite near here, and took me on board. David Elliman, who is one of the boys in our dormitory, has a short-wave radio and sometimes we tune it into the airport and listen to the controllers talking to the pilots. He can also pick up the police and the fire brigade, but nothing ever happens in Bournemouth so it's pretty boring.

We're in a new dormitory now, on the first floor above Warthead's office and the surgery. The new first years are now in our old dorm, so we told them how it's haunted by a window cleaner who was killed here when the school first opened. His name was Boris, and he fell from the roof and smashed his head open on the concrete outside. Now he haunts the dormitory by dripping water from his bucket on people when they're

16 Aside from a promotional visit in February 1971, it was.

sleeping. At Halloween we were planning to wait until late, then go over there and do that, but one of the teachers found out, so we couldn't.

It's probably just as well. They're such weeds that they'd probably all have had heart attacks and died. One of them, John Woodward, is named Mutant cos he's so short and talks a bit like a Dalek. Another has thick frizzy hair and glasses and acted like he was really tough, until the day Michael Nish hid around a corner from him, slammed a cardboard box on his head and pushed him down the stairs. He ended up with such a thick lip that he looked like Plug out of the Bash Street Kids. So now we call him Beano.

The only one we like is Wilky, who's a big Bowie fan, although he doesn't have any of your records yet. The worst of the lot is called Balland – short for 'Ball And Chain', because he was caught shoplifting at Waterloo Station on his very first day at school. The first thing Warthead said to him when we got to school was 'You're lucky you're here: I had a good mind to pack you straight off to borstal with a ball and chain', and the name has stuck ever since. He also looks like a fat albino toad.

A funny thing happened in assembly last week. Once a week, they let two of the older boys take assembly, where they can play a record or read something from a book, and then talk about how it applies to the school day. They usually play stuff like Cat Stevens and Don McLean, and we all end up with 'Vincent' stuck in our heads for the rest of the day. Last Wednesday, though, two of the fifth years played a song called 'Come To The Sabbat, Satan's There' by a group called Black Widow.[17] The woodwork teacher, Mr Yards, leaped up and snatched the record off the turntable before the second verse had even started, but of course everyone had a big laugh, and Danny Meath is convinced the song was played as a message to him, so he knows not to stray from the Evil Path. I'm not sure what sort of evil he thinks he can get up to in a place like this, though. Perhaps he could sacrifice the new French mistress. (*Vache!*)

17 From the CBS album *Sacrifice*.

You have so many new records coming out! I bought *For The Collector: Early David Bowie*[18] at Smith's last month, although I wasn't too keen on the songs. They sounded very different and very old-fashioned. 1965 seems so long ago. Do you even remember making those records? Jonathan James has the Mott The Hoople *All The Young Dudes* album. Your song is the best one on there, but I also like 'Soft Ground' and 'Sweet Jane'. *Space Oddity* and *The Man Who Sold The World*[19] have also been rereleased, and Mum wrote to say she bought me *The World Of David Bowie*[20] on Decca. I'm hoping the next time I write to you, I'll have heard all of them, and 'The Jean Genie' as well. Don't worry if you don't have time to write back to me. I'm sure you're really busy.

Yours sincerely

Gary

18 A four-track EP comprising songs recorded by Bowie during 1965–66.
19 Reissues of Bowie's second and third albums, previously issued by Philips and Mercury in 1969/1970.
20 A compilation originally issued in 1969, featuring material cut for (and on either side of) Bowie's 1967 debut album.

Bournemouth, Hants
Tuesday 19 December 1972

Dear David

Everybody's talking about how funny it is to hear 'The Jean Genie' and 'Blockbuster' side by side on the radio, especially as you are both on the same record label. Some of the kids are saying that you ripped them off – but others reckon they ripped you off. I was firmly on your side (of course). 'The Jean Genie' came out earlier and, besides, why would you need to nick things from The Sweet, of all people? Have you noticed how they've suddenly started dressing up glam on stage, with make-up and costumes and the guitarist pretending to be all poofy? Of course, everybody else is doing it as well – in fact, one of the teachers sat through *Top Of The Pops* a few weeks back, then walked away asking if they were ever going to have any proper men performing on the show again. Even worse, he was serious.

Anyway, it turns out that both 'The Jean Genie' and 'Blockbuster' nicked their riff from another record entirely, called 'I'm Coming Home', by The Deviants. One of the fifth years played it in assembly, then gave us a long speech about how he was sick of everybody arguing about David Bowie and The Sweet because it was disrupting Colditz at Christmastime. I reckon he was showing off. Have you ever noticed how older people always think the music they grew up with is superior to whatever's out now, regardless of whether it is or not? He also told us that The Deviants took the riff from an even older song, by The Yardbirds,[21] but he didn't have that one with him.

Our first lesson after that was Music, so we asked the teacher, Mr Skate, about whether people who write different songs with the same riff are stealing, if they're not aware of the other song... Is it subconscious? Or can coincidences like

21 'I'm A Man'. A variation also underpins 'Over Under Sideways Down'.

that really happen? He explained that as there are only eight musical notes (do, re, mi, etc), it's inevitable that they will often fall together in the same order. People who recognise a tune when that happens will sometimes then make a minor change, so it does sound different, but there are so many millions and millions of tunes that have already been written, that nobody can be expected to know every one of them. It was a very interesting lesson (a first!), but it does sort of spoil one of our favourite games while watching *Top Of The Pops*, screaming 'Rip-off' at every band that sounds like someone else.

Have you seen the special magazine that *Record Mirror* published about you? It was really good to find a list of all your old records – now all I need to do is find the records themselves. There's a couple of used-record shops near to Colditz that we visit most weekends. One's called Boccy Leckies (short for 'Boscombe Electrics'), where they have racks of singles and LPs, together with old record players and instruments; the other is called Steptoes, like the TV show, which is a normal junk shop, but they do carry a few albums. I have two Beatles LPs, *With The Beatles* and *Abbey Road*, which I bought there for 50p each, and The Rolling Stones' *Let It Bleed*, which was only 35p cos it was scratched. I don't know what the chances of finding any of your old records are, because they're all pretty rare. There is a copy of *Ziggy Stardust* at Boscombe Electrics for a pound, but it'll probably be gone by the time I get back there. It's still on my Christmas list, even though I now have four of the songs on singles.[22] Wish me luck.

Finally, guess what? My mum and stepfather have moved to Chelsea. I'm not very keen about moving to London, but they say it's important for my stepfather's business. So let him move there on his own... If I have to go to school 100 miles from home, he can go to work 40 miles away. But no, we have to follow him there. The only good thing is, I asked how far they

22 'Ziggy Stardust' was lifted for the B-side of 'The Jean Genie'. In all, RCA would release five of *Ziggy*'s ten songs as singles in Britain, with 'Rock And Roll Suicide' appearing in 1974.
23 Bowie's management company.

are from the Mainman offices[23] in Gunter Grove and it's only three streets away, so maybe I'll get to meet you! I will definitely write to you there and I can even deliver the letter myself during the holidays.

Happy Christmas to you, Angie and Zowie

Gary

Bournemouth, Hants
Wednesday 24 January 1973

Dear David

Happy New Year! Did you get the Christmas card I sent? I put it through the letterbox at the Mainman offices. I'm sorry I didn't get to meet you. I went to the offices twice, but there was always a lot of other people waiting outside and, as I didn't know any of them, I went home. Once when I was there, I overheard somebody say you were in one of the clothes shops at World's End, so I walked up there, but I didn't see you.

Were you in Granny Takes A Trip or Let It Rock?[24] I don't like Let It Rock, as there are always gangs of teddy boys hanging around outside. Don't they realise how gormless they look? That style went out of fashion centuries ago, even if the music is coming back a bit, but why anyone would want to walk around looking like Elvis Presley is beyond me, especially as most of the teds you see on the street are really old and fat. Have you heard the song 'My Generation' by The Who? There's that line 'Hope I die before I get old' – teddy boys should pay attention, although it's too late for most of them.

They're always shouting things out at passers-by, as well, and one day I saw a whole bunch of them break away and follow this hippy guy up the street, as though they were going to beat him up. I was with my mum on the way to the grocer's, so I didn't see what happened, but I wouldn't be surprised. And the police don't do anything, probably cos they'd be so outnumbered.

I hope your last tour went well. I still haven't seen you play, but maybe next time. I read in *NME* that you're off to America again soon. We had two American student teachers here last term, learning how the British prison system works. One was named Mr Romanovitch – we all thought he was going to be a Russian until he arrived. He had long hair and

---

24 Haberdasher Malcolm McLaren's Let It Rock subsequently changed its name to Sex and attracted a very different clientele.

round granny glasses, and we could hardly understand anything he said his accent was so thick. We nicknamed him Ivan, anyway.

We asked him what sort of music he liked, so he brought in his eight-tracks from his car. There was a band called The Eagles – Danny Meath nearly wet himself when he saw they had a song called 'Witchy Woman', so Larry took us out to his car and played it. It wasn't very good, but Danny's dead impressed anyway. He also had Jackson Browne (which sounded like something you'd hear on *The Old Grey Whistling Kettle*), Carly Simon, James Taylor and The Byrds, but not 'Mr Tambourine Man', which is the only one of their songs I know. Romanovitch said that this is the sort of music most American kids listen to, because things like T Rex and Slade and you are 'too English' for most Americans, whatever that means. I don't see what countries have to do with it – either a record is good or it isn't. But then Gnome's Head pointed out that almost every group and singer that we really hate – like The Osmonds, The Jackson Five, Elvis Presley and all that horrible soul stuff – comes from America, so maybe there is something in it, after all. Anyway, it sounds like you've got your work cut out for you over there, so good luck!

You were terrific on *Russell Harty Plus* on Saturday. We were allowed to stay up late to watch it. I wasn't sure what it was going to be like, because the outfit you had on made you look very stiff and uncomfortable, but the new song, 'Drive-In Saturday', was brilliant, and you sang Jacques Brel's 'My Death' as well. Mr Skate, the music teacher, has a double album called *Jacques Brel Is Alive And Well And Living In Paris*, and he recognised the song immediately.

He played us some of the record in class on Monday, and I can tell that you're a big Jacques Brel fan because, as soon as I heard 'Jef', I immediately recognised 'Rock And Roll Suicide', the 'you're not alone' section. I read somewhere that you sometimes play 'Amsterdam' in concert as well. Do you sing it in English or French? Mr Skate says Brel writes and sings completely in French, so the only versions of his songs that most English people know are translations, which often have very different words and meanings.

My David Bowie collection is as complete as it can be. Between Christmas and my birthday, on 30 December, I got all the LPs[25] that I needed, and I bought Lou Reed's *Transformer* with the gift token that my gran sent. My mum looked at the back cover photo of the man with that huge bulge in his trousers and asked me if Grandma would be pleased to know I'd bought a record like that. I think she was joking, though. We listened to the record when we arrived home and she laughed at some of the songs – when I asked her why, she said I was too young to understand. Everything I've heard by Lou Reed now I like, although it isn't much: 'Sweet Jane' on *All The Young Dudes*, and a song called 'Venus In Furs', which has a creaky violin sound all the way through it, that Alan Freeman played on the radio.

Oh, and who are The Thunderthighs? There's a rumour going around that it's you and Mick Ronson,[26] although as your names are already all over the record I can't imagine you need to come up with any pseudonyms.

The Man Who Sold The World surprised me. It was the last album I got, so I was expecting something along the lines of the records you made on either side of it, *Space Oddity* and *Hunky Dory*. Instead, it turned out to be a mad heavy-metal album, which is going to take a bit of getting into. 'The Man Who Sold The World' and 'Saviour Machine' are the best songs so far, although I do like 'All The Madmen'. It reminds me a little of 'Bewlay Brothers', although that might just be the funny voices. And doesn't 'Black Country Rock' sound a bit like Marc Bolan in places? It's funny to hear you doing that little quaver with your voice, although I noticed that The Kinks do it as well, on 'King Kong', so maybe that's what you were thinking of.

25 The reissued *Space Oddity* and *The Man Who Sold The World*, plus *Hunky Dory* and *Ziggy Stardust*.
26 Thunderthighs was an all-girl singing trio that dominated the sessions world of the early 1970s. Their most prominent/best-remembered appearance is on Mott The Hoople's 'Roll Away The Stone'.

Space Oddity is good, and I really liked *Hunky Dory*. I didn't know it was you who wrote 'Oh You Pretty Things' for Peter Noone! I thought you did a cover version because it was such a clever song. It was funny, I was singing along with it and was completely taken by surprise when you sing 'bitch' instead of 'beast'. Whose idea was it to change the words – yours or Peter Noone's? I also found out that you're playing piano on his record. It must have been interesting working with him, with your career moving up while his appears to be on the way down – Herman's Hermits weren't anywhere near as successful as they used to be, and none of his other solo records have done anything, either.

I was going to bring the LPs back to Colditz with me, but in the end I decided not to, in case anything happens to them. Our lockers don't have locks on them (so why are they called lockers?), plus our new housemaster, Mr Evans, is a real pig who confiscates everything he can and there's nothing we can do about it. His room must be like a cross between Aladdin's cave and Sainsbury's he's stolen so much from us. Any food and sweets he finds in our lockers he goes off with, even though there's nothing in the school rules to say we can't have things like that. Last week before we went to church, he thought Paul Banion had a packet of cigarettes in the top pocket of his school blazer so he grabbed at it, and ripped the pocket off! Of course, Paul doesn't smoke, so Evans then accused him of tearing his own pocket off and said he would dock Paul's pocket money until he gets it repaired. It's really unfair. But, even though we all saw what happened, there's nothing we can do about it, cos the other staff are always going to believe one of their own. I wish there was some way we could get back at him, but I don't know what it is.

'The Jean Genie' did really well on the charts, didn't it? Even if The Sweet did beat you to No.1. This week on the chart, Gary Glitter is No.5, Carly Simon is No.4, you are No.3 for the second week, Little Toady Osmond is No.2 and 'Blockbuster' is

---

27 The offending hit was Little Jimmy Osmond's 'Long Haired Lover From Liverpool'.

No.1. I can't believe Toady kept you off the top. It proves what idiots people are. He isn't even from Liverpool and he doesn't have long hair. But I suppose he couldn't call the record 'Short Haired Fat Obnoxious Creature From America',[27] could he?

Are The Osmonds taking over, do you think? Gnome's Head buys *Music Star* magazine and every week there's another article about them. I don't understand their appeal at all, they're so ugly and goofy, although 'Crazy Horses' was quite a good record if you like that sort of thing. But everything else they do is a load of bollocks. You should have been No.1 – but, there again, so should Paul McCartney's 'C Moon', which is the best record he's ever made.

Did you hear the other side, 'Hi Hi Hi'? It was banned by the BBC and I only heard it when Paul brought it back after the Christmas hols. The problem is, people think it's about drugs (high high high), but that seems silly, because you can read anything into a song's lyrics if you want to. The new Cat Stevens song is called 'Can't Keep It In' and we've already made up a new line about how his flies are broken. Then there's 'Do You Want To Touch Me? (Oh Yeah)' (no, thank you!) by Gary Glitter, 'Little Willy' by The Sweet and 'Come Softly To Me' by The New Squeakers,[28] all of which are disgusting if you think about it. Rather than ban records because they're dirty, it'd be better to ban them cos they're rubbish.

Wouldn't it be brilliant if the government formed a Ministry of Music, with people like you, Marc Bolan and Bryan Ferry in charge of it? Every time somebody wanted to release a new record, you would all listen to it and then decide if it was any good or not. If it's good it can be released, and if it's rubbish the guilty group is sent to the Siberian salt mines until they learn how to sing, play and write. I suppose the only problem would be, there wouldn't be many records released and the Top 20 would end up being the Top Three or something. But at least we wouldn't have to hear The Osmonds and David Crappidy and those horrible soul ballads any more.

28 Actually, The New Seekers.

Who do you think buys records like that? Apart from spazmos and retards, that is.

Do you have a new single planned? I think it should be 'Drive-In Saturday', because it's so different from any of your other songs.

Hope you are well. Good luck again with the American tour.

Best wishes

Gary

Chelsea, London SW10
Thursday 1 March 1973

Dear David

I almost met Dana Gillespie today. I was on Gunter Grove with some of your fans, and a huge car pulled up outside the offices. A girl climbed out, and Kathy (one of the girls who's always here) said it was Dana. A couple of the others ran over to try and talk to her, but she went into the building before they had the chance. We knew it wasn't you in the car, cos you're still in America – Kathy says you were playing in Memphis last night, and you're in Detroit tomorrow. Is it a long journey between the two cities? It looks like it in the atlas.

Did you mean it when you told the papers that you wanted to give up touring and make films instead?[29] I hope not – at least until I get to see you play. They also said that you collapsed from exhaustion after the final New York show, but then I read that you finished the show with the sound of gunshots, and that was why you collapsed, as though somebody had shot you.

What a strange end to the night that must have been for the audience: going home not knowing whether you really had been killed or not. I was wondering about how I'd feel if I saw that happen, and I can't imagine how awful it'd be, but then I started thinking about it from your point of view, and it occurred to me that it'd be a great way for somebody to 'end' their career, if they were to pretend to be shot on stage and then disappear. People say that's what happened to Jim Morrison of The Doors and Jimi Hendrix – that they didn't really die. They faked it so they could get back to living normal lives. It's a really interesting idea, because you read about normal people who disappear all the time in the papers. So I started writing a story about a rock star who did that. One of the hardest parts was coming up with a believable name for him, one that is as weird as 'Ziggy Stardust' but doesn't sound completely gormless.

29 Following two nights at New York's Radio City Music Hall, Bowie said exactly that to the press. Five months later, he proved temporarily true to his word.

I ended up naming him Tom Major (after Major Tom, of course), and after he's 'killed' he becomes a doctor. Finally he's recognised by one of his patients, so he announces he's making a comeback before she can go to the newspapers with the story. Everybody goes to the first show but, as it ends, a woman jumps out of the audience and drives a wooden stake into his heart because she thinks he's a vampire. That causes the audience to riot, because they think he's trying to fake his death again, and they don't want to let him go. I haven't written it all yet, so it might change along the way, but it's a good idea.

The papers also said that you're going to be making a film of *Stranger In A Strange Land*,[30] so I immediately found a copy in the Colditz library. I started reading it on the train home for half term. I'm not very far along yet, but I like it.

Did you know that there's another David Bowie out there? I was on the bus home yesterday, when we passed a cinema near Piccadilly Circus and, in big letters above the door, it said, '*The Image* starring David Bowie'. I jumped off at the next stop and ran back, but there was no information anywhere, apart from the fact that it's an X certificate.

I don't think it could be you, cos I don't think you'd make a film that you know most of your fans couldn't get in to see, and also because the papers are all saying *Stranger In A Strange Land* will be your first film. I know you had to change your name so people didn't mix you up with Davy Jones of The Monkees. You should make this other David Bowie change his, so he doesn't confuse your fans.[31]

Yes, it's half term, which means ten days away from Colditz, but I've only been able to go to Gunter Grove twice because my mum and stepfather wanted to do other things. We went into the West End one day, which was fun. I bought a Plasticraft set – it's a model-making kit, with different-shaped moulds that you pour a liquid plastic into, then embed different things into it. You should get one for Zowie, although

30 By science fiction author Robert Heinlein. The film was never made.
31 Ah, the innocence of youth. In fact this was the same David Bowie, seen in a brief (14 minutes), and somewhat surreal, art-house film shot back in 1969 by director Michael Armstrong. It was briefly revived in 1973 to cash in on Bowie's current success.

you'll probably want to wait until he's a little older, as it is a bit messy. You have to be careful not to spill the resin, because it sets like cement.

The box suggests using things like seashells and coins and making jewellery for people, but my mum told me not to bother on her account. She said you need to be a very special sort of woman to enjoy wearing jewellery made from inch-thick lumps of resin. So I'm making paperweights instead. I've made two so far – one with a Subbuteo player; the other, with a photo of you and Ronno that I cut out of *Music Star*. Unfortunately, it didn't come out very well, as the resin soaked through the paper and you can't even see what it's meant to be a picture of. Shame. The Subbuteo player looks good, though.

Another day, we went clothes shopping because I seem to have grown out of everything I got back in the summer. I saw some really far-out stuff in some of the shops which we went to, but of course rotten Mum wouldn't buy any of them for me. I ended up with two new pairs of school trousers and a pair of jeans, when I wanted a pair of flairs (I saw a really far-out pair of electric-blue ones). Thankfully we *didn't* end up at Tesco's – there's a new version of 'Space Oddity' going around school, with the words, 'The papers want to know whose jeans you wear, are they Levi's, Wrangler's, or Tesco's De La Mare?' and if anyone answers Tesco's, they get picked on for ever. I ended up with Wrangler's, so I'm safe. Phew.

I also need new shoes and I want some platforms, but Mum says I'm already so tall (five foot six) that platforms will make me look stupid. Plus, she says I'm so clumsy that I'll probably fall off them and break my neck. So I bet I end up with boring black lace-ups.

But she did get me one of your T-shirts, which has a picture of your head and shoulders on it, in red on white. I wore it when I went to Gunter Grove this afternoon, and one of the girls (Kathy, the one who recognised Dana) came over and asked me where it came from. We talked for a while.

She said that she'd met you once, and had also met Ronno, Trevor and Woody.[32]

She's 15 and really pretty. She says she goes there every day after school. She lives in Tetcott Road, which is the next street to me, so I asked if I could walk her home, but she was going out somewhere else with some of the others, so I couldn't. Maybe another time. I hope so. I'm going to go back tomorrow if I can, but Mum wants to go shopping again instead. I'm in London for another four days, though, so hopefully I'll get another chance.

Kathy also said your next single is going to be 'Drive-In Saturday'. I'm glad about that. I asked her what she'd heard about your next LP. She says you've recorded 'All The Young Dudes', as well as a bunch of older songs, like 'Prettiest Star', 'Holy Holy' and 'John I'm Only Dancing'. Woody told her that, although someone else standing near us said he'd read the same story in a magazine. Who cares? The record is meant to be out in April, and I can't wait!

Must go cos it's nearly time for *Top Of The Pops*, and who knows what stunning treats are in store?

Best wishes

Gary

---

32 Ronson, Bolder and Woodmansey – collectively, The Spiders From Mars.

Bournemouth, Hants
Thursday 12 April 1973

Dear David

I bought 'Drive-In Saturday' as soon as it came out, and I must have nearly worn out both sides, I've played it so often. 'Round And Round' is amazing as well. Jonathan James has the same song by The Rolling Stones, but your version is much more exciting. Ronno's guitar playing is fantastic. I listened to the Top 20 on Dave Lee Travis on Tuesday. 'Drive-In Saturday' came in at No.16 and was the highest new entry of the week. Gilbert O'Suckerpan is still No.1, though, and Dawn's 'Tie A Yellow Ribbon' is No.2, which reminds me of my idea for the Ministry of Music. That is exactly the kind of record I was thinking about – in fact, Paul Banion thinks it should have been banned anyway, because all that stuff about 'I've done my time' obviously glorifies crime and going to jail.

We go home for the Easter holidays tomorrow (Friday), so I can't stop, cos I have to pack. I'll write to you again as soon as I have *Aladdin Sane*.

Best wishes

Gary

Bournemouth, Hants
Tuesday 1 May 1973

Dear David

We came back to Colditz yesterday. It was brill when we all met up at Waterloo Station. First we heard that Mr Evans, the housemaster we all hate, has left. Then we heard a rumour that Nicky Jacks, who's this complete snob and only likes disco music (we call him Soul Boy) has meningitis and won't be back until after the summer holidays *at the earliest*. And then all of us who bought *Aladdin Sane* during the holidays ganged up and talked about it all the way back to Colditz.

It was really funny at first because, although we all said we had the LP, none of us wanted to believe that the others did, so first we had to ask things like, 'What did you think of the new version of "John I'm Only Dancing"?', or 'Which version of "All The Young Dudes" do you prefer – Bowie's or Mott's?' We were all trying to catch each other out, and couldn't discuss what was on the LP until we had all grokked[33] that we knew what we were talking about.

Because the album came out a week later than it was meant to (why?), none of us got it until right before coming back, but we all spent the entire last days of the holiday playing it over and over again. I read in *NME* (I think) that you had advance orders of 100,000, which is the first time anyone has done that since The Beatles. Congratulations!

To start with, don't worry, we all love it, although a couple of the others aren't sure it's better than *Ziggy*. I said it was and here's why. First off, it's a lot more varied. I love the way it slips between the really heavy songs like 'Watch That Man' and 'Let's Spend The Night Together', and the light ones, like 'Lady Grinning Soul' and 'The Prettiest Star'.

Aside from 'Drive-In Saturday', my favourite has to be 'Panic In Detroit', which is amazing! I can't believe how clever the

---

33 Apparently *Stranger In A Strange Land* made an impression!

arrangement is. Every instrument seems to be doing something different. I played it on headphones, and the drums and percussion are all over your head. So is Ronno's guitar, which reminds me a little of bits of the *Man Who Sold The World* LP. If you listen to the song with half an ear, it sounds like absolute chaos, but if you pay attention it doesn't matter which instrument you follow – everything makes perfect sense. I especially love the backing vocals! They remind me of The Rolling Stones' 'Gimme Shelter', cos again they are all over the place, but that's because they have to be – it's panic, after all.

After 'Panic In Detroit', 'Cracked Actor' left me feeling a little disappointed, but then I turned the album over and heard 'Time'. I was a bit embarrassed the first time, in case my mum heard you say 'wanking' and 'whore', but if she did she didn't say anything. The song took a little getting into, because you've broken it into those different movements, and the first part reminded me of 'Rock And Roll Suicide'. But then Ronno's guitar comes in and it goes off in a completely different direction. Who is Billy Dolls? I thought it might be Billy Murcia, the New York Doll who died last year, but Jonathan thinks it's one of the Bewlay Brothers. 'Whoever they are!' I replied.

'Prettiest Star' is amazing. You must love Angie a lot to have written such a beautiful song for her, and I bet she was thrilled that you recorded it again for this album, cos so many more people are going to hear it this time. If you released it as your new single, it'd sell millions. The backing vocals made me think of 'Drive-In Saturday' a little. They had that same updated-1950s feel. And the first time I heard Ronno's guitar solo it made the hairs on my arms stand up and gave me goose pimples! Sometimes when I listen to the album it's as much his record as yours.

Did you rerecord 'The Jean Genie'? It sounds a lot punchier on the LP than the single (although it could be my needle). Jonathan agreed with me, but said it might just have been remixed, which was really funny, cos this other boy named

Pollack The Bollock started arguing with him, saying that 'mixing' was the technical term for putting the songs in order! He's completely wrong, but he kept on arguing until, finally, Jonathan opened the train window and started to push the Bollock's head out. That's when Mr Yards came down the corridor and caught him. It was funny, though, because I don't think Yards likes the Bollock any more than we do, and he must have stood there watching for ages before he finally said, 'You'd be a lot better off waiting until there's a tunnel coming up, Jonathan. But as there won't be another one until we're nearly back in Bournemouth, you'd better let the boy go.' I wish all the teachers could be like him. And I wish he didn't teach Woodwork! I'm rubbish at it.

We arrived back at school, and the day kept on getting better. We found out that it's true about Soul Boy having the lurgy. We were even told to remember him in our prayers – although I was always under the impression that the Devil looks after his own, so I don't think there's any need for us to worry about him. I've always imagined hell to be a crowded disco playing wall-to-wall funk, so I'm sure he'll feel right at home.

Then while we were unpacking, Mr Vernon, who's our new housemaster, came in to introduce himself, before telling a whole bunch of us that Warthead wanted to see us. We went to his office, wondering what on earth we'd done, and spread out across his desk was all the stuff Mr Evans had confiscated from us over the school year!

There was my Plasticraft, some old issues of *NME*, a paperback of *Up The Chastity Belt* (you should read it, it's really funny) and my Bournemouth football programmes. Paul was given back a bunch of model aircraft and books, Gnome's Head got his copy of *Electric Warrior*, and there was stuff there that we'd completely forgotten about. Apparently, Evans left in such a hurry he didn't have a chance to scoop up all his ill-gotten gains. And that wasn't the end of it! The old crook had also kept a notebook, jotting down every time he'd fined us for breaking school rules – including a few he'd made up himself, like not whistling in the corridors, not turning the water off in the shower while soaping up, and not playing football on the hockey field. But he must have pocketed the money himself, instead of putting it into the school fund where fines are meant to go. So Warthead gave it all back to us! I got 68p back, Michael Nish got nearly a pound and Coconut got £1.76p!

We weren't given the cash (more's the pity – all our pocket money is kept by Warthead and his wife Gabby, and they dole it out as we need it), but we've all got much fatter accounts than we ever expected. I'd love to know what Evans did – there are rumours going around that he was messing around with some of the boys in one of the other dormitories, inviting them up to his rooms to play records and drink beer (and other things as well). The story I heard is that he was talking about music with Fatty Filer at the end of last term and, when Fatty said he liked you, Evans said that he knew how to play guitar the same way as you do. And we all know what he meant by that. Filer got away from him and went straight down to see Matron and told her what had happened. There's no way we'll ever find out if it's true, though, because Filer is one of those really stroppy fourth years who never talks to us. Besides, you never know whether you can believe stories like that. I think it's just as likely that Danny Meath put a spell on him, which is what he reckons happened.

Anyway, it's nearly lights out, so I'd better finish this up. I brought back some first-class stamps with me, so I'll post this to you tomorrow.

Best wishes

Gary

STOP PRESS!!!!!!!!!! I had to run down to Gabby's office to get this letter out of the outgoing mail box! At breaktime this morning, a few of us were in our common room playing records (*Aladdin Sane*, of course) when Wilky came in. He'd bought a copy of 'John I'm Only Dancing' during the Easter holidays and wanted us to hear it cos he said it sounded different. And he was right!

It's completely different, with more sax and a fantastic Ronno guitar freak-out at the end. None of us can explain it, but we told him to hang on to it cos it might be a really rare mistake. It looks exactly the same as my version, but when I looked at the writing scratched in the blank plastic around the label, his says 'B6BS-1956 A-2E', while mine says 'B6BS-1956'. Do you know anything about it? Is there anyone at RCA I can write to?[34]

---

34 The so-called 'sax mix' of 'John I'm Only Dancing' was recorded during the *Aladdin Sane* sessions and inadvertently issued when the original 45 was re-pressed during spring 1973.

Bournemouth, Hants
Friday 25 May 1973

Dear David

I didn't say anything to you about this before, because I didn't want to jinx it. But guess where I went last night? That's right – to Bournemouth Winter Gardens to see the best concert in the history of the world.

Warthead gave permission for a bunch of us to go to see you, as long as a teacher agreed to drive us there and pick us up afterwards. Mr Vernon said he would, so right after prep a dozen of us piled into Bessie the minibus and off we went. We reached the Winter Gardens at 7:30pm and there was already a long queue to get in, even though the doors didn't open until 8:00pm. We'd all bought tickets three weekends ago, when they first went on sale, which was just as well because there was a 'Sold Out' sign up on the box office.

A lot of the older kids were with us and they went off on their own, so that left Jonathan, Gnome's Head, Paul and I, because we were all sitting together. We were worried that we were going to look really out of place. In all the pictures we've seen from other concerts you've played, the entire audience seems to be done up like Ziggy or Aladdin (or Ronno), and all we had were our regular casual clothes. So all last week we were planning little additions that we could keep hidden until the others were out of sight. Gnome's Head had a black and gold headscarf that he stolen from his sister; Paul made a silver mirror from the lining from a pack of Park Drive, which he stuck to his forehead with Cow gum (of course, it kept falling off); and I tried making an earring out of a paper clip and a small crucifix, but it kept falling out as well. Jonathan went completely over the top, though. Under his shirt he had a T-shirt, which he'd ripped across his nipples, then glued some nylon (which he stole from his mum during the holidays!) across the hole! Then he poured an *entire* tube of silver glitter over his head! And after all that there was only about half a dozen other people who'd dressed up for the show. Everybody else looked so normal that Jonathan put his shirt back on, and Paul left his mirror in his pocket. (I'd already given up with my earring.)

We all bought souvenirs. I bought a blue and white silk scarf for 50p and an eight-page programme for 30p; Gnome's Head and Paul picked up badges (which I don't really like); and Jonathan went mad and bought one of everything. His mum had given him £3.00, which he has kept hidden in his shoe since we returned to Colditz (so it wouldn't be taken away and put into his account), and he spent the lot!

Our seats were near the back of the stalls, but we could see the stage perfectly. There were some idiots in front of us who stood up as soon as you came on, so we did the same, and by the end of the show I was standing on my seat. It was so exciting waiting for you to come on, the audience was really loud and enthusiastic, and when the lights went down and the Beethoven intro music began, everybody was howling and screaming. You could tell even then that the sound quality was going to be perfect. After reading the reviews of the Earl's Court concert, we were a bit worried about that, but there was no need.

We knew 'Hang Onto Yourself' and 'Ziggy Stardust' would open the show, but everything else was a complete surprise, especially the medleys.[35] I loved the bit where you climbed up the speakers during 'Free Festival', and 'Moonage Daydream' was the best thing I've ever heard. It went on for ever, and Ronno's solo at the end of the song sounded like galaxies exploding.

The costume changes were as far-out as I'd heard, and the only song that was unnecessary was 'Width Of A Circle', which went on way too long. I suppose it was meant to give you time to change into the next outfit, have a sit-down and a cigarette. It was nice that Ronno was given a break, as well, during Mike Garson's piano freak-out in 'Aladdin Sane'. I just wish you wouldn't do that mime where you pretend you're behind the

---

35 'Wild Eyed Boy From Freecloud'/'Oh You Pretty Thing'/'All The Young Dudes' and 'Quicksand'/'Life On Mars?'/'Memory Of A Free Festival'.

sheet of glass, trying to find the opening. At junior school we had a class called Free Expression, which was their way of trying to persuade us that it wasn't poofy old dancing, and that was one of the routines they used to make us do. Then, at the end of term, we had to put on a show for the parents and teachers, and that was part of it. Thankfully I escaped it, by enrolling in the version of *Pirates Of Penzance* (I played the Major-General). I was half expecting you to suddenly stand stock-still and wave your arms in the air, 'like a tree in the breeze'!!!!!!!!

The end of the concert was completely mental, especially 'Panic In Detroit'. I really wish I'd thought to bring a pen and write down the songs as you played them, because already I can't remember the order they were in. But I know that, no matter how many concerts I ever go to (and we're already trying to work out how to go to your Southampton show next month), this one will always be one of the best.

Best wishes, and good luck with the rest of the tour

Gary

Bournemouth, Hants
Tuesday 3 July 1973

Dear David

The tour is finally over (or it will be after tonight) and you must be absolutely knackered! I worked out that you've been on the road almost nonstop for more than 18 months, you've played all over the world and you've made one of the best LPs ever. I wouldn't blame you if you simply went home, locked the door and refused to get out of bed for the rest of the year! Will you get any chance for a rest before the next American tour starts? I hope so!

We didn't get the chance to see you again. Nobody knew exactly when you were playing! I wrote all the tour dates down in my diary when they were first announced, and you were playing Southampton on the 18th and Portsmouth on the 19th, but then we heard that you'd cancelled Portsmouth and moved Southampton to a bigger venue on the 19th. Anyway, did you know, you played Bournemouth on 25 May and Southampton on 19 June both this year and last year? Was this deliberate, or is it a really strange coincidence?

Not that it mattered where or when you were playing, because I wouldn't have been allowed to go. I was caught smoking in the cricket pavilion the week before – I wasn't the only one, but everybody else had finished theirs when Mongy (the mad scientist Physics teacher) came round the corner, as I was getting the last drags out of the butt. So I was put on the Restricted List for the weekend, and got fined.

Talking of concerts getting cancelled and moved around, my penfriend Dave lives in Leeds, and I received a really funny letter from him this morning, telling me about the concert you played at the Rollerena there on Friday. You were meant to have played the university the weekend before; Dave says you pulled out because 'the dressing-room mirrors weren't big enough or some such pop-starry thing'. There was a bit of an outcry, so you did the two shows at the roller-skating place instead.

Dave went with his girlfriend and another couple and, during the show, a girl in front of them climbed on her boyfriend's shoulders to get a better view. Dave's mate's girl, instead of asking her to get down because they couldn't see any more, went and pulled her off his shoulders and they rolled away across the floor, hissing and spitting at each other like two cats. Dave says his mate looked at him with one of those 'What shall we do?' looks, so Dave said, 'You'd better go and separate them.' Which he did, before they were all thrown out for brawling. And the two girls spent the rest of the concert casting hate-filled looks at each other! I loved Dave's last line, though. He wrote: 'And as for Ziggy? I don't think he even noticed.'

We didn't see any fights at the Bournemouth show, but Paul reckons he saw a couple having sex a few seats away from us. I bet that was uncomfortable! He says that when he joins the RAF he's going to have girls chasing after him all the time because they won't be able to resist the uniform. I told him if that was true, traffic wardens would be the sex gods of the world, but they always look really old and sad so he may need to rethink. I haven't really decided what I want to do when I'm sprung – it still seems so far away – but something to do with music would be good. I'd like to run my own second-hand record shop, but I'd probably end up keeping all the records for myself.

I really thought 'Life On Mars?' was going to go straight in at No.1 this week. I was listening to the Top 20 and it was getting really exciting as they counted down to the Top Five, because they were teasing us by saying you had the week's highest new entry. 'Honaloochie Boogie' was second highest, at No.14. Jonathan James read that you rewrote Ian Hunter's lyrics for the song, to make it more commercial. Is that true? And Linda Lewis, one of the backing vocalists on *Aladdin Sane*, was No.15! I don't think much of the record, 'Rock-A-Doodle-Doo', but it's good to see her getting the recognition. I also hope she's on *Top Of The Pops* this week, because I'm curious to see what she looks like.

George Harrison was No.10, then Paul Simon, T Rex ('The Groover' must be their worst record EVER!!!!!!!), Dave Edmunds, that stupid Snoopy Versus The Red Baron song was No.6, Fleetwood Mac were No.5 with the 'Albatross' reissue (I remember that from the first time around – I must be getting old). I said to Danny Meath that it was between you and 10cc for No.1, but he thought it'd be Peters And Lee, as old people have more money than kids and are probably buying hundreds of copies each just to put all the pop stars in their place!

You were finally in at No.4, which isn't bad, especially as the song is two years old and most people already have it on the *Hunky Dory* LP. Plus, you were only playing a little bit of it on tour. Did you know it was going to be the new single when you rehearsed the medley? If I were you, I'd have played the whole song, then told the audience to make sure they went out and bought it every night. Anyway, 10cc were No.3, Peters And Lee were No.2, which meant that Slade are still No.1, with their worst record ever (although the B-side, 'Kill 'Em At The Hot Klub Tonite', is OK). I'll listen to the Luxembourg charts tonight and see if you do any better there.

If I finish now, I can get this letter into the last post, so I hope you are well and feel rested soon.

Best wishes

Gary

Bournemouth, Hants
Wednesday 4 July 1973

Dear David

You've retired??????????????
I don't know what to say! We were still celebrating hearing that 'Life On Mars?' is No.2 on the Luxy[36] chart, behind Slade, when Kid Jensen broke the news at ten o'clock. I don't think I slept a wink all night thinking about it.

Coconut reckons it's all a publicity stunt, but I don't agree with him. It's like saying Don Powell crashed his car and killed his girlfriend[37] as a publicity stunt. You only have to look at the chart and see you're No.2 to know that you already sell enough records and sell out so many concerts that there'd be no point in doing something just to get your name in the newspapers. It's already in there quite enough. Plus, if you say something like that, you have to follow through, cos if you then carry on as normal your fans will feel betrayed and you'll end up not selling anything to anyone.

But what are you going to do now? Will you still make records? I hope so! It feels like the end of an era, though, and what happens to glam rock now that you're no longer around for everyone to rip off? Won't all the bands who've jumped on the bandwagon this year be confused! It's funny because last night, before we heard the news, Gnome's Head and I were talking with Bilge Rat, who is one of the third years (his name is Anton Gilbert but, if you only use his first initial, it becomes an anagram), about the way glam has been completely taken over by people who've no business even pretending they are part of it.

As far as I'm concerned, glam is things like you, Lou Reed, T Rex, Roxy Music and bits of Mott The Hoople and The Sensational Alex Harvey Band, who put on a show but perform songs with depth and meaning as well. All the other

36 Radio Luxembourg.
37 Slade drummer Powell was involved in a serious car accident that same evening.

groups, like Sweet, Slade and Wizzard, I call glitter rock. To people who don't understand music, there might not seem to be a difference – it's all men in make-up, after all. But glam is real. Glitter isn't.

Alex Harvey's version of Jacques Brel's 'Next' is amazing. He doesn't simply sing the song, he lives the words, and that's what music should be – real life twisted like a reflection in a fairground mirror, boys dressed as girls, but still looking like boys. Do you remember The Kinks' 'Lola', which was a No.1 in 1970? In a way that song summed up everything glam is – sleazy clubs, champagne and wide-eyed innocents not knowing who or what they were dancing with ('She walked like a woman and talked like a man'). Glam is about discovering yourself, through the example of people like you and Marc Bolan wearing make-up and glitter on *Top Of The Pops* and causing adults to have spazzy fits, *not* because they didn't like the music but because they didn't like the way he looked.

What's funny is that these are the same people who had arguments with their parents about Elvis Presley and The Beatles, and who shouted 'Right on' a lot! You hit the nail bang on the head in 'All The Young Dudes' – 'We never got off on that revolution stuff'. That kind of thing was ideal for the 1960s generation, but not for ours. We want something more than Mick Jagger blabbing on about streetfighting men. The world is a mess and it's going to keep on getting messier, no matter how many songs people sing about it. Musicians should forget trying to solve the problems in Northern Ireland, the Middle East and Vietnam, and pay attention to what's going on in our own lives.

The last Kinks album was called *Everybody's In Showbiz, Everybody's A Star*, and that's true. Whether they're famous or not, people should behave as though they are, and live out their fantasies in their normal life, because if you can't be honest to yourself and about yourself, what's the point? Sometimes people can take it too far, which is what *A Clockwork Orange* is about

(I've not seen the film, but I have read the book). But that's what *The Rocky Horror Show* is about, as well. I went to see it on the King's Road during the last school holidays and it was amazing – *Ziggy Stardust* meets *The Wizard Of Oz*. Was Frank N Furter based on Ziggy, do you think? (Or vice versa?) Except it wasn't the kids who killed him, but the conservatives (Riff Raff and Magenta), who wanted to return home and get back to 'normal' rather than press on with the fantasy.

Is that the way it always has to go? I was reading *A Wop Bop A Loo Bop* by Nik Cohn,[38] and it seems that rock history is a never-ending battle between the straights and the freaks, with the freaks leaping ahead (Elvis in 1956, the Stones and The Beatles in 1963, the hippies in 1967, glam in 1972), and then the straights trying to claw them back down, first by attacking them in the papers, then by dressing up as freaks themselves, so that the freaks don't look so freakish after all.

That's who the glitter groups are, the bands who know how to make big hit singles, but they don't have a clue about dressing up. You see a picture of Marc Bolan or The Spiders From Mars and it's easy to believe they wear the same clothes whether they're going on stage or digging in the garden. But nobody believes Roy Wood puts on all his make-up to go trolling round Sainsbury's buying beans and frozen veg. He gets away with it because everybody – from schoolteachers and parents to the record companies and the radio stations (let's not forget the BBC is controlled by the government) – wants him to, because he takes our minds off people like you, who are really doing something that challenges what society thinks is normal.

I saw an album by The Edgar Winter Group the other day, and they're wearing silver and glitter and rhinestones,[39] trying to fool us into thinking they're glam. The danger is they probably soon will be, because what will anyone have to compare them with? It sounds like Roxy Music are splitting up,[40] T Rex, Alice and Slade have completely lost it, and now you've 'kicked it in

38 The first (and still the greatest rock history) ever told.
39 *They Only Come Out At Night*.
40 Synth peacock Brian Eno quit for a solo career that same summer.

the head at 25'... Well, 26 actually (were you planning that when you wrote 'All The Young Dudes'?). Which is fine for you – but what about us?

I really hope you reconsider when you've had a chance to rest for a few days!

Best wishes

Gary

Chelsea, London SW10
Saturday 11 August 1973

Dear David

I'm sorry about that last letter I wrote. I went a little over the top on you. You can't be held responsible for the way other people use (or abuse) what you've made possible. In fact, in a way, maybe retiring was a good move because it forces people to make their own decisions rather than follow other people. Although it looks like you've started a new trend anyway. Have you noticed how many other people have retired since you took your final bow? Ray Davies of The Kinks, Rod Stewart, Jethro Tull and The Everly Brothers have all given up![41]

And it was reassuring to read in the music press that rumours of your retirement are exaggerated, and that you've simply given up playing regular concerts. Is it true that you're already planning to play the Marquee Club in October? I suppose it's probably too late to join your fan club and get tickets, isn't it? I'm not sure why I've never joined, but, between your diary[42] in *Mirabelle* (why did you pick a girl's magazine; it's so embarrassing going into Smith's every week to buy it?!) and the coverage in the press, I always wondered what other benefits there would be. Now I know!

That was an excellent interview you did with Charles Shaar Murray in *NME*. So many rock stars simply talk rubbish, and a lot of journalists let them get away with it. You sounded like you'd given some thought to the things you wanted to say.

I especially agreed with you when you said that there should be stars for every occasion, and that people should be able to pick two or three, depending upon what they needed them for. I used to think having favourite pop stars was the same as having a favourite football team, but it isn't. You pick

---

41 Or so it seemed. Davies recanted within days, while Rod Stewart (having announced his next solo LP would be his last) apparently immediately forgot ever saying such a thing. Tull's demise was simply a bad-tempered reaction to a few bad reviews, and did anyone even care about the Everlys in 1973?

42 A weekly column penned by publicist Cherry Vanilla – of dubious value to historians, but immense importance to the fan base. Where else would they discover how David liked his toast prepared?

a team for whatever reason, and it doesn't matter how shitty they get, you're stuck with them. There's an old man at Dean Court who I talk to at half-time sometimes. He's been supporting Bournemouth since he was a boy, back in the 1920s, even though they've never won a sausage and never look likely to.

He says his love of Bournemouth has lasted longer than any other relationship in his entire life, including two marriages and half a dozen jobs, and he still doesn't know what he sees in them. But he could never change and start supporting another team, even though he has tried. He said he started going to see Southampton instead, back in the 1950s, but returned to Bournemouth because he realised he was spending every game waiting for the half-time scoreboard to come up, so he could see how they were doing.

I don't think most pop fans have the same loyalty. I consider myself to be one of your biggest fans, but I've often wondered what would happen if you made an LP I didn't like. Would I have to stay a fan out of loyalty? Like if a tree fell on your head and you went disco-shit. Would I listen? Would I still care? I suppose I'd probably wait and see what the next one was like, but I wouldn't be out buying it on the day of release.

When I first came to this school, in September 1971, Atomic Rooster and Curved Air were really popular groups, and everyone went out and bought 'Devil's Answer' and 'Back Street Luv'. Today, you hardly ever hear those groups mentioned any more, because everybody's moved on. The only people who seem to have stayed loyal are Beatles fans. One of our teachers, Mr Pinkney, saw them play a concert in 1963 and, ten years on, he still reckons they're the best group in the history of the universe. I wonder if people will be saying the same thing in 1983 about the groups and singers who are that popular today. Mr Pinkney laughed his head off when I asked him about that, and said the only people who'll still care about Suzi Quatro, Mud and Gary Glitter will be their grandchildren.

Everyone else will have found new stars, like you said they should – or else they'll have gone back and rediscovered old stars, which sounds a lot like what you are doing with the new LP. Is it really going to be *all* 1960s cover versions? I hope so, because I really liked your version of 'Let's Spend The Night Together' (on *Aladdin Sane*). It was much heavier than the Stones' original, and a lot dirtier as well. My stepfather heard me playing it and went mental. He walked in for the bit where you go, 'They say that we're too young' and the guitar makes that loud grinding noise, and said it was the filthiest thing he'd ever heard and he was surprised shops were allowed to sell things like that to kids. He really is an idiot.

I expect you'll be recording some Velvet Underground songs as well? Try 'Venus In Furs' – it's such a bizarre sound on that record, but with modern technology you could make it even weirder. You should record some Iggy Pop songs, too. I have his *Raw Power* LP and it's incredible. I read some reviews where the journalists were complaining about the sound, saying it was muddy and dense, but that's what makes it special – the fact that there's not another record on earth that feels like that. And that's important.

There are so many groups who sound the same, and who make records that have the exact same noises and special effects on them, and then something like *Raw Power* comes along and it doesn't sound like anything – except, maybe, a lift full of fat people falling down the shaft...for 40 minutes. I don't think it's necessarily a record you play for fun – it's more a statement of what is possible if people would only have the courage to follow their own ideas, rather than cling on to someone else's. I wish more people would realise that that is far more important than having hits – it's what keeps music alive. In years to come, when (as Mr Pinkney said) Suzi Quatro has been forgotten, *Raw Power* will still be there, blurging out its nasty noise and people will still be putting it on and saying, 'Bugger me'. Again, a star for a certain occasion.

Anyway, that's all, so I hope you get this letter – I'm writing c/o the Chateau d'Heureville studio – did you know Elton John's *Honky Chateau* album was named after the same place? Maybe you should cover 'Rocket Man' as well!

Best wishes

Gary

Bournemouth, Hants
Wednesday 26 September 1973

Dear David

Well, here I am, in Group Three at last. It seems so strange to think that I was only a first year when I started writing to you. Now there's a whole new intake of the grotty little things, and this bunch are even worse than the last. I'll soon be 14 (in December), so I try not to have much to do with them – we let Group Two (last year's firsts, of course) take care of them and make sure they remain in their lowly place.

Aside from that, things haven't changed much. We still have the same boring routine of the same boring lessons, and we've been moved into another dormitory – the worst one of them all, because at one end there's a flight of stairs that leads down to the flats where the live-in staff stay (that's Warthead, the deputy head and all the housemasters). Some of their windows look directly into our dorm as well, so not only do we have to look like we're behaving ourselves, but we have to *sound* like it as well, which means no playing loud music in either our dorm or our common room.

Of course, it's completely a matter of trial and error if something is too loud, and I bet you'll never guess what I was playing the first time I was busted? 'Width Of A Circle'? 'Watch That Man'? 'Panic In Detroit'? No, it was 'The Laughing Gnome', and I don't know who was more embarrassed – Mr Vernon for rushing up the stairs convinced we were having a heavy-metal riot, or me for being caught happily singing along with the chorus. It must be really strange for you to see it going up the chart like it is, after five years of total obscurity. It's No.14 this week and it's bound to enter the Top Ten next week, although I don't think we'll be seeing you do it on *Top Of The Pops* tomorrow. Maybe they'll have Pan's People dance instead. That'll be amusing.

Did you know it was coming out when you set the release for 'Sorrow' – your 'real' new single? It is confusing; I was in Smith's and asked if they had your new single, thinking they'd know what I meant, and they'd already taken 'The Laughing Gnome' off the shelf and rung it up before I even had a chance to say, 'Not that one.' I bought it anyway, to keep the collection complete, but I wonder if people who are less fanatical than me might feel a bit cheated when they hear it? There again, it'll probably be a shock to get 'Sorrow' if you're expecting to pick up 'The Laughing Gnome'. I'm assuming your version isn't going to be quite as wet as the Merseys' original, is it?

I'm really looking forward to hearing *Pin-Ups* when it comes out next month. It's an interesting idea doing all covers, and narrowing them down to one period of time is really smart. I saw a track listing for Bryan Ferry's album, which is *also* covers-only, but it's all over the place – 1940s, 1950s and 1960s. I suppose it's a complete coincidence that you both came up with this idea at the same time, isn't it, although I love the idea of you getting together and plotting these things, just to keep people wondering.

I remember nearly all of the songs you've covered, and I have the originals of 'Shapes Of Things' by The Yardbirds, 'I Can't Explain' by The Who and 'Where Have All The Good Times Gone' by The Kinks (the B-side of 'Dedicated Follower Of Fashion') – Boccy Leckies have boxes full of old singles for 5p each, so I've been picking up as many as I can. I'm going to try to find all the others; I looked them up in *Rock File*[43] and they were all big hits. If they don't have them at Boccy Leckies, I'll get them from the Vintage Record Centre in Caledonian Road at half term. I went there quickly during the summer holidays and it's the best record shop in the world!

I found copies of your American singles, 'Changes' and 'Time' – but can you believe they released that as a single? When I saw it had been edited, I was convinced they'd have cut off the opening verses, so when I played it I was amazed to hear them

43 The first in a series of five annual editions edited by Charlie Gillett, a precursor of the Guinness *British Hit Singles*. Essential reading for the adolescent fact fiend.

in all their glory. Someone told me the word 'wanking' doesn't mean anything over there, but I'm sure 'whore' does and, even in 1973, that's not exactly the kind of word you expect to hear blaring out of the radio, is it?

There again, any country that has the name 'Randy' probably deserves what it gets. I feel so sorry for someone like Randy Jackson of The Jackson Five, coming to England for the first time and having everyone crease up laughing when he announces, 'I'm Randy.' 'That's nice, young man, but it's probably a good idea to introduce yourself first.'

Anyway, I'd better go, as there's a school outing to the cinema to see *That'll Be The Day* in Bournemouth. I hope it's as good as it's meant to be!

Hope all is well

Gary

Bournemouth, Hants
Saturday 20 October 1973

Dear David

I'm writing this on Saturday afternoon in the dining room, as I'm not allowed out this weekend – or any other weekend for that matter. And why? Because I did a bunk Thursday evening to see you play at the Marquee. I surrendered myself to the law late last night and have been in chains in the dungeon ever since.

BUT IT WAS WORTH IT!!!!!!!!!!!!!!!!!!!!

It started on Wednesday during Woodwork. Gnome's Head, Nish and I were talking about the Marquee concerts,[44] and how much we hate being at boarding school, because if we weren't we'd have been able to go. I was still thinking about it the next evening so, after tea, I bunked out, cut up through the woods and made it to Boscombe train station. There's never anybody on duty there during the evenings, so I sneaked on to the platform, and within ten minutes the London train came! They probably hadn't even noticed I was missing back at Colditz either, so I knew I was OK as long as a ticket inspector didn't get on board.

The journey took ages, because it was the slow train and stopped at virtually every station between here and London. I thought about changing at Southampton, but there's always inspectors on the fast train, so I decided I was better off where I was. I was at Waterloo Station by ten o'clock, which is when I started having second thoughts a bit, as I only had 60p on me. Thank goodness I remembered to wear my parka, though, so I wouldn't freeze. Of course it was raining.

I was going to tell my parents I was there, but I knew they'd make me go back to jail, so I waited till all the lights were out in the house and spent the night in the garden shed. It was freezing cold and I hardly slept, plus I was starving to death, but I survived the night, and in the morning I sneaked out and had breakfast on King's Road. Then I walked into the West End,

---

44 Bowie took over the Marquee for three days (18–20 October) to shoot a performance for American TV's *Midnight Special*, punningly titled The 1980 Floor Show.

which took hours, and finally arrived at Wardour Street around one o'clock.

Even though it was raining, there was already a huge crowd of people there, so I knew that, even if anyone did think of looking for me there, they'd never find me. I managed to join up with a bunch of kids who were a bit older than me, who didn't have tickets and were trying to find a way of sneaking in. Of course we were caught by the gorilla on the door, so we walked around to the back of the building so we could hear what was going on inside. We stood around there for a while when this American guy, who was one of the film crew, started talking to a couple of the girls – and then he stepped aside and said that if we were all to run in while his back was turned he'd never notice. So that's what we did!

It was amazing! Even when there was nothing happening on the stage, which was most of the time, the entire room was alive with excitement. I saw Angie and Tony DeFries,[45] and tried to get Ronno's autograph, but he disappeared into the dressing room before I could get through the crowd. Wayne County was standing right by us, though, in a bright red nightdress, with a huge blond Afro and a metal handbag with 'Something Queen' written on it, so I went over to ask for his autograph and ended up talking to him for ages. He said that he's making an album with you and Ronno, and that you're trying to work out what songs you want to put on it. One idea was to do a bunch of cover versions of songs that didn't get on to *Pin-Ups*, but you don't want to do that so soon, so you're going to record his own songs instead.

While we were talking, Cherry Vanilla came over and asked Wayne who his 'little friend' was. So he introduced us, and she was wonderful as well. A few other people had wandered over to talk to them, and ask questions about you, so Cherry told how she first met you when she was in London with *Pork* ,[46] and that after you'd been to see their show, they went to see one of yours, back in the days when you had long hair and still played acoustic guitar.

45 Bowie's manager, visionary head of the Mainman company.
46 The Andy Warhol play, staged at the Roundhouse during 1971.

Then the next time they saw you, a year later, you'd turned into Ziggy and they barely recognised you! Cherry also said that you don't write your diary in *Mirabelle*, because she does it for you! That's so funny, as it reads like you were writing it. I suppose that's why you employed her, though, because she can make it seem so real. Anyway, don't worry, I won't tell anybody – and I'll make sure I keep reading it as well! Wayne said you might be making a record with Cherry. I hope so.

The other person I talked to was Scott Richardson. I didn't know who he was, but I saw him talking with some other fans so I walked over, as he was telling them that he's also making a record with you! No wonder you wanted to retire from live work, with all these other projects flying around! Apparently it was him who suggested you record the two Pretty Things songs? He looks amazing, sort of a space-age James Dean in this far-out Sterling Cooper canvas outfit, and he mentioned that he used to be in a band called SRC, who I've never heard of. But, as soon as I can break out of this place again, I'm going to look for their records.

Was it Carmen or The Troggs who played first? I only caught the end of the show and wasn't sure. Wayne said that there had been plans for both him and Cherry to do some songs as well, but the TV people were running behind and they had to cancel. I tried to get to the front of the stage when you came on, but the crowd was too thick. I saw most of it, though, and it sounded amazing. The songs from *Pin-Ups* were really impressive, and it was hilarious when you introduced 'I Can't Explain' as 'The Laughing Gnome'! I wonder what would've happened if you'd sung the song?

I assume the '1984' song is from the rock opera you're writing around the George Orwell book? We read that in English class earlier this year and, when I heard you were planning to make it into a musical, my first reaction was 'How?' But if Lou Reed can make an entire LP about divorce and suicide,[47] then *1984* doesn't seem too far of a stretch. Plus,

47 *Berlin*, issued earlier in the summer.

now I've heard one of the songs you've written for it, it's going to be really good.

I also really liked the version of 'I Got You Babe' you did with Marianne Faithfull. What a fantastic outfit she was wearing – I thought it was a regular nun's habit until she turned around! Her voice has really changed since 'As Tears Go By' (which somebody told me she sang the day before; I can't believe I missed it), but she looked really good.

They pushed us out of the club really quickly at the end, so I didn't get the chance to say goodbye to anyone, which was a shame. I went back around to the back door, but there were so many people there that I knew I wouldn't have a chance of seeing anybody, so I left and went to Wimpy's for dinner. That was when the sheer enormity of what I'd done sunk in – I'd bunked off school, and I know from when other boys have run away that the entire place goes into complete chaos. There would probably be teachers driving all around Bournemouth looking for me, Warthead would have phoned home and the police – and I'd be in for the biggest bollocking of my life!

I did think about trying to sneak on to a train going back to Bournemouth, creep back into school and then deny that I'd been anywhere at all, but I didn't think that would work. So then I wondered what *you* would do under similar circumstances, and the answer hit me like a thunderbolt. I should make the most dramatic return I could! So I walked to Leicester Square and turned myself into the police!

I asked if they were looking for a boy who'd run away from a Dickensian workhouse in Bournemouth to see David Bowie. They didn't say yes or no, but they took the school's phone number and called, arranged for somebody to come and pick me up – and then they made me sit in the waiting room.

They were really nice to me. They gave me a cup of tea and some biscuits, and a policewoman came over and asked if I'd run away for any particular reason, like bullies or the teachers. I almost told her no, that I'd wanted to see David Bowie, but then I thought if they asked how I got in, or reached London in the first place, I might get into even deeper trouble. So I told her I was homesick, but hadn't had the guts to call home, so I simply walked around London for the day.

Warthead finally arrived at the police station in the middle of the night, and I could see from his face that all he wanted to do was beat the shit out of me. Thankfully, the policewoman talked to him before he had the chance, and he barely said a word to me all the way back to Bournemouth. He told me to sit in the back seat and try to get some sleep, but of course I was still so excited after the concert that that was the last thing I was going to do. Then, when we reached the school, I was told I had to sleep in the sick bay, so I didn't disturb the rest of my dormitory. You should have seen their faces when I appeared at breakfast this morning! And you can imagine how jealous they all were when I told them where I'd been!

After breakfast, I was called into Warthead's office, with about five other teachers and our housemaster, to be told how worried everyone had been (a likely story!) and that, if I had any problems, the only way to solve them was to talk to somebody about it, not to run away. Then, just as I was convinced I'd got away with it, Mr Vernon said, 'Of course, if we find out you didn't run away because you were unhappy, but because you wanted to go to a pop concert, that would be another matter entirely.' I don't know if he overheard me talking at breakfast, or if somebody grassed me up, but it turned out they knew exactly where I'd been.

So I've been placed on the Restricted List, which means I can't leave the school buildings for the rest of this half term (which thankfully is only another week), and then for next half as well, until they think that I've learned my lesson. I've also been fined and Warthead says I have to write a letter of apology to British Rail and tell them I'll never bunk a ride on a train again!

He even asked me if I had any souvenirs from the concert, so I said I didn't (because I know he was looking for something to confiscate), which is only half a lie – do autographs count as souvenirs? Especially as he won't have heard of either Cherry, Wayne or Scott. I've also been told that I'm not allowed to watch *Top Of The Pops* or read *NME* any more, because they're obviously bad influences on me, and when I returned to my cubicle I found all the posters had been torn down off my locker and thrown away! I am to be a Pop-Free Zone. Thank goodness I keep all my records in the common room, mixed up with everybody else's, because they'd probably have been taken away as well.

Anyway, as you can imagine, I can't wait for half term – but in the meantime thank you for a fantastic concert!

Gary

PS If this reaches you looking a bit folded up, that's because I'm writing it secretly and will have to hide it in my shoe until I can think of a way of posting it. Hopefully, Gnome's Head or someone will take it for me when they go out tomorrow.

PPS Who or what is Boz Scaggs?[48]

---

48 It was reported in the press that Bowie and American singer Scaggs were planning to record an album together.

Bournemouth, Hants
Wednesday 31 October 1973

Dear David

Amazing! I arrived home and absolutely nothing was said about my adventures last week. I wonder if the school didn't really phone, figuring it'd be embarrassing to call up and say, 'Hello, we've lost Gary.' Or maybe it's being kept back to use against me at some future date. You can never tell with parents.

Anyway, I've been home for a week (and it's back to Colditz on Monday, so we miss Bonfire Night – typical!), and I've spent most of my time at the Vintage Record Centre. I love that shop: so far I've found original singles of every song from *Pin-Ups* except 'See Emily Play' and 'Sorrow' – the guy there said a lot of people have been asking for that since you covered it. 'See Emily Play' is on a Pink Floyd compilation called *Relics*, and I may have to get that instead. I also bought the first SRC album. It was a bit more expensive than I hoped it'd be, and I wasn't really sure about getting it, in case it was rubbish. Thankfully, it's OK, a lot like really early Procol Harum, only without the Extremely Serious Expressions. I can't wait to hear the album you're making with SR himself.

Of course I've also bought *Pin-Ups* and your 'Sorrow' single, with Jacques Brel's 'Amsterdam' on the B-side. What was it like to meet him when you were in Paris back in May? It must be strange being able to meet your heroes so easily, knowing that they probably know as much about you as you do about them. I know it was very different when you met Andy Warhol.[49] Apparently he simply took photographs of your shoes and hardly spoke to you, even though you'd written a song for him. That's so rude and ungrateful, but I bet he wouldn't have acted like that if you'd been as famous then as you are now.

Did you tell Brel you've been playing his songs in concert, and that you'd recorded 'Amsterdam'? I'm glad you've finally

49 At the Factory, New York, in late 1971.

released it and it's gratifying to see the single doing so well, because I was worried people might take your 'retirement' the wrong way and stop buying your records. It was No.4 this week. Maybe this'll be your first No.1? I also picked up Brown Furry's[50] 'A Hard Rain's A-Gonna Fall'. I've not bought up the album yet but, from what I've heard, yours is truer to the spirit of the originals. I love Bryan Ferry, but he sometimes tries too hard to *be* Bryan Ferry, if you see what I mean. Did you see the film on *Top Of The Pops*? He's sitting at the piano, but he's doing his best to look smooth and sophisticated, even in a dirty T-shirt. And it sounds like he really works hard at the songs, to get the mood and arrangement just perfect, whereas *Pin-Ups* sounds like a band simply kicking into a bunch of their favourite oldies, relaxing and having a fun time – which is important, because that's exactly what the originals sounded like.

You read interviews with Pete Townshend these days and he's always so full of himself and how important he is, but play 'I Can't Explain' or 'Anyway Anyhow Anywhere' and you know such lofty thoughts were the last thing on the group's mind when they made those records. The same with the two Pretty Things songs, 'Rosalyn' and 'Don't Bring Me Down'. I read that at one point The Pretty Things were even wilder than the Stones, and their records certainly sound it... And, talking of the Stones, what do you think of *Goat's Head Soup*? 'Angie', in particular? Everybody's saying it's about your Angie, although it's more likely that Jagger/Richard just picked the name because it is all over the place at the moment, thanks to her. You watch – if Cherry's album does as well as it should, they'll probably have a song called 'Cherry' as well.[51]

My favourite song on *Pin-Ups* has to be 'Where Have All The Good Times Gone', though. The Kinks' version is wonderful, but you really bring a new dimension to it. It has that same kind of grinding feel to it as 'The Jean Genie', and you make the lyrics seem really wistful and nostalgic, whereas The Kinks sounded more sarcastic. Did you have a firm reason for

50 Bryan Ferry.
51 The Cherry album never happened, but the Stones did a song anyway, a cover of the reggae classic 'Cherry Oh Baby', on 1976's *Black And Blue*.

ending the album with that song? My theory is, partly you're asking why life today isn't as simple/pure as it was back when those records were first out, but you're also presenting *Pin-Ups* as the latest instalment of the story you began with *Ziggy Stardust* – the clock's still ticking down the five years, the world (as seen through *Aladdin Sane*) is falling apart, and now you're focusing in on the two lovers in 'Drive-In Saturday'.

Pin-Ups is intended as a kind of *Desert Island Discs* compilation album for them, which is why you've filled it with songs that are looking forward to their time, even as they're looking back towards ours – things like 'Shapes Of Things', 'See Emily Play' and 'Everything's Alright' – and the album itself ends with 'Anyway Anyhow Anywhere'. Then 'Where Have All The Good Times Gone' comes in, which is them singing back to the record. And that's why you have Twiggy (Twig The Wonder Kid) on the cover, because – again, as 'Drive-In Saturday' makes plain – she is one of the few images from our time that has survived into theirs.

What are your next plans? I know you've been recording for your next album, but have you started work yet on *A Stranger In A Strange Land*? You've killed Ziggy, but how fitting that you should be reincarnated as his brainy brother!

Finally, remember I told you about the girl Kathy who I met at the Mainman offices a while back? I've seen her around a few times since then, so last week I asked her out. We're going to go to the Marquee tomorrow night to see Skin Alley, because they have a track on the same side of the *Glastonbury Fayre* album as you do.[52] I don't know if it'll be any good because that's the only song I've heard by them, but it beats staying in to watch *Top Of The Pops*!

Wish me luck!

Gary

---

52 A 1972 three-LP compilation based around the previous year's free festival. Bowie contributed an unreleased *Ziggy*-era version of 'The Supermen', and Skin Alley offered 'Sun Music'.

```
Bournemouth, Hants
Tuesday 8 January 1974
```

Dear David

Happy birthday – belated! Sorry for not writing sooner, but last term at school was hectic, because we were taking our end-of-term exams. Thankfully all the fuss about my 'trip' to London had blown over by the end of the half-term holiday – I arrived back in the jug again expecting my punishment would carry on, but nothing was said, and I wasn't on the Restricted List any longer. Maybe the staff had been at the Christmas spirits.

How was your Christmas? Mine was dull. I was hoping to see Kathy again, but she didn't call and she doesn't have a telephone, and, the couple of times I went round to her place, I'm not sure whether the guy who answered the door even spoke English. So I spent most of the time touring London record shops. I wish the old Mainman offices were still open, although I suppose New York makes more sense, now that you're into making films. Are you still going to do *A Stranger In A Strange Land*? Or has *Octobriana*[53] taken its place?

I also went down to Trident Studios, where you are recording The Astronettes' album, but the only person I saw was the guitarist from Queen – big deal! I saw them supporting Mott at the Bournemouth Winter Gardens last year, and I really wasn't impressed. They looked good and the singer can do some amazing things with his voice, but the songs were boring heavy-metal plods and the last thing we need is another Silverhead.

The only new group I've heard that I like is Cockney Rebel. Their album *The Human Menagerie* is brilliant. If you haven't heard it yet, you should get a copy now! They're a glam band, but they have a full orchestra behind them – although it's nothing like that dreadful classical rock-concerto thing that Deep Purple did a few years back. The orchestra is playing with the band; it's more like the strings you had on *Space Oddity*, but

---

53 Based on Peter Sadecky's comic strip, *Octobriana* was to star Amanda Lear in the title role, but the project ultimately fizzled. As did *A Stranger In A Strange Land*…

much more dramatic and symphonic. Plus, Steve Harley, Rebel's lead singer, is just about the only person I've heard who's honest enough to admit that they were inspired to go glam by the bands that were there before them.[54] A lot of the others (Queen included) expect us to believe that they've always looked and dressed like this, and it's pure coincidence that everybody else is doing it as well. Did you hear that Larry Lurex single last summer? That was Queen under a different name, and it shows how original they really are. Not at all.

You probably hate it, but my favourite record right now is Alvin Stardust's 'My Coo-Ca-Choo'. It reminds me a bit of 'Spirit In The Sky'; the guitar is very similar. But the record has an amazing sound, really dirty and sinister, and Stardust looks terrific. I keep reading things about Gene Vincent, the old 1950s rock 'n' roll guy – how he dressed in black and had a gammy leg that he used as a stage prop. Alvin Stardust is kind of what I imagine he'd have been like, although instead of having a bad leg he has a really bizarre way of holding his microphone. I know it's probably all image (Coconut swears the first time he saw Stardust, on *Lift Off* during the holidays, he was wearing all pink), but I love it.

I also really like the B-side of Slade's 'Merry Xmas Everybody', 'Don't Blame Me'. After all we hear about bands ripping each other off, this one goes for the throat so hard that you know it's a total piss-take. It starts out exactly the same as T Rex's 'Jeepster', then turns into 'Baby Please Don't Go' halfway through. Everyone I've played it to reckons it shows how quickly Slade are running out of original ideas, but I think it's brilliant.

However, I'm deeply ashamed to admit that I also had high hopes for Leo Sayer. The first time I heard 'The Show Must Go On', and saw him on *Top Of The Pops* in the Pierrot costume, it reminded me of the first time I saw you, because he was doing something that seemed so different from everybody else. So I rushed out and bought his LP *Silver Bird* with one of my

54 In 1974, Harley credited Bowie's *Ziggy Stardust* shows with giving him the impetus to form his own band.

Christmas record tokens. And what a load of shit it is – a heap of poxy old ballads, with every song slower and gushier than the one before.

I took it back to the shop the same afternoon and swapped it for ELP's *Brain Salad Surgery*. I got the free flexidisc in *NME* before Christmas, so at least I knew what to expect, although they could spend some more time on their lyrics. In English today, Paul ripped off one of ELP's lyrics, rhyming 'sadder', 'madder' and 'get me a ladder' in a poem, to see what would happen. He ended up with a 'C'. He should now tear the page out of his English book and post it to Greg Lake.

Not long now until your new single comes out. I was also interested to hear that you've recorded one with Lulu. You're really into reviving the 1960s, aren't you? It's good that you're doing a couple of your old songs, rather than some of hers. When I first heard about it, all I could think of was the two of you duetting on 'I'm A Tiger' maybe, or 'Boom Bang A Bang'. 'The Man Who Sold The World' and 'Watch That Man' are much better choices. Her oldie, 'Shout', was on the radio recently, and it was hard to believe it was the same Lulu who made all those horrible records at the end of the 1960s.

Is there any news on any of the other album projects I've heard about? Ronno, Wayne, Cherry, Scott, The Astronettes, Steeleye Span, Adam Faith?[55] What about the live album from the Hammersmith concert? I know it's called *Bowie-ing Out*, and there'll be a film to go with it, but that's about all. I was hoping it'd be out for Christmas, but I suppose with *Pin-Ups* and then the new single coming out so close to each other, we're going to have to wait until the summer.[56] That probably makes sense anyway, because all your fans will be on their summer holidays, and will be able to get to the pictures easier. I hardly ever get to go during the school term, but at holidays I always try to see a couple of films.

55 The Ronson and Steeleye Span albums alone emerged, both boasting minimal Bowie involvement – three songs on Ronson's album and some asthmatic sax on one song on Steeleye's.
56 In fact, the film and accompanying soundtrack album were not released until 1983, as *Ziggy Stardust: The Motion Picture*. An edited version was, however, screened on US TV during 1974.

I really enjoyed *That'll Be The Day*. It's the first film I've seen that makes the 1950s seem like they might have been fun – I hate so much of the music that I've heard from that time, and it really pisses me off that I was born two days before the 1960s started. What awful timing! If mum had kept her legs crossed for another 48 hours, I'd have been fine.

I also went to see Pink Floyd's *Live At Pompeii*, but it was one of the most boring things I've ever seen or heard. That surprised me, because I quite liked bits of *Dark Side Of The Moon*, and I love *Relics*, which is that collection of old singles and album tracks (including 'See Emily Play') I told you about. The *Pompeii* thing, though, was just background music with a lot of cymbals. Truly dreadful. As far as Pink Floyd goes now, I'd like to hear more stuff by Syd Barrett. Apparently he was only with Floyd for their first two albums, then left to go solo. I can't say I blame him. He probably heard them rehearsing 'Set The Controls For The Heart Of Something Indescribably Pointless And Boring' and figured there was no point in even offering them songs like 'Bike' or 'Arnold Layne' any more. Has he heard your version of 'See Emily Play', do you think? It's the one song on *Pin-Ups* where you moved away from the original arrangement and made it more of a Bowie song, and it does stick out a little bit. You might have been better off saving it for the *Son Of Pin-Ups* album, with 'White Light White Heat', 'God Only Knows' and 'Ladytron'.[57] I couldn't believe it when I read you'd recorded that one, by the way, but I know it's going to be amazing.[58]

When is your new album coming out? According to *Record Mirror*, it's called *Revenge: Or The Best Haircut I Ever Had*. What a fantastic title!

Best wishes and, again, belated Happy Birthday!

Gary

---

57 These and several other songs were all rumoured to have been taped during the *Pin-Ups* sessions. In fact, the only one they tackled was 'White Light', which Bowie then handed over to Mick Ronson. 'God Only Knows' was recorded with The Astronettes, but remained unreleased until the mid-1990s. 'Ladytron' was never even considered, although journalist Charles Shaar Murray did report seeing the sheet music in the studio.
58 See above!

To Major Tom

Bournemouth, Hants
Tuesday 29 January 1974

Dear David

Just wanted to drop you a quick line to say I almost heard 'Rebel Rebel' on Radio 1 today! Except they didn't play it.

There's a bug going around the school and I caught it, so I was kept in bed all day, with my tranny and three other sickies for company. Anyway, Gnome's Head reckoned that, while I was having my temperature taken by Matron (101 degrees! George Orwell would be thrilled), they said on the radio that they were going to be playing the new David Bowie single. But, because none of us has heard it, we weren't sure whether we'd recognise it – which ended up hysterically funny for most of us, and really embarrassing for Coconut, because every time something we'd not heard before came on, he'd shout, 'Shut up! This is it!'

Which means we sat there patiently for hours, only for Gnome's Head to finally admit he'd heard it wrong, and it was Marc Bolan's 'Teenage Dream' that they were playing, not the new Bowie. If we hadn't all been feeling so sick, we'd have pummelled him to a pulp. Still, at least we know you're not going to have any competition in the charts, as virtually everything they played today was sheer crap. I do like 'Teenage Dream' – very grandiose and dramatic, and it doesn't sound anywhere near as desperate as some of his recent singles. And I don't mind The Hollies' 'The Air That I Breathe' (Coconut reckons that's Ronno on guitar – is it?). But have you ever spent an entire day listening to Radio 1? It's completely soul-destroying. Not only do they keep playing the same records you've been hearing all week, they often play the same records you've been hearing all day. The only highlight was the chart rundown, and that turned out to be a load of rubbish as well. 'Tiger Feet' is still No.1, 'Teenage Rampage' is No.2, The New

Seekers are No.3. The only bright spot is that Lulu's 'The Man Who Sold The World' is in at No.13, so well done.

It's a terrific version of the song: very different to the original and one of the best cover versions you've ever had. Did you hear Simon Turner's 'The Prettiest Star'? I know Angie liked it (probably because it was written about her), but I don't think it was a patch on the original. The Lulu record, though, is really rocking, and your sax playing is the best ever. I don't normally like saxophones – they always sound like croaky old geese to me, half coughing, half honking. But you make it play a melody properly.

The other record I sort of like is 'Dance With The Devil' by Cozy Powell, although Daniel Moppett, who's one of the dayboys in my class, told me that it was ripped off from Jimi Hendrix's 'Third Stone From The Sun', which he found on one of those old *Backtrack* albums. Anyway, it's really hard to keep on liking a song once you realise how unoriginal it is, although – having listened to the entire Hendrix album – I do think Cozy stole the only bit worth stealing. I quite like a couple of Hendrix singles (I have 'Purple Haze'), but I don't understand why people go on about his guitar playing so much. Most of it sounds like he's still tuning up, and he's not a patch on people like Ronno, Jeff Beck or even Marc Bolan – the end section of 'Elemental Child' is my favourite guitar solo EVER.

Moppett reckons you wrote 'Ziggy Stardust' about Hendrix, and he's probably right, but I had a great time winding him up by arguing that you were really talking about Paul McCartney – because not only does he play left-handed, but he also has a far more 'snow white tan' than Hendrix! And the line about the kids killing the man works better, because of that rumour in America that Paul was dead. In other words, the kids really did kill him.

Moppett thought he had me with the 'Weird' and 'Gilly' bit, because there were three other Beatles, but only two in the Hendrix Experience – so I told him it was Linda McCartney and

Denny Laine, the only members of Wings to have stayed in the band since the beginning. And the cat from Japan was Yoko! It really was funny, because by the end he was believing me. And then Bilge Rat walked in and ruined it, by picking up the record sleeve and saying, 'Hendrix is phenomenal! Did you know Bowie wrote "Ziggy Stardust" about him?' The bastard – I should go and replace all his Genesis records with copies of *Silver Bird*.

Are you living in America now, or just visiting? What is it like over there? I've only ever seen it on telly, but it must be pretty exciting. Everything looks so much bigger and more modern than over here, although aren't you worried about all the crime? Or did you take your bodyguards with you? I know I would have. What's your house like? Do you have a big car? If you do, I hope it's one of those really flashy ones with the fins, and a television in the back.

Have you been at all hit by the energy crisis? We were really hoping that school would have to go on a three-day week like all the shops and factories, but it didn't work out like that. We have to freeze our nuts off and sit in the dark because they've turned the heat down and taken away half the lightbulbs. We're not allowed to have more than one teaspoon of sugar for our tea and breakfast cereal, and we've been told not to waste paper in our exercise books. Stop making us do algebra, then! That'd save pages.

Even worse, all the music papers have completely shrunk in size – *Sounds* has even stopped printing its colour posters. What's going to happen to the 1980 Floor Show now? Is the energy crisis as bad in America as it is here? Every news story in last week's papers seemed to be about another band cancelling tours because of the shortages – although, as the main ones seemed to be The Allman Brothers, Joe Walsh and Steely Dan, you could say that every cloud has a silver lining. But it'd be awful if your show went the same way, after all the work you've put into it.

Anyway, must go. Matron said she'd be around to check up on us before tea, and I'm really hoping I'll be allowed to get up and have something to eat. Apart from a bowl of soup (I almost wrote 'soap'!) at lunchtime, they've been starving us to death all day.

All the best

Gary

Bournemouth, Hants
Thursday 21 March 1974

Dear David

I picked up the new *NME* and I can't believe what I read on page three – 'BOWIE COMEBACK?' I know it's only a rumour, so I almost didn't write this letter, but then I realised that if I don't, and the rumours are true, you might never realise what a HUGE MISTAKE you are making by going back on tour in America before playing Britain. Did you think maybe we wouldn't find out that you've GONE BACK ON YOUR WORD? Or that we'd think it didn't count because it's only America? Well, you're wrong and here's why.

1) Just look at the American chart in any of the music papers. Americans don't like you and they don't care. The only proper hit you've ever had there was a reissue of 'Space Oddity' in 1972, whereas Britain has given you nine.

2) America doesn't understand glam rock and never will.

3) Your British fans deserve better, and so does your music. T Rex and Slade have both tried to make it in America and, not only did they FAIL and lose their British fans as well, they also became so obsessed with making records they thought Americans *might* like that they forgot to make ones the British *would* like, and lost all the magic that made them so special in the first place. Do you want the same fate to happen to you? BECAUSE IT WILL!!!!!!!!!!!

Have you ever even heard any American glam bands? I'm not talking about the ORIGINATORS like Iggy, Lou and Wayne County. I mean the ones who are coming out now, thinking that simply slapping on some make-up and a pair of platforms is enough to disguise the fact they're still playing the same mindless rubbish they've already played.

Suzi Quatro would be just another boring rocker chick without Chinn and Chapman to write her hits for her, and

The New York Dolls look like they raided their mums' wardrobes for clothes, and their dads' Rolling Stones collections for ideas.

Jobriath's not bad, because at least he's copying from the right people (you, Cockney Rebel, Roxy Music), but the only genuinely original American band is Sparks – 'This Town Ain't Big Enough For Both Of Us' has to be one of the best records of the year so far, while the song 'Equator', on their *Kimono My House* album, has some of the best saxophone playing you're ever going to hear. And why are Sparks so good? Because they came over here and formed a band that doesn't look like a bunch of unemployed Foghat roadies. And now you're apparently putting together an all-American band for an all-American tour.

Hopefully you'll come to your senses, reform The Spiders From Mars and tour a country where people *want* to see you. But, if you don't, I hope you are happy in OBSCURITY. I'll still be buying *Diamond Dogs* when it comes out, but don't be surprised if I'm the only person who does. You have been warned!

Gary

Bournemouth, Hants
Sunday 28 April 1974

Dear David

I don't know where to start this letter, so much has happened since I last wrote to you. In fact, it all happened last week. First I bought *Diamond Dogs* and I love it, then I got Ronno's *Slaughter On Tenth Avenue*, which is excellent as well. And last night I went to see him play at Hammersmith Odeon AND GOT TO MEET HIM AFTER THE SHOW!

He autographed my LP cover, then he pointed at my *Aladdin Sane* T-shirt and said, 'Oh, so you like The Sweet as well?' He was only joking, but afterwards I felt a bit of a gorm for wearing it, like you would if you wore a Roxy Music T-shirt to an Eno gig. The reviews of his Rainbow shows were right: if Ronno is to make it on his own, he has to get away from the 'David Bowie's guitarist' label, and people trotting around wearing old shirts like that probably don't help. But I wasn't the worst. There were other people dressed as Ziggy Stardust and Aladdin Sane, and I only saw a few of them wearing the same clothes Ronno wears on the cover of his LP.

He'll do it, because he recorded an album that you can enjoy listening to, rather than a bunch of old guitar-wank (which is what most guitar players' solo records end up as). But he needs to get away from your shadow first, and that might prove difficult. The ex-Beatles are still the ex-Beatles, and they will be if they live for ever. Bill Wyman and Roger Daltrey are both trying solo careers, but the only people who care are Stones and Who fans, and there are probably thousands of other examples – in fact, can you think of anyone who's been able to use a well-known role in one band as a stepping stone to success on their own? I'm drawing a complete blank, but there's always the exception to prove the rule, and I really hope Ronno will be it.

When the concert dates were first announced, I didn't think I'd be able to go, but on the first day of the holidays I went down to the box office and they still had tickets. The gig was amazing. He opened with 'I'm The One', which surprised me a little because it's probably my least favourite song on the album. Next was a song that I thought, at first, was going to be Mott The Hoople's 'One Of The Boys', but it turned into one I didn't recognise.[59] There were some others I didn't know as well, but he played all of *Slaughter*, and his guitar playing was amazing all the way through. 'Only After Dark' was excellent as well. I see it was co-written with Scott Richardson. The sooner you get to work on his album, the better.

Ronno's solo in the next song[60] was one of the best I've ever heard him play. Of course the crowd went mad when he did 'Moonage Daydream', but I really enjoyed 'Slaughter On Tenth Avenue' as well, because it proves he can play more than rock guitar. I'd love to see him again, but his Bournemouth gig is next Wednesday, and we don't go back to school until the Monday after. Oh, well. Maybe next time.

I really wanted to ask him if he'd heard *Diamond Dogs*, but there were so many people there that I didn't get the chance. None of the reviews I've read understood the album at all, I don't think, but I reckon it's fantastic. It's so 1974, and it makes almost everything else I've heard this year sound hopelessly old-fashioned (apart from *Slaughter,* of course). Guy Peelaert's cover is as phenomenal as anything in *Rock Dreams*, and is that really you playing guitar on a lot of the tracks? I'll admit I'm biased and still think Ronno is the best guitarist ever, but you come close.

I was really excited about buying the album, because of 'Rebel Rebel' not having anything new on the B-side – 'Queen Bitch' is a terrific song, but it doesn't say anything about what you're doing now. So waiting for the record was a bit like waiting for Christmas, when you know what one of your presents is but not the rest. On the day of release I was at Town

---

59 Actually 'Leave My Heart Alone'.
60 'Angel No.9'.

Records in World's End (we're on our Easter holidays, of course) an hour before the delivery truck came. I'd paid for my copy of the album before they'd even put them out on the racks and, while I was waiting, I found a ton of other stuff in the second-hand box, including Lou Reed's first LP and Mick Farren's *Mona* LP. It opens and closes with two really wired versions of the old Bo Diddley song, and when you hear it you can imagine that the 1960s simply never happened. Rock 'n' roll just leaped from the passion of the 1950s to the glamour of the 1970s, without a single note of hippy music in between.

Of course I played *Diamond Dogs* first when I got home. And second, and third. There's so much going on in and around the songs – the mad guitar between 'Sweet Thing' and 'Rebel Rebel', and that heart-attack moment at the beginning of 'Rebel', where the drums first come in. 'Candidate' has some of the most visual lyrics I've ever heard (even if I am still trying to decipher some of them – why no lyric sheet this time?). And, as for 'Chant Of The Ever Circling Skeletal Family', I can't believe you only let it go on for two minutes. It's completely insane and totally contagious, and it should be given an entire side of an album to itself. Imagine, 20 minutes of the 'Chant', spiralling on for ever (of course, there'd have to be a stick groove at the end of each side). It'd be the greatest record ever made!

I can tell which songs come from the 1980 Floor Show/*1984* project[61] – 'Big Brother', '1984' itself (it sounds different from the one you did at the Marquee – wasn't there another section, something about a dodo?[62]) and, of course, 'We Are The Dead'. It's funny you chose to write that song, because that's my favourite scene in the entire book, where Winston and Julia are in the rented room talking, and suddenly the screen comes to life. Considering television was still so new when Orwell wrote that book, and generally regarded as a novelty that would never catch on, it's amazing that he was able to predict a day when it'd be watching us as avidly as we now watch it.

61 Aborted after Orwell's widow, Sonia, refused permission.
62 The live version was medleyed with another song, 'You Didn't Hear It From Me'.

But, although you've kept the thread of the *1984* story, you've added so much more. The whole Halloween Jack scenario is fascinating. Presumably there's been a nuclear war, and the album is set in its aftermath – 'five years' after *Ziggy*, perhaps? So 'Diamond Dogs' sets the scene, then 'Sweet Thing'/'Candidate' close in on the lives of the survivors, as they try to find some kind of normality amid the wreckage. The image of the shop selling bulletproof papier mâché masks (in 'Candidate') is terrific.

The best thing about *Diamond Dogs*, though, is that it remains true to what you are best at – glam rock, with the emphasis on the ROCK. 'Rebel Rebel' is especially clever, because, while it's obviously about the 'très butch little numbers' who you introduce during 'Candidate', it's also a total celebration of glam. So many other groups are waving goodbye to it, because they think they're too important for it now, or because it's been overrun by poseurs and fakers. But you understand that glam is more than a bunch of men in make-up, that it has a spirit that will completely outlive the bands who are playing with it now. I truly believe that there will still be glam bands around in ten years' time, which isn't something you could say about Mersey beat, psychedelia, heavy metal or any of those other bandwagons. Glam is real life; the others are manufactured.

Then again, I do wonder sometimes who will be left to keep making the records. Roxy's last album, *Stranded*, is half really good, but half pretty boring, which proves that Eno was a lot more important than Brain Fury lets on. Gary Glitter's turned into a total wimp and if he really wants us to 'remember him this way', he'd better hope we all have short memories. And, once past 'Teenage Lament', Alice's *Muscle Of Love* was even worse.

The Sweet seem to think they're the new Deep Purple (as though we don't hate the old one enough already) and, as for Marc Bolan, what is he playing at? Aside from having the crappiest LP title of all time (*Someone Someone And The*

Somethings From Somewhere,[63] how breathtakingly original!), he's also gone hopelessly disco-shit. After hearing 'Teenage Dream', I was hoping he might have pulled out of the crap-dive his last few singles took, but the LP is just Fat Boy Funk without a solitary original tune or good idea in sight. The music scene right now is so bad that I even like half the new Queen album (the second half, once they've run out of Led Zeppelin riffs to rip off).

Diamond Dogs, on the other hand, is unmitigated brilliance from start to finish, even if it did cost an unbelievable £2.50. Which is why I can't figure out why your new single is 'Rock And Roll Suicide'/'Quicksand'. Surely everybody who could possibly want those songs will already have them? Especially now that singles have gone up as well – from 48p to 50p, and some places are now charging 53p! You ought to put out '1984' or 'Rock 'n' Roll With Me' instead, and have a song on the B-side which we haven't heard before. Otherwise, people might think it's a waste of money and a waste of vinyl.[64]

How's life in America? The only American news we're getting over here has been Patty Hearst joining the SLA, and being caught on film at the bank robbery.[65] It's such a beautiful story, the pretty rich girl turning her back on the family fortune, and becoming a freedom fighter – even if the papers are calling her a terrorist. I suppose it simply depends which side you're on. I've got a collection of *Commando* war comics and, every time there's a story about the French Resistance, the Nazis call them terrorists, like we see the IRA, or the Americans see the SLA. But if you support the things those groups are fighting for, then they're not terrorists at all. They're heroes.

What's really inspiring about the SLA is that they understand the power of image. Glam-rock guerrillas! Have you seen the photograph of Patty Hearst with the machine gun, in front of the SLA flag? It's so powerful, like a film still or a rock poster. Give her a guitar and she'd sell a million records on the strength of the photo alone! The SLA knew that, as well. They saw all those

63 Actually, *Zinc Alloy And The Hidden Riders Of Tomorrow*.
64 Early 1974 saw the rising price of oil precipitate a vinyl shortage, itself responsible for the rising cost of records.
65 American heiress Hearst was kidnapped in February by a group calling itself the Symbionese Liberation Army (SLA).

posters of Che Guevara that are hanging up everywhere and thought, 'We can do that.' Plus, it doesn't hurt that Patty Hearst's so good-looking, because that's a lot of Guevara's appeal as well. Most people don't have a clue who he was or what his politics were; they just like the image. You said it with the opening line of 'Panic In Detroit': 'He looked a lot like Che Guevara'. If he'd looked a lot like Harold Wilson, nobody would even remember him any more.

Being a rock star must be a bit like being a terrorist, except you're using songs instead of bombs. But you're still fighting to make your voice heard, at the same time as trying to create a little world that you are in control of. I've read interviews where you say that's what you did with *Ziggy*, except you went further and created a person to live in that world as well. And when you retired, it was because that world had been taken away from you by the record company and your fans. I remember you telling one journalist that your career had been mapped out for you until 1975, but by retiring you had changed that situation completely. You were taking back control of your world and starting again; otherwise the people who claimed to love you might have destroyed you.

That's partly what you were talking about in 'Cygnet Committee', isn't it, when the love machine goes haywire and starts killing the people it's meant to be protecting? It cares so much about something that it forgets to pay attention to what that something itself might be feeling. In the song, you are obviously looking at the hippy movement of the late 1960s, but the meaning can be changed to any situation where people are so blinded by success that they don't see their failure.

A lot of the people we call terrorists today are people who realise that, and are trying to overthrow the system, which they believe has lost sight of its own purpose...hopefully to replace it with a new one. The problem is, the society they are struggling against can only see their idealism as fanaticism, as though having such powerful beliefs that you're willing to die for them is some sort of character flaw. Better to sit back and accept the status quo. Don't try to change things, don't try to fight things – just let it happen. And hope to high heaven that the leaders who are telling you this aren't as fanatical in their own beliefs as the so-called revolutionaries are in theirs.

What a stupid world we live in!

Gary

```
Bournemouth, Dorset⁶⁶
Thursday 14 November 1974
```

Dear David

Hi, Gary Weightman here. I haven't written for a long time, because I really wasn't certain that I liked what you were doing any more. But I bought your double live album, *David Live*, last week, and have played it at least once every day since then.

The music press has been full of stories about how you've gone disco, and redoing 'John I'm Only Dancing' as a funk song. Part of me was horrified, because that's my past you're stomping all over as well as your own, you know. But part of me was sort of resigned to the inevitability of it all. Marc Bolan has gone disco, Elton John has gone disco, John Lennon has gone disco. Why should you be left out? Besides, I have to admit that 'Knock On Wood' sounded amazing on the radio – a lot better than I was expecting. So, finally, I went out and bought the LP.

I'm still getting into it. Bits are excellent, the *Diamond Dogs* tracks really work well and, of course, with Mike Garson on piano, 'Aladdin Sane' is always going to be fantastic. The new guitarist, Earl Slick, is good as well, although it must be really difficult for him trying to follow Ronno. But I did notice that you've rearranged both 'Moonage Daydream' and 'Width Of A Circle' to put less emphasis on the guitar solos, while the new arrangement of 'The Jean Genie' took me completely by surprise. And the audience, as well, from the sound of it!

Opinion at school is divided. A lot of the younger kids, who got into you later and maybe don't know the songs as well, are really excited by it and, maybe, they have an advantage over those of us who've been with you since *Ziggy*. For them, growing up on the press image that you are some kind of rock 'n' roll chameleon, changing with every record, this is one more LP, one more new sound. But, having lived with your music for the last two years, I've always been able to pursue a single line

---

66 Bournemouth was moved from Hampshire to Dorset as part of summer 1974's reshuffle of local government boundaries.

of thought through it. *David Live* represents the end of that sentence, and the beginning of another, with songs like 'Knock On Wood' and the new versions of 'Dudes', 'The Jean Genie', 'Rebel Rebel' and 'Panic In Detroit' pointing you in a whole new direction. Which is where I begin to wonder about it. What I've read about it certainly makes it sound interesting, although I had to laugh when someone told me you'd recorded a 'new' version of 'Can You Hear Me', because we've not heard the old one yet![67]

There's not much news to tell you at this end. I'm in Group Four now, which means a new dormitory and a new housemaster (Mr Pauly, a really weird bloke who likes Elton John and Randy Edelman far too much to be healthy). As far as lessons go, our classes are now being directed towards our CSEs and O-levels, which are now less than two years away, although it still seems a little early to be worrying about such things. Next week we have our first meeting with a careers officer, who'll apparently be working with us for the next two years to help ensure we make the right choices for our exams and chosen careers. As if a 14-year-old has any idea what he wants to be doing in 40 years' time. Most people I know have trouble figuring out what they want to do this weekend.

Then again, half our class have already made up their minds that they want to join the armed forces; Danny Meath still wants to be a tramp; there's another one who is bent on becoming a priest (or, maybe, he's just bent – rumours are flying!); and we're trying to convince Gnome's Head to tell the officer he wants to work in a garden centre because, with a name like that, where else could he go?

I'm undecided. My stepfather reckons I should join his company, because he could find me a good job with career prospects, but he must be joking! If he sent me 100 miles away to go to school, imagine how far he'd send me to go to work. I'd probably end up working in an office in Timbuktu. I'm still really keen on a second-hand record shop, but I don't

67 An outtake from the 1973 Lulu sessions.

know if telling a careers officer that you want to spend your life surrounded by scratchy old records is a particularly good idea. Besides, if our teachers are anything to go by, he'll tell me that a shop's a shop, and I don't need a lecture about how my education is costing a lot of money and it'd be ungrateful of me to throw it all away on the broken biscuits counter at Woolworths. Perhaps I'll tell him I want to go on to college. That'll give me another two years to decide and – who knows? – maybe I should marry an heiress.

The highlight of the term was, believe it or not, the school Christmas play. We put on *Oliver* for the school governors, parents and other local worthies. Sikes, Nancy and Fagin were played by teachers and Matron (none of us kids looked criminal enough for those parts), and Oliver himself was this nauseating little first year who seems proud of the fact that his balls might never drop. When he first started here, he was known as the Ball-less Wonder, which changed to the Walrus Blunder at some point, so it was hysterical to see him listed in the programme with 'Walrus' as his middle name. I'd love to see him explain that away to his parents!

Paul and I were anonymous among Fagin's little boys, which was fine by us, while Danny was the Artful Dodger, and he was absolutely brilliant. Through all the rehearsals he played it straight, but on the night he magically transformed into the Black Artful Dodger, sweeping on stage in a black cloak he'd borrowed from the staffroom and changing virtually every one of his lines into either a spell or an incantation. When Sikes knocks down Nancy at the end, Danny rose up on tiptoe, raised his cloak above his head and let rip with more Latin than he ever let on he'd learned in class! If Sikes had turned into a frog on the spot, I don't think anyone would have been surprised.

The other highlight was the way Fagin's pet crow kept turning into different things. Every time we had a scene change and the birdcage was in sight, there'd be something else in there – a doll, a football boot and a picture of David Cassidy.

We never found out who was doing it, but I'll never forget Mr Skate in a false beard, singing 'I'm Reviewing The Situation' to a stuffed toy penguin. Even he looked like he was going to crack up for that one. So it was complete chaos and a total success, and if that's what school plays are like I wish I'd done them every other year as well!

I've been to a few gigs since I last wrote, but not as many as I'd have liked. I really wanted to see Cockney Rebel. Paul Banion saw them play at the Farnborough Air Show of all places during the summer, and reckons they were terrific. But now they've broken up, so I'll never know. I might go to see Queen, but only if their next album is as good as the new single.[68] I found out yesterday that Mott The Hoople's latest tour[69] has been cancelled because Ian Hunter had a nervous breakdown. I even missed Sparks when they toured – Coconut was jammy enough to see them in Croydon and he's still talking about the show. Have you heard 'Never Turn Your Back On Mother Earth' yet? Alongside 'Rebel Rebel', it's my favourite single of the year by far – it's such an unusual song, and if you listen to it carefully the second verse could be about Major Tom, the lament of an astronaut, regretting that he ever went into space.

I was wondering, did you ever find out what was going on with that weird version of 'John I'm Only Dancing' that I mentioned a few letters back? Because I've found another one! I bought an American 'Not for sale' single of 'Rebel Rebel' from Vintage, and it's COMPLETELY different from the single and the LP versions, even though it says 'From the *Diamond Dogs* album' on the label. The guitars are run through all these weird effects, and there's an echoey 'la-la-la' backing vocal, a bit like the version on *David Live*. Except this isn't live. The catalogue number is DJHO 0287 (APBO 0287).[70] Do you have any idea at all?

Finally, I'm really excited about the movie you're writing with Marc Bolan,[71] and I'm really looking forward to the BBC

---

68 'Killer Queen'.
69 Their first with Mick Ronson.
70 This alternate take, with Bowie playing all the instruments, appeared briefly in the US in May 1974. It later resurfaced on the *Sound And Vision* box set.
71 In July, Bolan told the *Sun* newspaper that the pair were planning to co-direct. Bowie was writing the screenplay, Bolan the music.

documentary.[72] I hope they put it on soon, and at a reasonable time. If we can't see an entire concert (do you have any plans at all to bring it over here?), at least we can catch the highlights!

Hope all is well

Gary

PS As a fellow Syd Barrett fan, have you noticed the similarities between 'Wombling Merry Christmas' and 'Arnold Layne'? And there was me thinking the hairy little beasts only collected waste paper.[73]

---

72 Alan Yentob's *Cracked Actor*.
73 The eponymous hero of Pink Floyd's debut single steals ladies' underwear from suburban washing lines.

Bournemouth, Dorset
Monday 27 January 1975

Dear David

I cannot BELIEVE you never brought the Diamond Dogs tour home. Yes, we were allowed to see *Cracked Actor* on BBC2 last night, even though it finished way past our bedtime. Warthead realised that if he didn't at least allow the fourth and fifth years to stay up and watch it, he'd have a riot on his hands.

The live footage was spectacular. I loved the juxtaposition of 'Sweet Thing'/'Candidate' with the Hollywood street scenes – that was really effective. The interviews with the fans were eye-opening, as well. I still don't think Americans understand glam rock, but they certainly know how to be WEIRD! The specimens Alan Yentob[74] sought out were so far gone that it wasn't even funny! My favourite one was the kid who said you're from your own universe. 'Which universe is that?' 'The Bowie universe.'

Some of your comments were really funny, like the crack about the waxworks museum in the middle of the desert.[75] But I was puzzled when you told the interviewer that you never wanted to be a rock 'n' roll star. If that's true, then why did you join a rock 'n' roll band?

It'd have been different if you'd started out in life as a vet or a policeman, and suddenly been elevated to international fame and fortune because somebody heard you singing in the shower one day, released a tape without your knowledge, then stole your home movies to show on *Lift Off*. But to physically commit yourself to a career in music, work long and hard for umpteen years, and then say you never wanted it to happen is like taking a job as an accountant, then wondering why you're stuck working with numbers. And, besides, even if *you* didn't want to be a star, what about Ziggy? He certainly did!

Or maybe you were just taking the piss. I did like the way you seemed to be giving completely irrelevant answers to very

74 The show's director.
75 'You'd think it'd melt.'

straightforward questions, only for them to make sense at the end. The American TV guy they showed right at the beginning of the programme didn't seem to understand, though, which was one of the funniest parts of the whole show.

The concert footage was utterly fab. The version of 'Rock And Roll Suicide' was far superior to the one on *David Live*, and I liked the way they pulled footage from the *Bowie-ing Out* film. 'My Death' sounded amazing. It was also interesting that the longest live clips from this tour were of songs that aren't on *David Live* – 'Time', 'Space Oddity' and 'John I'm Only Dancing'. Another taste of what we missed!

Is 'John I'm Only Dancing' going to be on *Somebody Up There Likes Me*?[76] And, more to the point, is it indicative of how the album sounds? Hmmm, and we thought *David Live* was a departure! Still, at least it's something to look forward to! I can't believe how bad the charts are these days. Was it because I was so much younger then that everything seemed exciting in 1972–73? Even the old Mud, Sweet and Gary Glitter records sound like classics compared with what they're doing today, while the new groups coming through are horribly watered-down versions of things that weren't very good the first time around.

I'm not even going to mention The Bay Shitty Rollers (but I did – damn), Pilot (who are a poor man's 10cc) or any of the others. But, apart from Sparks, SAHB[77] and, hopefully, whatever Steve Harley does next, the entire country seems to be sinking into a sea of unfunny novelty records, mediocre disco-shit and sentimental ballads. Somewhere in Tin Pan Alley, there is a Versificator[78] machine that must be stopped! You're so lucky you're in America right now and, if you get a chance, go to see SAHB. I saw them on the last tour and it was amazing – if you've heard the last album,[79] you'll already know 'Anthem' is one of the most beautiful pieces of 'rock' music ever written. Live, it was even better. They end the set with it, going out with the girl singer, a drum roll and bagpipes, and

76 The album's working title, as announced in the UK press.
77 The Sensational Alex Harvey Band.
78 A mechanical songwriting instrument created for George Orwell's *1984*, capable of turning out mindless hit jingles without any human intervention whatsoever.
79 *The Impossible Dream*.

I couldn't believe the size of the lump in my throat! It really was moving – and I'm not even Scottish!

On the other hand, I can't believe how appalling Elton John's version of 'Lucy In The Sky With Diamonds' is. It's bad enough getting all these wishy-washy reggae records from real Jamaicans clogging up the charts, without rubbish like that being flung at us from our own shores as well. I love reading in the music papers how reggae is going to break really big in the next few months, but everything I've heard has either been stupid nursery rhymes, like 'Black And White', or bad covers of songs which were sentimental rubbish to begin with. The only decent reggae artist I've ever heard is Judge Dread...and he's English, from Chatham, like me.

Have you read George Tremlett's biography of you yet? I really enjoyed it. There was so much info that has never been in the music press. Now I know who Hermione is, as in 'Letter To Hermione'.[80] What a wonderful name that is – the only other one I can think of is the actress, Hermione Gingold. I especially enjoyed everything he wrote about your early days, before the *World Of David Bowie* album, and even before the Pye singles! I always thought 'Can't Help Thinking About Me' and so on were your first records, but the book mentioned an even earlier one, 'Liza Jane' by The King Bees.

As soon as I read that, I went up the Vintage Record Centre to see if they had a copy in stock. 'Oh God, you've been reading that bloody book as well, haven't you?' the bloke behind the counter said. If you have a spare copy of it (or any other of your early records), I'd love to buy it off you.

Anyway, that's enough from me. I just wanted to let you know what a success *Cracked Actor* was, and to wish you luck with 'Young Americans'.

Best wishes

Gary

---

80 Ex-girlfriend and Feathers bandmate Hermione Farthingale. She inspired several Bowie songs following their break up, including 'She Shook Me Cold' on *The Man Who Sold The World*.

Bournemouth, Dorset
Sunday 23 February 1975

Dear David

The weirdest thing just happened, and you're kind of responsible for it.

Jonathan James and I returned from a trip into Boscombe yesterday afternoon, convinced that we were the first kids in the school to have bought 'Young Americans', only for 'Soul Boy' Jacks to walk into our common room while we were playing it, and announce it was the best record you'd ever made. I've mentioned him before. He's that mardy bastard a year above me, who has never said more than three words at a time (usually 'Fuck off, Weightman') to me in all the years we've been here. He had meningitis a couple of years ago and were all hoping he'd not come back, but he did.

Anyway, as far as we were aware, he's never listened to one of your records in his life. You're not black, you're not American and you don't have some hyper-obscure 1960s soul single being raved about on the Northern Soul circuit, which is the only music he's into. But he doesn't simply like 'Young Americans', he went out and bought a copy, which means it's now nestled into the same box of 45s as Chairman Of The Board, Motown and Gloria Jones. And, as Jon said, if you can convert him, you can convert anyone!

Loved your new look[81] in the ads in the music press – real James Dean stuff. But I do think 'Young Americans' was an unusual choice for a single. It's so long and, although it has a tune and a chorus, it doesn't really have a hook. I wouldn't be surprised if it didn't do particularly well on the chart, although the Top 20 is such shite these days that that's probably a good thing. Would you really want to spend your time flotching around with the likes of Sweet Sensation, Johnny Wakelin and Syreeta? I can't remember the last 'new' record I rushed out and bought (except for 'Young Americans', of course), although I'm picking up lots of second-hand records, trying to catch up with everything I missed in the past.

My new favourite shop is Unlimited Sound on the right-hand side of the North End Road, as you're walking down towards Fulham. It's the place Ian Hunter calls Brian's in *Diary Of A Rock And Roll Star*, although I didn't know that at the time – they told me after I'd bought a copy of Mott's *Wild Life* album for a quid. I was dead chuffed; you hardly ever find their old records around any more, and this is the one that no one at school had even *seen* before, let alone heard.

From there I went up to Roundabout Records, at the top of the road by Olympia, and found the 'Midnight Lady' single[82] and, to prove that these things come in threes, the next day Vintage Record Centre had a copy of *Brain Capers*. I also picked up Ronno's 'Slaughter On Tenth Avenue' single – a bit late in the day, I admit, but for some reason I completely forgot about it even being out. His new album's out at the end of this month, and apparently it features the version of 'White Light White Heat' that you recorded at the *Pin-Ups* sessions. Are you singing on it or is it just him? I'm going to the Hunter-Ronson gig in London on 31 March, and I can't wait.

Best wishes

Gary

---

82 Another Mott oldie.

Bournemouth, Dorset
Sunday 13 April 1975

Dear David

I've had *Young Americans* for two weeks now, but didn't want to write until I'd had a chance to really get into it. The title track has completely grown on me, and I love 'Fame' – if all soul and funk music sounded like that, I'd like a lot more of it than I do. I read somewhere that the song is based on an old James Brown song called 'Footstompin'', so I asked Soul Boy about it and he says it's by a band called The Flares, who I've not even heard of. But what a suitable inspiration for a man who's been known to wear some wildly bottomed trousers in his time!

What was it like working with John Lennon? Of all The Beatles, he's the only one who seems to have maintained a sense of Beatle-ness about him. Paul, George and Ringo are always on telly, and churning out records without seeming to care whether they're any good or not. But, even when I don't like his records, John seems to still care about what he's putting out, which is how he can come out with something like 'Number 9 Dream', which is so lush and beautiful, while George sticks out rubbish like 'Ding Dong'. I'm not crazy on what the two of you did with 'Across The Universe'. But 'Fame' more than makes up for it.

Anyway, Soul Boy's quickly turning into one of my best friends, which is so strange because we used to hate each other. It's amazing what a common interest in a certain kind of music can do – what he doesn't know about soul and funk isn't worth knowing, he reads *Black Echoes* as religiously as I read *NME* and, although I don't have a clue what he's going on about half the time, he has some really amazing records.

Have you ever heard Funkadelic and Parliament? They're pretty much the same band, but the singer, George Clinton, takes it in turns to release records under the two names. They're a lot heavier than the Philly stuff that is all over the radio these days – in fact, one of their songs, 'Maggot Brain', is heavier than a lot of heavy metal as well. They also did an album, called *Osmium*, that is kind of funky folk rock. It's a really weird band, but there's a lot more to get your teeth into than you'd know from reading the regular music papers, who seem to treat that whole scene as some kind of amorphous blob with the occasional 'character' popping up to amuse the masses with tales of excess and unreliability. I'm really getting into Sly And The Family Stone as well (the only record I'd heard before was 'Family Affair').

A couple of weekends ago, Soul Boy, Jonathan and I went to a disco Soul Boy's been going to for years now, in Bournemouth. He tells the school that he's going to the church youth club in Walkford, which is about ten miles away (there's a train straight there), and most weeks he really does go – a bunch of kids from the school are members, and I've just joined. But once a month he catches a train in the opposite direction and goes to the disco, where everybody knows him and the DJ even lets him help out choosing records to play! It's a great place to pick up girls as well, he says, especially now that summer's coming and Bournemouth is filling up with grockles. We stayed there till almost half past ten, and when we got back to school we said we'd missed our usual train and they believed us!

I can't say I liked every record they played, because a lot of them were rubbish from the chart, which the holidaymakers request. But Soul Boy still got in a few good ones, and I plucked up the courage to ask a girl to dance when The Isley Brothers' 'Summer Breeze' came on. I'm a hopeless dancer, but it was really fun.

Anyway, we both agree that 'Fame' is the most convincing white funk record ever made, and had a fabulous time laughing about all the other bands who are going to be following in your footsteps. And, I suppose, Marc Bolan's. Although his last couple of albums really haven't been very good, you can tell he was obviously thinking along the same lines as you, but without the courage to make the same massive leap. His popularity has really sunk, but while he can still have hits with records that sound like the old ones, I don't think he'll ever completely throw away the formula and go all out with something new, which is a shame. He really is the father of the whole glam rock thing, and he's still one of the most inventive people around. It'd be terrible if he sunk into oblivion, to be remembered only for a couple of 'oldies but goldies' on Radio 2.

There again, it must be difficult for anybody to simply throw away everything they've achieved in the past and begin again. You can kind of get away with it, because of that 'rock chameleon' image. Even though that tag is simply used by lazy journalists so they don't have to explain what you're doing and why, it completely set you up to be able to keep moving around. You listen to recent records by Slade, though, and you can tell they're desperate to move on – soft rock ballads, correctly spelled song titles, the lot. But, as long as people want to hear Noddy screaming, they have to keep making records like that, because the alternative is to risk falling out of the charts for ever.

That's why I really admire George Clinton. He understood right at the start that if a band becomes really popular their audience can hold them back and make it impossible to change or move along. So he formed two bands: one to do one thing, the other to do another. Apparently there's a whole rivalry among his fans – some love Parliament and hate Funkadelic, and vice versa.

You were working along the same lines a couple of years ago, weren't you? The Arnold Corns project was one example. (Did I tell you I picked up the Mooncrest reissue of 'Hang Onto Yourself'? It's really strange, but I do like it.) Even more to the point was that period when you seemed to be either recording, or getting ready to record, with everybody you could, so that every idea and musical fantasy you had would have a home, and it didn't matter if people bought it or not because you'd always have something else going on at the same time.

So you had the whole Mainman stable of Mott, Lou Reed, Iggy And The Stooges, Dana Gillespie, Scott, Wayne And Cherry,

The Astronettes, Lulu, Adam Faith, Amanda Lear...and I'm sure I'm missing some others out... And if you put them all together, like you said in that *NME* interview around the time of *Pin-Ups*, you'd end up with the ultimate Superstar – a multifaceted creature that would boil down into a complete human being.

It's interesting that it's only since you stopped working with (or talking about working with) all those people that you've started to move around so much musically. Mott and Lou Reed only lasted an album each before they went off on their own courses, and your only songs on Dana's album turned out to be the ones you recorded in 1971.[83] I don't know what happened with The Astronettes or any of the others, but (please correct me if I'm wrong) it does look like they're never going to happen, and maybe now you're having to channel all the ideas you had for them into your own music.

It's a shame, because the Lulu album could have been a real gem. I remember reading an interview where you were saying that she had the greatest soul/R&B voice around, and you wanted to make a record with all the best soul musicians backing her up. But that's sort of what you've done with *Young Americans*, and I'm wondering if the Lulu record had happened and you'd got all those songs and ideas out of your system, what would your own next LP have sounded like?

I really wish you'd made the album with Wayne County as well. After all the rubbish that's been thrown at us in the name of glam these last couple of years, Wayne would have out-glammed everyone. Including you! The music scene has become so safe again. It needs someone like Wayne to come along and shake everything up, if only to remind people that music is meant to be something more than reissues of Bobby Goldsboro's 'Honey'.

The only new band I've seen that even vaguely deserves to be called glam (or, at least, has any understanding of what glam should be) is this little group I saw playing in Putney over Easter. They're called The Doctors Of Madness. I saw them listed in the

83 Gillespie's *Weren't Born A Man* album featured versions of Bowie's 'Andy Warhol' and Gillespie's own 'Mother, Don't Be Frightened'.

gig guide in *NME* and it's such a neat name that I knew they were either going to be absolutely amazing or totally shit.

They probably won't get anywhere, but if you can imagine *Diamond Dogs* crossed with Cockney Rebel's *Human Menagerie*, with a mad violin player and really good costumes (the bass player dresses as a skeleton), playing old Bob Dylan songs at eardrum-piercing volume, that's what they sound like. If you ever start looking for a new group to produce, you should catch them. (They play a lot of their own songs as well.)

The other gig I went to was Hunter-Ronson at Hammy Odious,[84] and it was amazing. First on was a band called Jet. A couple of them were in John's Children with Marc Bolan, and their guitarist is Davy O'List from The Nice and the early Roxy Music. Their sound wasn't too good, so it was hard to tell what a lot of their set was, but their new single, 'Nothing To Do With Us', was OK.

Hunter-Ronson, meanwhile, did most of *Play Don't Worry* and Hunter's album, which was perfect. Have you heard Hunter's album yet? A few of the reviews have said the song 'Boy' is about you and, if you follow the words really carefully, I'm sorry to say, it could be. I don't always like his 'real-life' songs – I get the feeling that he's trying to create a band mythology himself, rather than letting the public do it, as you did with *Ziggy* and *Aladdin Sane*. But 'Saturday Gigs' was a magnificent record, and 'Boy' is equally good. I also love the way the new album opens with him saying, 'Hello', because it follows on perfectly from the 'Goodbye' at the end of 'Saturday Gigs'.

The highlight of the show, though, was 'All The Young Dudes', when Mick Ralphs and Ariel Bender both came out on stage to play. Everybody goes on about The Yardbirds having three world-class guitarists (Clapton, Beck and Page), but in years to come I hope Mott are remembered in the same way, because their guitarists were/are just as good – and the songs were better!

84 Hammersmith Odeon.

The Yardbirds made some good singles (including 'Shapes Of Things' and 'I Wish You Would'[85]), and I do understand why they're considered so influential. But have you ever tried sitting through one of their LPs all the way? The Clapton one with Sonny Boy Williamson is so boring, and even the 'famous' one with the cartoon cover[86] is more a matter of high ambition, low success rate. You can almost hear the group sitting around in the studio wondering what cleverness to get up to next, but I really don't think the songs were that good. It'd be like having Queen rerecord their second album, but only let them play 1930s blues songs.

Mott, on the other hand, didn't make a bad album their entire career, and no one could ever doubt how great Ralphs, Bender and Ronson were (although Ronno certainly messed up 'Play Don't Worry' on *Whistle Test* last night!). I still remember how upset I was when I heard the band had broken up, although if the new Mott line-up (apparently they're shortening their name to just 'Mott' – that'll be confusing) is even half as good as Hunter-Ronson, we may well be better off with two bands than we ever were with them! Fingers crossed!!!

Anyway, I must go. Soul Boy and I are halfway through making a killer funk cassette ('Fame' is on there, of course!) and I want to get down to the common room before he fills it up with 'Maggot Brain'.

All the best

Gary

PS You may want to have a word with the mailroom at RCA. I mailed my last letter to you there – and they sent me back a photo of Ronno! No complaints, but I do wonder who his fans are getting photos of. Henry Mancini,[87] maybe?

---

85 Both covered by Bowie on *Pin-Ups*.
86 The so-called Roger The Engineer.
87 Fellow RCA artist.

Bournemouth, Dorset
Sunday 18 May 1975

Dear David

This'll make you laugh! I went to see The Bay City Rollers yesterday! Gnome's Head, Paul, Soul Boy and I were bored and broke, so we wandered down to the Winter Gardens to watch the Roller Girls having hysterics on the street outside. Plus, some of the girls from the youth club were going and we were hoping to meet up with them. We didn't, but while we were walking around Paul noticed a stream of girls disappearing into the building through a window, so we joined the queue, in we went...and found ourselves in the ladies' bog!

We were more embarrassed than anybody in there. They slapped our backs and hustled us out into the main hall, which was so chaotic that security had completely given up trying to keep people in their seats – a far cry from when we saw you there! So we dived into the crowd, I found a tartan scarf to wrap up in, and we had a fabulous time joining in the screams and chants ('E-R-I-C, he's the only one for me!'), and by the time the Rollers themselves came on we were enjoying ourselves so much that we didn't even laugh. Plus we'd probably have had our heads kicked in if we had – some of those Roller Girls are SCARY. Even better (or, more humiliatingly, depending upon whether it's the cold light of day or not), we knew the words to virtually every song they played and, by the time the show was over – in less than an hour! – I don't think I've ever been so exhausted (or hoarse) in my life.

Don't worry, I'm not about to defect to the tartan menace and, once we were outside again, I don't think any of us really wanted to admit how much fun we'd had. When we did, of course, then it was wild hysterics and singing all the way back to school, and so what if we were given a mighty bollocking when we returned so late? We saw the Rollers and lived. And we loved every minute of it.

However, that's not why I wanted to write to you today. I don't know where he got them from, but a friend in London mailed me a package of LPs (which arrived yesterday), all by you and all ones we'd never heard of... *His Master's Voice*, *Dollars In Drag* and *Live At Santa Monica Civic*. They weren't cheap – the whole lot cost £12, and I know they're bootlegs, but after listening to them I really don't understand why you've never released any of this stuff yourself. The Santa Monica show, from 1972, is fantastic – a double album (the complete gig, I think), with the best version of 'My Death', you and an acoustic guitar; an amazing 'Waiting For The Man'; and some really funny chat before a couple of songs.

Dollars In Drag is taken from the 1980 Floor Show – although 'Sorrow' caught me by surprise, as I'd swear you didn't play that. Was there another show that I missed?[88] Both sides of the Arnold Corns single were on there as well – it'd have been better if they'd put on tracks that hadn't been reissued, but I'm not complaining. After 18 months of hearing me go on about what a superb gig it was, it's nice that everyone else can finally hear what all the fuss was about!

My favourite one of them all, though, is *His Master's Voice*, which was recorded at the Hammersmith retirement show. It's only one disc, so obviously a lot of the gig is missing, but the 'Wild Eyed Boy'/'Dudes' medley is there, 'Moonage Daydream' with Ronno exploding on guitar and 'The Jean Genie'/'Love Me Do' with Jeff Beck, and it winds up with your retirement speech – which gave me goose pimples the first time I heard it. The way the audience went so completely quiet, and then burst out howling and screaming as you went into 'Rock And Roll Suicide', has to be one of *the* all-time magical moments in music history, especially as you led them so far down the garden path when you started out saying thanks to the roadies, the lighting crew and so on.

I know bootlegs are illegal, and that you probably aren't at all happy to know I have them, but if you (and all the other

---

88 'Sorrow', complete with a complicated dance routine featuring Amanda Lear, was filmed on the third day, without an audience.

artists who've been bootlegged) only knew what it means to us, as fans, to be able to hear things like this, you'd be a lot happier. Who knows when *Bowie-ing Out* will finally be released, or if the 1980 Floor Show will ever turn up on British telly? We could all die (or at least grow up, get married and be too old to care) before things like this are officially issued, if they ever are.[89] It's much better that we hear them now, while we're still enthusiastic, than in ten years' time, when all the magic is long forgotten. One of our teachers was talking about The Rolling Stones' new *Metamorphosis* outtakes collection, and he said he'd have been a lot more excited if it had come out while he still cared about The Rolling Stones. And when I showed him your bootlegs, he said the same thing.

I know that you, Mainman and RCA all have your own reasons for not releasing things like this, but I really can't imagine what they are. It can't have anything to do with the performance, because all three are excellent. An article I read, I think it was in *NME*, said that bootlegs take away sales from a band's proper releases, but that's rubbish as well. We've already bought all the proper ones, and if you did release all these yourself next month you know we'd buy them all again, just to keep the collections complete. Plus, it's a miracle that somebody taped the shows and made them available – if they hadn't, think of the fantastic music that would have been lost for ever![90]

Some bootlegs are a total rip-off – there's another one of yours called *Soft In The Middle*, which simply bundles up a bunch of old singles and a couple of really lousy-sounding live tracks. But some official record company releases are rip-offs as well, so surely it's up to the fans to decide whether they want the record or not? I'd love to hear your private thoughts about bootlegs, and if you've ever bought any yourself.

Finally, any news on what your next single is going to be? I know I said 'Young Americans' probably wasn't going to do

---

89 *His Master's Voice* finally came out, heavily remixed, in 1983 as the soundtrack companion to *Ziggy Stardust: The Motion Picture*; *Santa Monica* received an official release in 1994.
90 In fact, all three came from broadcast sources – the American *King Biscuit Flour Hour* (*Santa Monica*), ABC TV (*His Master's Voice*) and NBC's *Midnight Special* (*Dollars In Drag*).

very well on the chart, but even I was surprised that it only reached No.18. I'd still go with 'Fame' if I was you, although I have a horrible feeling it'll be 'Across The Universe'. Please don't!

All the best

Gary

PS We had the annual end-of-term football match (boys versus staff) last weekend and, not only did we stuff them (7–0!), but the only way we persuaded them to even turn up for the second half, 4–0 down, was to taunt them with your very own 'Starman' – suitably amended, of course: 'There's a staff team hiding over there, they thought that they could beat us, but now they're just shit-scared.' Hot stuff, eh?

```
Picture Postcard - Polperro, Cornwall
Thursday 7 August 1975
```

Dear David

You'll be thrilled to know that you may only be No.33 on the national chart, but at Seaview Holiday Camp in Polperro, Cornwall, you're up there with Typically Tropical and 'Give A Little Love'[91] on the Social Club jukebox. Could life get any better?

Having a great holiday – will write again next week.

Gary

---

91 The latest Bay City Rollers 45.

```
Polperro, Cornwall
Tuesday 12 August 1975
```

Dear David

Hope you received my postcard last week. I'm still here, having a really fun time, but I have an hour to kill before going out for the evening, so I thought I'd drop you a quick line and tell you all about it.

We left London the same day school finished. I arrived home in time to unpack my school stuff, repack my swimming costume and turn back around. Under the optimistic delusion that they'd be getting an extra day's holiday, my parents booked us on to the night coach from Victoria Station. It left at 11:45 and – after 12 hours of zero sleep, singing drunks and a mysterious early hours stop in Salisbury – we reached Seaview, at which point they went to bed. So much for the extra day...

We're here for a fortnight, which is excellent because London is UNBEARABLE at the moment. I'm sure you've heard about the heatwave that has been going on all summer – in fact, it's the only subject we ever hear about now. A couple of days ago, the temperature reached 90°F,[92] the hottest day on record since 1940, and they reckon it's only going to get worse. At least here we have a swimming pool and the sea, although I have to be careful because I sunburn so easily.

There's no music scene at all down here, but there are people here from all over the country, so at least we can all go through withdrawal together. I've hooked up with a bunch of kids from Manchester who are here without their parents (jammy sods), and we've spent the whole time exploring the countryside (not much), looking for record shops (not one, although I did find a copy of NME at the newsagent's in Looe, the nearest big town) and seeing how many pubs we can buy cider in without being asked our age.

So far, we're running more or less even. The funniest moment was when this kid named Jiggy (that's what he says his name is,

92 32°C.

although it's probably Nigel or something) was thrown out of the Treble A Club (an ultra-slick adults-only room at another holiday camp) for not being 18 – and he's the only one of us who actually is!

The other big amusement for the first few days was seeing who could monopolise the jukebox the most. There's a group of girls here who arrived in full Rollers gear and have been wearing it ever since. At first we thought they were wearing the same clothes every day (clothes-peg-on-nose time!), but then we began to notice subtle variations in the tartan, and it turns out they brought complete wardrobes full of clothes with tartan sewn on. They have two chalets, which they've covered in Rollers scarves and posters in the windows, and one of them has a cassette playing the Rollers nonstop. But that doesn't stop them from descending on the club and pouring five-pence pieces into the jukebox – I know 'Give A Little Love' and its B-side like the back of my hand now, and I'm wondering if this isn't my instant karma punishment for sneaking into that Rollers gig.

The only chance we had of blotting it out was to get to the club first and put 'Fame' and 'Right'[93] on as many times as we could, but somebody complained about hearing the same songs so often, because when we went back a few nights ago both your record and the Rollers' had been removed from the jukebox! So now we all sit there and sing very loudly and badly along with 'Barbados', T Rex's 'New York City' and Jasper Carrott's 'Magic Roundabout'(the B-side of 'Funky Moped' – it's not particularly good, but there is something hysterically funny about a dozen voices suddenly bellowing, '"Piss off," said Dougal,' at the appropriate moment).

We also Bowie-ed out the disco in Killigarth on Tuesday. I asked the DJ which of your records he had, and he pulled out virtually every single since 'Starman'. So I requested 'The Jean Genie', then we took it in turns for the rest of the evening to ask for the others. He never figured out what was happening, either, so every second or third record that played was one of yours.

93 The B-side.

Polperro's an interesting place – have you ever been there? It's a fishing village that is completely untouched by the outside world, except for the holiday camps. I've also been hanging out with a girl, Jan (she looks like a young, slightly less skinny Twig The Wonder Kid), who lives here. Her brother Colin works at our camp. She says that when the tourist season is over the whole village curls up and hibernates, and the only excitement during the winter is when a storm comes in off the channel and the whole place rushes down to the harbour to pull all the fishing boats in.

I asked her if she's ever been to a gig. She said The Wurzels have played a few times, but the only real band she's ever seen was – guess who? You, at Torquay Town Hall, in 1973! She'd like to move up to London when she's 16 (at the end of the year), but doesn't know anybody there. I told her to hang on until next summer and I'll be there full-time.

Yep, this time next year, I'll be a working boy…or, at least, an unemployed one. I had a huge row with my stepfather about what I'm going to do when I leave school. Of course, he waited till Mum wasn't around before starting on me. He said either I take the job he's offering me or I find one myself. Either way, he's not going to have me cluttering up the house doing nothing, and he'll throw me out on the street if I don't find something. I told him to fuck off, and that I'd rather live in the gutter than have to spend all day every day staring at his ugly face, and we haven't spoken since. To be honest, I'm really not sure what I'm going to do now, but at least it's given me an incentive to get as many CSEs and O-levels as I can. The trouble is, the way things are going, there might not be any jobs for me to do, no matter how many I get. And the careers officer still hasn't taught us how to sign on the dole, which may be the most important lesson of all.

But it might not be that bad. I rang Soul Boy last night – he left school at the end of term and he's landed a job already, making tea at a press agency in Islington. I'm meeting him on his lunchbreak when I get back to the smoke, to visit a record shop he's found on Upper Street.

I hope 'Fame' keeps moving up the chart. Anne Nightingale on Radio 1 just played Rod Stewart's new album in its entirety, and I have a sneaking feeling that the song 'Sailing' is going to be massive. Did you know Tim Renwick, your guitarist on 'Space Oddity', plays on the original version, by The Sutherland Brothers And Quiver? It's amazing – look around hard enough and there's probably a Bowie connection to every band on earth.

All the best

Gary

PS I know artists don't have any control over who does cover versions of their songs, but surely you could have done something to stop The King's Singers?[94]

---

94 The vocal group had just released an *a cappella* version of 'Life On Mars?' as a single.

Bournemouth, Dorset
Tuesday 4 November 1975

Dear David

CONGRATULATIONS!!

5 'Hold Back The Shite' – Trammps
4 'Rhinestone Crap Boy' – Glen Campbell
3 'I Only Have Eyes For Poo' – Fart Arsefumble
2 'Love Is The Slug' – Roxy Music
1 'SPACE ODDITY'!!!

And it only took six years!

It's the first full day back at school after half term, and I couldn't imagine a better welcome back present than seeing you finally get to No.1. Where did the BBC get that film they showed on *Top Of The Pops*? Was it from the first time the single was out? It was really strange to see you looking so young, and the version of 'Space Oddity' that played with the film was completely different as well.[95] Are you going to do any other television shows? I'd love to see you on *Supersonic,* although I don't think you'd particularly enjoy the experience. It's a completely mad show that revolves around the producer, Mike Mansfield, cueing in ever-more-bizarre special effects and stage props to accompany whichever band is on next – think *Top Of The Pops* if the stage designer came out of Christmas panto. You know how Gary Glitter always does that look of shock and surprise when he's performing? The last time he was on *Supersonic*, I don't think he was faking it, and now everyone's running around school going, 'Cue the papier-mâché dragon.'

School is really strange this year – and not only because of *Supersonic*! It's my last year, of course, so everything is geared towards the exams, with mountains more prep and, suddenly, teachers taking everything really seriously – and expecting *us* to,

95 The footage was excerpted from Bowie's then-unreleased 1968 film *Love You Till Tuesday*.

as well. But at the same time we have so much more freedom. I'm still going to the youth club most weeks, and now I know how Soul Boy was able to swing it so he could go to the disco without anyone minding. We've been told that, so long as we behave ourselves and don't do anything to disgrace either the school or ourselves, we should use our free time to find our way around the outside world.

I don't think this means we have licence to smoke, drink and shag our way through Bournemouth (in fact, we've been told it definitely doesn't). But Warthead had half a dozen of us in his office before half term, the more 'responsible' members of our class, he said (how little he knows!), and told us that, while boarding school tries to offer us a miniature version of the world outside, there are lots of experiences it cannot duplicate that we'll be facing on a daily basis in a little over six months. Therefore, if we can guarantee that our schoolwork won't suffer, he's prepared to give us a little more leeway when it comes to weekends and evenings. Of course, he left us in no doubt what will happen if we fuck up (or, at least, get caught fucking up), and he also swore us to secrecy, telling us to treat this 'freedom' as a privilege, not a right. The first sign of a foul-up and we'd be on the Restricted List before we could blink.

He wasn't joking, either! Within a week, Danny Meath got himself thrown out of three pubs on the High Street, before a fourth called the police, who brought him back to the school and he was barred from going out for the next three weeks. The weekend before half term, Coconut wound up in casualty having his stomach pumped after going on a pub crawl of his own and mixing every drink imaginable. Michael Nish came close to getting expelled for going on a shoplifting rampage, and right now Paul Banion is convinced he's got one of the girls at the youth club up the spout, because he used the wrong-size johnny. I told him I didn't think they came in different sizes, but he reckons the barber sold him Mr Fat Bastard size by mistake, and it kept falling off. And they wonder why I don't really hang around with them any more when we go out! I'm no angel, but at least I'm not stupid. Right now, Jonathan James and I are the only ones who've got through unscathed, and we're going to make the most of it, believe me!

Anyway, what a fantastic couple of months this has been for you, what with 'Fame' getting to No.1 in America, a new single ('Golden Years') already set to come out and a namecheck in the new Judge Dread single[96] – OK, so it's in the same breath as The Osmonds, but at least it wasn't with Little Jack Horner! I was also excited to see RCA have finally released 'Velvet Goldmine' on the B-side of 'Space Oddity'. What a wonderfully sleazy song that is, although is it really a *Hunky Dory* outtake, like it says on the sleeve?[97] It sounds completely different to anything else on the album – apart from possibly 'Queen Bitch'.

I assume the title is another tribute to The Velvet Underground. I finally heard more than a handful of isolated songs – Jonathan James came back from the summer holidays with the double album with the multiple lips on the cover[98] and, while I still think some of the songs are impossibly weak, 'Venus In Furs' and 'Black Angel's Death Song' are amazing.

They remind me a little of The Doctors Of Madness, who I mentioned to you a while back. I've seen them a couple of times since then. They're still playing pubs and things, but they're getting more and more of an audience, and somebody told me that their manager is Justin De Villeneuve – who also manages Twiggy! A small world, isn't it?! I don't know if you've had a chance to hear them yet, but next time you're in England you really should. I think you'll like them.

The other reason 'Space Oddity' did so brilliantly is because it ties in with *The Good Life* on the box. Have you seen it? It's about a couple living in Surbiton who throw away their old life and become self-sufficient, growing their own food, raising livestock in their back garden and so on. It's really funny, but underneath the comedy – and this is why it's so successful – it's

---

96 'Big Nine'.
97 It was later revealed to be a *Ziggy Stardust* outtake, remixed by RCA without Bowie's involvement or permission. 'An extraordinary move', he mused.
98 The 1973 compilation Andy Warhol's *Velvet Underground Featuring Nico*.

about the need to escape from all the pressures of the modern world and to cut yourself off in a world of your own. Sounds familiar? Their way of life becomes their tin can, and their neighbours are ground control, for ever trying to bring them back to earth. And I don't think it's coincidence that the husband's name is Tom, either.

Changing the subject, have you been to any of Ronno's gigs with Bob Dylan? I was amazed when I heard he was doing the tour – I bet Ian Hunter must be going mad with jealousy! I've never been much of a Dylan fan, although I liked a few of his old singles, and *Blood On The Tracks* was pretty good. I wonder if Ronno will be on his next album as well as the tour?[99] That could be interesting.

I don't know if you've heard, but there's a new music paper started up. It's called *Street Life* (like the Roxy song), and it's meant to be a British version of *Rolling Stone*, in that it covers things outside of the music scene – politics, sport, books, etc. There's only been one issue so far, but apart from jumping on the same Springsteen bandwagon as everybody else (what is the fascination? So what if he owns a lot of leather jackets – he still looks like an unemployed woodwork teacher), it was a lot more open-minded than *NME*, *Sounds*, *Disc* and so on.

One of the groups they covered was The Sadistic Mika Band, who were the first Japanese rock band ever to appear on *Whistle Test*. They were pretty good – I don't think I'd go out and buy one of their albums yet (they've made three), but the interview says their next one is going to sound like The Velvet Underground and that could be worth hearing. So many British and American artists have failed at recapturing that sound, after all. The only record I've heard that threatened to even come close was the ACNE[100] live album last year, although I don't know if that counts, being as two of them were ex-Velvets to begin with. Plus, if Eno's latest album[101] is anything to go by, he's not especially interested in rock songs any more.

99   Sadly, Ronson appears only on the live *Hard Rain* LP.
100 Kevin Ayers, John Cale, Nico and Eno, newly signed to Island Records in spring 1974 were rumoured to be considering forming a full band, inevitably viewed by some journalists as a Velvets reunion. In fact, the partnership recorded just one live album together at the London Rainbow, *June 1st, 1974*.
101 *Another Green World*.

A couple of bits are up to *Tiger Mountain*/*Warm Jets* standards. Everything else, though, seems to be vague instrumentals that don't really go anywhere, and have too many sound effects in them to be good background music. I played my copy a couple of times, then took it back to the shop and bought John Cale's *Helen Of Troy* instead. Alan Freeman played 'Leaving It All Up To You' on the radio a few Saturdays ago, and the old blues song 'Baby What You Want Me To Do' sounds really evil. My favourite, though, is 'Pablo Picasso'. It's a cover, but it sounds exactly like a John Cale song should sound – really menacing and churning. I hated his last album, *Slow Dazzle*, but this one's at least as good as *Fear* and *Paris 1919*.

Anyway, I'd better get on. Now we're in the fifth year, we're getting more prep every evening than we've had in the last four years put together. Tonight is Physics and French. I wonder if they come up with these combinations deliberately, or if some sort of mad computer hatches them?

All the best – and, again, CONGRATULATIONS!!!!!!!!!!!!!!!

Gary

Bournemouth, Dorset
Saturday 29 November 1975

Dear David

Just a quick note to tell you how excited I am about *The Man Who Fell To Earth*.[102] I saw the clip of it during your interview on *Russell Harty Plus* last night and, while the few minutes they screened probably weren't very representative of the entire film (and you barely spoke!), it looks like it's going to be good.

I do wish you'd made *Stranger In A Strange Land*, as that is now one of my all-time favourite books, but maybe if this one does well that'll be next. I'm glad you're writing the soundtrack to it, even though it's not going to be a rock film in the same way as *Stardust* or *Slade In Flame* (my two current favourites). It'll be interesting to hear you writing music that falls outside of the conventional rock and soul mould.

I really thought the interview would be cancelled because of Franco's death – I know there aren't many satellite hook-ups available, and I'd have thought that the death of a world leader would take some kind of precedence over a 'mere' rock star.[103] So it was great to switch on and find the show go ahead as scheduled. Apart from the interview, they also showed your *Soul Train* appearance, performing 'Golden Years' – were you really drunk when you filmed it? Now I'm hoping someone will show us the *Cher* show![104] From what I've read, that sounds completely over the top.

Is it true that you're going to be playing some London shows next summer? I can't believe it's two years since your last concerts here. I loved the bit in the interview when Russell Harty asked if you think you're a better musician after two years away from touring, and you looked at him like he's mad (which he probably is). And when he asked you what your new look will be, you said, 'I'll be a lot fatter.' He probably believed that as well.

---

102 Bowie's first starring movie role.
103 Normally, it would have, but Bowie refused to give up his pre-booked satellite time, so the interview went ahead.
104 On November 23, Bowie appeared on Cher's US TV show duetting with the hostess on a string of mainly MOR standards, medleyed with 'Young Americans'.

I don't think Russell Harty is particularly good at interviewing musicians – he never seems to be really sure who they are or what they're doing. Did you ever see Alvin Stardust when he was on? He told Harty that he thought it was a puppet show, and that Harty himself was a little dog, like Basil Brush. It was hysterical. Harty looked like he was going to explode.

I didn't like the way he brought up that interview with your mother.[105] Everybody has problems with their parents (some of us more than others!), so why is it that, because you're famous, it suddenly becomes some big news story? You really put Harty in his place when you told him to mind his own business, though. Well done.

Finally, what do you think of The Spiders From Mars (or, at least, Trevor Bolder and Woody Woodmansey) getting back together? I was a little surprised that you're letting them use the name, although it'd be perfect if you produced their record or wrote some songs for them. After all, they were half of the Greatest Group Ever! I'm not expecting miracles from it, but I'll probably pick up the single when it comes out.

If I don't write again before, Happy Christmas!

Gary

---

105 Bowie's mother was interviewed in the *NME*, revealing that the pair rarely communicated any longer.

Chelsea, London SW10
Friday 2 January 1976

Dear David

Thank goodness that's over. I hate Christmas, I hate New Year and I'm not keen on my birthday, either. There's nothing on telly, and you can't slope off to your room to play records because it's a 'family' day, and the house is always full of revolting relatives you've never heard of, who sit and ask things like 'How's school?' (shit), 'What exams are you taking?' (as few as possible) and 'What are you going to do when you leave school?' (smoke heavily, scrounge off the government and piss my stepfather off). Plus I received a Christmas card from my girlfriend (Jan in Polperro) saying she won't be able to write to me any more because her new boyfriend doesn't like it. Happy Christmas, the miserable cow.

None of my mum's side of the family ever visit us, but my stepfather's lot can't keep away. He runs the company with his brother Kevin, so he's always around, with his ugly fish-voiced wife Toni and two of the most revolting children you've ever seen. At Christmas, though, his mother, a sister (Aunt Stella, who my mum hates almost as much as I do) and others I've never even met descend on us, hand me a few badly wrapped presents – vests, socks, the usual gubbins – and then sit and complain about everything. Stella has asthma and, I swear, if I hadn't already started smoking I'd do it just to spite her.

And it gets worse. I picked up a ton of records that I've not been able to play because I need a new needle for my record player, and Rumbelows are out of stock until next week, by which time I'll be back at school. So, if you've heard any of the following, please take pity and let me know what they sound like.

Roxy Music – *Siren*
Supertramp – *Crisis? What Crisis?*

Peter Hammill – *Nadir's Big Chance*
Sparks – *Indiscreet* (produced by Tony Visconti!)

I was going to take them round to Soul Boy's to listen to, but he'd probably hate most of them, so we've been going out to gigs instead. We've been to a bunch, mainly at the Marquee – and I might as well have made him suffer Peter Hammill, because most of them were rubbish as well. Out of sheer curiosity (and because Alan Freeman played a track that wasn't bad), we went to see Brand X, Phil Collins' side-project. Dreadful, a really noodly jazz thing, and Collins wasn't even playing with them. Giggles weren't even good for a laugh, and The Pink Fairies were SO disappointing. I love the albums, but that was then. This is now – stodgy, endless guitar solos, crappy songs I didn't recognise and an audience full of bikers who were themselves so bored that they spent more time staring at Soul Boy and me than they did watching the band. We left before the gig was even over.

Christmas Eve, we went to see The 101ers at the Hope and Anchor in Islington, figuring that with a name like that they're either George Orwell students or *Diamond Dogs* fans. Actually, I don't think they're either – just another slightly retro rock band, old before their time. Did you ever see that movie about the 1972 London Rock 'n' Roll Festival? They could have been one of the backing bands in that, completely anonymous, plodding along. They reminded me of The Rubettes without the berets. Or the hits. It's strange, there's a bunch of new bands coming through in London – people like Ducks Deluxe, Eddie And The Hot Rods and Dr Feelgood – who play with a real intensity, like they're really pissed off at something and music's the only weapon they have against it. And then there's this battalion of others, with The 101ers at the forefront, who seem to think it'll be 1974 for ever, and that if they play loud enough no one'll notice that their songs all sound the same.[106]

The best band we saw the whole time was The Heavy Metal Kids on New Year's Eve. Have you heard their album yet? It's

---

106 101ers frontman Joseph Mellor later re-emerged as the Clash's Joe Strummer.

wonderful. The singer, Gary Holton, reminds me a bit of Steve Marriott, one of those little Artful Dodger types (he was in a school production of *Oliver* as well) with a superb voice. He can sing soul, rock, even a bit of reggae, but what I like best is that he doesn't seem to be taking any of it at all seriously. He's always messing around on stage, dressing up funny, taking the piss out of the band and the audience. I was talking to him in the bar before the show, and he told me that they'd just toured America and had a 'luvverly' time winding up kids who saw them play, then complained that they weren't heavy metal. He'd tell them that they were, and it was everybody else who'd got it wrong. I didn't realise that they took their name from William Burroughs – and it turns out that The Doctors Of Madness did as well.

The trouble is…perfect band names, dreadful inspiration. I tried reading some of Burroughs after you talked about him in an interview, and I couldn't get into it all. Things really don't need to be that complicated. If you're going to write something, whether it's a story, a book or a poem, then write it. Simply using random phrases and sentences might make you look clever but, if it doesn't mean anything, what's the point? I really wanted to ask Holton if he knew what Burroughs was on about, but I couldn't think of a polite way of phrasing the question. Maybe I should have written it down, cut all the words up and then reassembled it on the bar in front of him: 'Burroughs what have about do whatsoever any you on idea is?'

After the Heavy Metal Kids gig, we went down to Trafalgar Square to see in the New Year, but it was too crowded to be any fun. Plus the law was getting really heavy-handed. Every time someone even looked like they were drunk, a couple of cops would grab him and throw him in the back of a Black Maria. By the end of the evening, it must have been like the Black Hole of Calcutta in there, they locked so many people up.

The tube home was disgusting, of course. The District Line is never that reliable at the best of times, but that was the worst ever. Finally I gave up waiting for a Fulham Broadway train and went to Sloane Square instead, walked home and was given a bollocking because I was meant to be home early so we could all see the New Year in together, blah-blah-blah. Hurrah, Andy bloody Stewart's *Hogmanay Show*, with my stepfather farting out his single glass of champagne and my mother wondering where it all went wrong. At the rate this holiday's going, I'll be glad to get back to school. At least there they *admit* that you're a prisoner.

Still, I did sort out one thing, sort of. Soul Boy reckons if he's still at the press agency in July, he might be able to get me a job there so, next time the careers officer comes to tell me that I really should consider the options my stepfather has so generously made available (would you believe the bastard wrote to the school to tell them about it?), I can tell him to stuff it.

How did you spend your Christmas? I read the interview you did in *Playboy* (I had to go to three shops before I found one that would sell me the magazine!) and I was surprised to read so much about your family. I knew you had a brother, Terry, but I didn't know he was in an asylum, or that others in your family had also been there. I've been wondering if *Aladdin Sane* was somehow based upon that, but people can read far too much into song lyrics, and it's daft asking songwriters to explain what the song is about, because if they could do that in a few easy sentences why would they have gone to all the trouble of writing the song?

I read Anthony Scaduto's biography of Bob Dylan earlier this year, and I don't know how Dylan could stand having people analysing every word he writes and building their own fantasy Dylans around them. If I were in that position, I'd never want to write another song again! Or maybe I'd go completely instrumental, although the nutters would probably start analysing the notes as well. Can you imagine having somebody like A J Weberman following you around, going through your dustbin in search of new clues about the meaning of a song you've forgotten even writing?

My own theory is that most rock stars live lives that are as ordinary as everybody else's, but because they're famous those ordinary things seem a lot more interesting. That's why the teenybopper magazines make such a big deal about favourite colours, favourite cheese, favourite swear word and things. Everybody has a favourite colour, but because a pop star *is* a pop star, his or her favourites seem far more exotic.

When I was younger, I used to pick up magazines like *Popswap* and *Music Star* if they had articles about you in them, but I stopped because there never seemed to be any real information – unless, of course, you need to know what Woody Roller's shoe size is. The last issues I saw were full of Slik, the next Great Scottish Hope, but every time I see a picture of them, all togged out in their baseball uniforms, all I can think of is Iron Virgin – remember them? One of those wonderful pseudo-glam bands of a couple of a years back, also Scottish, put out one OK single called 'Rebels Rule' and strolled around wearing American football outfits. Didn't work then, won't work now... Don't give up your day jobs, boys.

Anyway, the only mags I read now are *NME*, *Zig Zag* and, occasionally, *Street Life*. You still can't believe a lot of what they print, but at least they try to find out interesting things about the people they cover – plus writers like Mick Farren and Charles Shaar Murray are always worth reading. Or, at least, they understand that rock music is more than simply musicians playing music, and that it has a mythology that is all its own. Mick Farren's *The Tale Of Willy's Rats* is a great book if you're interested in that sort of thing. It's fiction, but it taps into the spirit of darkness, mystery and decay that is always lurking just behind the smiling face of pop – Altamont, Charles Manson, faked deaths, covered-up murders, the lot. Did you hear Golden Earring's 'Ce Soir' single? A famous rock star is killed on stage by a sniper hired by his manager, and sales go through the roof. Shades of Eddie Cochran... I expect you've heard the story that Gene Vincent reckons he was still alive after the accident, and only died after receiving certain secret visitors? Then there's the stories about how Jimi Hendrix was murdered, and Buddy

Holly's plane was shot down, while Jim Morrison didn't even die but ran off to Africa to become a mercenary. Rimbaud has a lot to answer for.

People concoct these stories because it's a lot easier to accept a mysterious death than it is to know your idol pegged out in the same mundane manner as any 'normal' person. Jimi Hendrix could make his guitar speak, they say – so how come he wasn't capable of clearing his own throat? Or, what if Morrison had taken a shower instead of a bath? Throw in a few layers of conspiracy, then a flaky girlfriend and some shadowy associates, and suddenly a simple passing becomes a web of intrigue. And, even if it doesn't – well, maybe that's why people think drug overdoses are so glamorous, because rock stars do it and what could be more glamorous than a rock star? I loved the film *Stardust* for that reason – watching it, you realise that there was nothing glamorous at all about the way Jim MacLaine lived or died, but the fact that he was a white-suited recluse rattling around this sprawling Spanish castle made people think there was. In instances like that, it's not even a matter of projecting an image – the trick is to maintain a perception. And snuffing it on live television, of course, reinforces it.

The other film I really enjoyed, along the same lines, was *Phantom Of The Paradise* – a rock version of *Phantom Of The Opera*, of course. The soundtrack is appalling, but I love the idea of a rock star faking his death, then haunting his fans… I wish they'd taken it even further, and given us a rock remake of *Theatre Of Blood,* that Hammer film from a few years back, with Vincent Price as a Shakespearean actor who fakes his death so he can strike out at the critics who slagged him the worst. How perfect! Can you imagine, the staff of *NME*, *Record Mirror* and *Melody Maker* being snuffed out one by one by a vengeful failed glam rocker? Coming soon, *The Curse Of Jobriath*.

Even *Ziggy* taps into that fascination in a way, the 'What if?' sort of scenario. The kids killed the man, the band broke up – but what would have happened if they hadn't? WE WOZ CHEATED, and that's the belief that lies at the core of the mythology. Rock 'n' roll has a life force of its own, and rock 'n' rollers are simply the vessels through which it is projected. Break the vessel and the spirit lives on. And the best rock 'n' roll writers are the ones who not only live in hope of figuring out where it's going to turn up next, but also try to trace the places where it's already been.

They don't even have to die any more. Go mad, get religion, become a recluse – anything, so long as people can look back at the career and be left to wonder 'What if?' That's why there's so much interest these days in people like Vince Taylor (even The 101ers were playing 'Brand New Cadillac'), Syd Barrett, Scott Walker, Peter Green. If Vince hadn't turned into Jesus, if Syd hadn't gone round the bend, if Peter hadn't wanted to give all his money away to charity…

Pay attention, and you can see the process in action today. Remove yourself from the commercial mainstream, either physically (death, damage, retirement) or creatively (in years to come, people will worship *Metal Machine Music*), and sooner or later you'll be the stuff of legend. I'll bet you anything you like that, in years to come, Iggy Pop will be held up as a lost saviour of rock 'n' roll. So long as he doesn't make the mistake of staging a comeback – which doesn't seem very likely right now! – his immortality is assured.

Back to reality… There's an intriguing interview with Nicolas Roeg[107] in the new *Street Life*, where he describes your *Man Who Fell To Earth* character as being based on Howard Hughes(!). Makes a change from the Legendary Stardust Cowboy, doesn't it! The soundtrack music sounds interesting. The journalist called it 'a simple melodic instrumental based around organ, bass and drums', all of which you played yourself. Will any of the music be appearing on *Station To Station*?[108] I'm very curious about the album – I read in *NME* that the album features appearances from Alice Cooper, Peter Frampton, Bobby

---

107 Director of *The Man Who Fell To Earth*.
108 Bowie's soundtrack was ultimately replaced in the film by music from former The Mamas And The Papas frontman John Phillips. Elements of Bowie's themes ultimately appeared on his 1977 LP, *Low*.

Womack and Ronnie Wood, plus Bruce Springsteen's keyboard player. What an amazing combination – I just hope it works![109]

It must have been funny working with Frampton. Were you friends at school, or was the age difference too much? I simply can't imagine you working with Alice Cooper, though. His approach to music seems so different from yours. I always think that you write the songs first, and then create the theatrics to go with them, whereas with Alice it seems like he comes up with the visuals first, then writes songs to fit them.

Some friends saw his *Welcome To My Nightmare* concerts last year and said that they were excellent, some of the best theatrics ever. But they also said you need to see the show before the album even starts sounding good. I suppose, in a way, that's how you're working at the moment, writing the movie soundtrack. The difference is, movies are around for ever, whereas concerts are one-off experiences and, once they're over, you'll never see them again, whether you have the album or not. Still, I'm looking forward to seeing what the two of you come up with.

Happy New Year – and all the best for 1976.

Gary

PS Any idea how long it's going to take for them to send back tickets for your Wembley shows? I sent in for two for the Saturday show (8 May) back on 6 December, and STILL haven't heard anything. But I bet they've already cashed my postal order!

---

109 Springsteen's keyboard player (Roy Bittan) was the only one who made it onto the disc.

Bournemouth, Dorset
Saturday 27 March 1976

Dear David

This'll probably be the last letter I write to you for a while – exams start in earnest in a couple of weeks, and it's been virtually nonstop revision for weeks now. For all the good it'll do. Either I'll remember this stuff or I won't, and I'll either pass the exams or I won't. I'm taking eight CSEs and eight O-levels, all in pretty much the same subjects. I'm not sure why I've got to double up like that, I suppose it's a safety net or something... a CSE Grade 1 is equivalent to an O-level pass, so I could end up with 16 identical results, or I could turn out to be the greatest academic failure in the school's history. Wish me luck!

I've got my ticket for Wembley, at last. Now all I have to do is keep my nose clean for the next couple of weeks. Unlike the last time I saw you, I'm doing everything legally this time. We're so near the end of term – and my entire school career – that I barely even had to ask permission to come up to London for the weekend, just promise that I'd do Saturday morning's prep on the Sunday evening when I get back. Even better, I'll be staying at Soul Boy's for the entire time, so I don't have to tell my parents I'll be in town.

I was thinking, in a way, we're in much the same boat. Rehearsing for a tour must be a lot like revising for exams, going over all the stuff you've done during the past few years, making sure you remember everything and then hoping your mind doesn't go blank on the big day. I wish there was an O-level in Applied Bowie-onics, though – I know I'd pass that. Fancy swapping jobs for a few days? I'll come up to Wembley and sing all your songs, and you can come down to Bournemouth and sit my O-level Maths.

I've tried to find a healthy balance between revision and recreation, but it's been difficult. I've been going out with a girl at the youth club most of this year. Her name's Nicola and she really is gorgeous – even Paul Banion, who fancies himself as something of a ladies' man, is secretly jealous. But because she's getting ready for her exams as well, we've probably only seen each other half a dozen times this year, and I don't know what we're going to do after I leave school. I'm trying to convince her to come up to London with me for your show, I'm sure we'll be able to get a ticket somehow, but I don't think she will. If nothing else, her father wouldn't give her permission. He's ex-air force, so you can imagine the type.

Aside from that, the most exciting thing that's happened was Coconut, Jonathan and I getting chased through Bournemouth town centre by a gang of teds a few weeks ago. It was pretty terrifying at the time, because they were a lot older than us, but they were also grockles (which is why they were after us – we made the mistake of thinking they were deaf as well as stupid northerners), so we knew all the little short cuts and alleyways between the disco and the railway station. We got on to the train as it was pulling away, and left them on the other side of the ticket barrier, shouting insults. By the time we were back at school we'd turned a frantic flight into a major bundle from which, of course, we emerged triumphant. Well, it's only a slight exaggeration!

What music are you listening to at the moment? Aside from your own, of course! I'm really not finding much new stuff that gets me going – Nicola and I spent an evening slow-dancing to Cliff Richard's 'Miss You Nights' a few weeks ago, so I've developed an embarrassing attachment to that, and Pluto Shervington's 'Dat' is annoying enough that it's bored a hole straight into my skull. I'm not at all big on reggae, but every so often, once a year or so, something will come along that I find completely addictive. Rupie Edwards' 'Ire Feelings (Skanga)' falls into the same category.

My favourite new band, though, is probably Supercharge, who are that rarest of creatures: a decent English funk band!

But they have a really warped sense of humour as well. They'll be playing a straightforward show, then suddenly lurch into the most amazing Drifters parody, dedicated to the etiquette surrounding taking a piss in the kitchen sink. It's called 'She Moved The Dishes First' – of course! I first saw them at one of the free gigs in Hyde Park last summer, then a couple of times in pubs since then, and they get funnier every time. They're even responsible for my other favourite song of the moment – they do a hilarious piss-take of 'Save Your Kisses For Me',[110] which has opened my ears to what a perfectly constructed song that really is. Utterly mindless, utterly bland, but pressing so many of the right pop buttons that it's absolutely inescapable.

Don't worry, though. I'm not turning into a total Top 30 chart-fodder freak. I'm listening to a lot of old Bolan again – 'New York City' was such a jewel that it sent me all the way back to *Electric Warrior* and *The Slider*, and I've been tracking back from there, rediscovering the earlier albums and having a great time. I have to ask you, though. You know how Marc is prone to tell the odd whopper every now and then? I read an interview with him where he's talking about 'New York City' and saying he really did see the woman with a frog in her hand there, except it was a 90-year-old witch with an enormous toad, walking down Park Avenue. And you were with him at the time. It's such a wonderful story that I do hope it's true. Maybe you could write a song about it as well!

What else? The Doctors Of Madness' first album is finally out and I'm playing it constantly. You should try doing History revision to 'Mainlines', 17 minutes of psycho violins and dead rats. It'd be perfect if we were studying the Middle Ages. I love Ducks Deluxe (Sean Tyla has to be one of the most captivating frontmen around); The Heavy Metal Kids are as entertaining as ever; and Dr Feelgood are everything I ever wished the early 1960s had sounded like – *Pin-Ups* on

110 The Brotherhood Of Man's 1976 Eurovision Song Contest winner.

speed. Finally, if you haven't already, you have to hear The Winkies! The album was produced by Guy Stevens, and the similarities between The Winkies and early (*Wildlife*-era) Mott are amazing. In fact, I'm off to play it again now, so I hope all is well... See you on 8 May!

Gary

Bournemouth, Dorset
Sunday 9 May 1976

Dear David

Station to station indeed – I'm writing this on the train back to Bournemouth, after coming up yesterday to see you at Wembley. It was a spectacular show, as good as any I've seen this year. The new band was so tight; in fact, I prefer the live sound to the album! Stacey Heydon nails the songs down a lot harder than Earl Slick did,[111] and Tony Kaye's playing is much more interesting than Roy Bittan's.[112] Is there anybody at all associated with Bruce Springsteen who *isn't* completely overrated?

Great set list as well. 'Station To Station' and 'Stay' were already my favourite tracks on the album, but the live versions made them sound like The Brotherhood Of Man. I loved the way you steered clear of all the big hits, at the same time as making sure there were enough familiar songs in there to keep everybody happy. 'Fame' worked a lot better than I ever imagined it would, and it was wonderful to hear 'Waiting For The Man' as it *should* be done, as opposed to that ridiculous semi-metal corpse Lou Reed's been dragging around lately.

Would you believe I missed the film that opened,[113] because I ran out to hit the souvenir stalls while the crowds were otherwise occupied. But even from there you could hear a massive, collective 'Bleaugh' go through the entire venue when the razor blade went through the eyeball.

The audience was exactly as you'd expect, Ziggied up to the nines, with a few Halloween Jacks and Young American clones rattling around for good measure (God, where did people find some of those suits?). But you could almost hear their jaws drop when you came out on stage looking like you did. Even though we've all seen the photos from the American dates, there was a vague belief that you'd do something different/special here – first British gigs in almost three years and all that. Plus,

111 The hitherto unknown Heydon replaced Slick early on in rehearsals for the tour.
112 Bittan was unavailable due to commitments with Bruce Springsteen/E Street Band. He was replaced by the former Yes keyboard player.
113 Buñuel/Dali's *Un Chien Andalou*.

things often look more extreme in real life than they do in pictures. I love the slicked-back hair, by the way. Kind of vampiric...although have you noticed how they never have blond vampires in the films?

Of course, the look tied in perfectly with all that 'fascist dictator'/Nazi salute business that's been engrossing the papers these last few days. Now, I don't know what really happened – I wasn't at Victoria Station when you came in (although riding around in an open-top Mercedes probably wasn't the best idea you ever had under the circumstances) – and, the fact is, Britain probably *would* benefit from a fascist dictator. Preferably one who not only made the trains run on time (this one was 20 minutes late leaving), but who also did something about the buffet snacks. Do you know anyone who's ever bought one of those little slices of fruitcake, except for a dare?

Seriously, though, it's fascinating the way that the concept of fascism has now become inextricably linked with Hitler and the Nazis, which is a point you made that got overlooked completely. If you read any history of prewar Britain (with the O-level coming up, I've read several), there was a school of thought that advocated a kind of benign fascism that had nothing to do with genocide, repression and invading Poland, but was concerned purely with pulling the country out of the Depression and the post-World War I trough by fostering a pride in being British, which translated, in turn, into a pride in yourself.

Fascism – and communism come to that – was simply an attempt to create some kind of alternative to the crass capitalism that was already taking over. We call it Americanisation today, of course, and it's an even bigger problem than ever, probably because those alternatives did fail so badly. But it wasn't fascism that failed; it was the bullshit that was added to it by the Nazis, because it's the bullshit that has survived, whereas the actual doctrine is long forgotten. There's not a single mention of genocide in *Mein Kampf*, any more than *Das Kapital* is filled with handy tips for conducting pogroms.

My grandfather, and a lot of people of that generation, insist that the worst thing Britain ever did was to do away with National Service, and the fascists' politics – at least before Mosley[114] started hanging around with Hitler – were an extension of the belief that some kind of enforced regimentation is necessary, to stop people from reverting to useless blobs of protoplasmic slime. The idea was for people to start taking pride in their appearance again, and pride in being members of society – no more unemployment, no more slacking off, no more selfishness. Fascism was about everybody working for the common good, rather than shooting off at a thousand different tangents, none of which was at all compatible with what was good for society in general. It'd probably have been pretty vile living under a regime like that, but there's no denying that the theory – all for one and one for all, and all that – is so sound that it's virtually idealistic.

Also, no matter how people think of the Nazis' politics, you have to admit they knew how to put on a show – or, at least, they knew how to employ people who knew how to put on a show. And, looking at your stage set, I know you know exactly who I'm thinking about: Albert Speer, Leni Riefenstahl. I got to see *Triumph Of The Will* for the first time a few weeks ago, and all I could think of was: 'The world's first rock movie'. Like that, the sheer scale of your show was mind-blowing. I know it was just a regular stage lit up with a few fluorescent tubes, but it completely dwarfed anything I've ever seen, including Ziggy. There, the theatricality was in the costumes. At Wembley, it was even in the shadows – which was precisely where Speer intended it to be way back when.

My own interpretation of your fascist controversy is that you were trying to do the same thing with politics as you did with sexuality back in 1972, when you stirred up that whole 'Is he or isn't he gay?' furore. Everybody had always seen homosexuality in terms of either black ('He's queer') or white ('He's straight'), and then you came along with a wife and a kid and began

114 British fascist figurehead Oswald Mosley.

talking about the shades of grey in between. You opened the whole subject up to mass debate (pun not intended), and it really did make a difference. Homosexuality stopped being something that was kept buried – it's no coincidence that openly gay characters have started popping up even in mainstream TV shows and, while neither whatshisname in *It Ain't Half Hot, Mum* nor Mr Humphries[115] are exactly positive role models, at least they exist.

It really wouldn't hurt to have the same thing happen with politics. The system is totally in disarray. Labour isn't working (another dreadful pun – and I didn't even intend that one!); the Liberals are so wishy-washy that they probably don't even wear matching socks any more; and the Tories are simply saying the precise opposite to whatever the government comes up with. Besides, you'd have to be deaf to want to vote for that Thatcher woman – she sets my teeth on edge every time she opens her mouth.

And, in the face of all that, people wonder why the far right wing is getting so strong. Because they're the only ones who have anything remotely resembling a plan of action, whether you like what they stand for or not. I can't stand them but, rather than encourage some kind of open debate about why they are so appealing to some segments of the population, people would rather shout them down. And, of course, that's exactly what happened to you, everyone rushing to condemn without considering for a moment that not only is the issue not a matter of black and white but there might be something in the grey area that's worth talking about.

This whole resurgent Nazi thing could be cleaned out immediately, if only people were willing to try to explain the wrongs of the past, rather than simply cover them up, pretend they didn't happen and stifle anyone who says otherwise. Because that prompts those people to say it even louder, and because they know they'll get a reaction. It's the rebellious kiddie syndrome. The more the parents say 'Don't do that', the more

115 John Inman's camp mens' outfitter in TV's *Are You Being Served?*

the kid is going to do it, to get a reaction. Half the people walking around 'admiring' the Nazis today would run a mile if they came face to face with the real doctrine – they're simply picking up on the elements that are going to get the strongest reaction, and running with them.

Do you remember a couple of years ago, when one of The Sweet went on *Top Of The Pops* dressed as a gay stormtrooper, with a swastika armband and a Hitler moustache? Everyone thought it was really funny, and it was. But try that today and see what happens. Yet, does anybody even care that American dimes are decorated with precisely the same insignia as Mussolini used to strut around with? It's called a *fascis* and, while it's been around since the Roman Republic (just like the swastika's been around since ancient Indian times), that's hardly the most convincing role model for democracy and freedom, is it?

There again, neither's America. Look at what happened to The New York Dolls last year. Over there, they look at communism in the same way as we look at Nazis, so the Dolls dressed in red, used the hammer and sickle for a backdrop and wound up horrifying half the country. What they didn't realise was, holding up a nation's biggest nightmare for all to see doesn't cure it. It reinforces the phobia and wedges another few tons of kneejerk paranoia and ignorance in between the two extremes – again, as you found out. On the bright side, though, I hope you appreciated the irony of the anti-fascists themselves becoming a bunch of total fascists: 'Ve do not agree vith vot you are saying. Recant or ve vill exterminate you.'

I know history is always written by the winners, but wouldn't it be nice if they'd occasionally let the neutrals have a go? How long before they really start doctoring the history books, and rewriting the archives to make sure everything fits in with current thinking? People go on about *1984* as though it's some kind of magical date where everything goes to pot, but that date is simply the year in which Winston Smith's story happened. The process had begun long before – and, looking around, sometimes

I wonder if it's not already under way. You were right when you said this country needs to have a revolution. But people took it the wrong way completely. We need the revolution to *stop* the country from turning into a totalitarian state, not to create one.

Anyway, enough of that. I really enjoyed part one of *The David Bowie Story* on Radio 1. They had a lot of new information in there, and some interesting music as well. It's really going to reawaken interest in your older records again, so have you thought any more about arranging for them to be reissued? I must admit I was pleased to see *Images* released over here last year – I bought the American import when it first came out, and was thrilled that it rounded up all the Decca material. Now, if only you'd do the same with the Philips/Mercury songs, and the earlier singles as well!

Talking of which, there's a question I've been meaning to ask you. I picked up an American copy of 'Space Oddity' (the one on Mercury), and was wondering how come 'Wild Eyed Boy From Freecloud' starts a few lines into the song. I know the Yanks love their singles to clock in around the three-minute mark, but this was a B-side, and it loses half the story! Ridiculous.

Well, we're only a couple of stops away from Bournemouth, and I've rambled on for far too long, so I'd better wrap this up. Thanks for a fantastic show, an inspiring album, a terrific new single – and please don't make us wait so long to see you again!

All the best

Gary

Chelsea, London SW10
Monday 2 August 1976

Dear David

Well, that's that. I left school for good on Friday but I don't think the sheer enormity of the event has quite sunk in yet, despite spending the last week having huge farewell parties at school, at the youth club, at school again and then round at Soul Boy's on Saturday night. There were a couple of moments on Thursday and Friday, though, when it sort of hit home. Teachers who'd always been total bastards were suddenly being nice, reminding us to stay in touch because they always like to hear how 'old boys' are doing...but the real 'Oh my God, I'm free' moment came Friday, before we left for the station, and one of the kids in my class came over, shook us London boys firmly by the hand and said, 'Have a good life.'

My first reaction was to laugh and make some kind of joke, and then it dawned on me that he was being serious, and I'll probably never have to gaze upon his ugly mug ever again. Ever. Or any of the others'. I've spent the last five years with these people, and suddenly it's over. In one of those moments of completely inexplicable panic, I rushed around and got everyone's addresses and phone numbers, 'In case I'm ever in your neck of the woods' – I know I probably won't be, but it's sort of reassuring to know that there's some way of contacting them if I ever want to.

Of course, I'm not free of all of them. Gnome's Head and Paul are already planning to move to London, and we've been through too much together to simply cut off completely. There's a couple of others who are already living there, so we'll probably bump into one another occasionally. And if I ever become really schoolsick (the opposite of homesick, I suppose), I could always head down to Waterloo Station on the first day of term to say hello. Yeah, right.

No, I'm out of there and I'm glad of it. Tomorrow I'm off to the DHSS to see about signing on for the first time, and then it's the Job Centre to see what limitless opportunities await an ambitious, efficient, smart and intelligent school leaver. Then they can tell me what's left for me. It does seem a bit retarded trying to find a job before I get my exam results through, but they probably won't make much difference anyway. There's a million people on the dole, so what chance do this year's school leavers have?

My rat-bastard stepfather has finally given up on drawing me into the family business. I told him that I don't care who he's married to, I've never considered him family and never will, so it's a bit late to start pretending now. And, oddly, my mum agrees with me, although not in those same words. She said I'd be a lot better off being left to stand on my own two feet, rather than being pulled out of one closeted environment into another. If I don't have a job by Christmas, maybe we can re-examine the situation, but until then he should leave me alone. I could tell he was furious, but there's one thing about my mum – when she puts her foot down over something, it stays down. Thank goodness for her.

At least I'm in London, though, rather than stuck out in the provinces somewhere. The first few days, all I could think of was Thin Lizzy's new single. That first weekend, I met up with Soul Boy at Fulham Broadway and we went for a celebration coffee and burger at Dino's, right by the station, and there was, indeed, a jukebox in the corner, the nights are getting warmer (in fact, they're already boiling hot), summer's here and the boys are back in town! I love that song so much right now! There's always something to do, even if it's hanging around record shops or going to gigs. Tomorrow night, we're off to the Nashville to see The Stranglers, who Soul Boy reckons are so awful that they're hysterically funny – he described them as a cross between The Doors and Les Dawson. The Daws. I can't wait.

What are you up to now? Have you finished the Iggy album yet? I was surprised to hear that you're doing it, as it seems years since you were actively working with another artist. Then again, it's certainly going to be a challenge (for you as producer and us as listeners), at least if Iggy's last album is anything to go by. I scoured London for weeks to find *Metallic KO* – it finally turned up, of all places, at that little record stall in the arcade on the King's Road. And was it worth it? I dunno. The sound quality is atrocious – some of my worst bootlegs sound better. But live Iggy is so hard to find, and it was a historic show. Side two, when the riot gets going and the Angels are throwing things at the stage ('eggs, jelly-beans, grenades' – I love that line) is almost frightening to listen to, but at the same time it's completely irresistible.

It has that same aura of horror as the Stones' *Gimme Shelter* film, where you can feel the tension building, long before things start to happen – even on side one, which was recorded at a completely different show. It's a funny feeling, then, to listen to *Metallic KO*, then read reports in the music papers about how 'violent' some of the bands playing around London at the moment are. All the papers go on about how The Sex Pistols pick fights with their audience, but then you wonder what sort of audience they get. A few dozen kids who are there to see the show? Or a few hundred Hell's Angels who've descended on the place explicitly to kick the shit out of the band? Whenever I've seen them, it's definitely been the former – art-student types, trainee hairdressers, the sort of crowd who used to follow Roxy Music around, together with a smattering of curious scruffs who tend to drift away long before the show is over. Metallic KO? More like a big, soft, fluffy one.

Finally, did you see the Viking space probe photographs from the surface of Mars on the box last week? It looks like one of your old questions has finally been answered, doesn't it?[116]

All the best

Gary

116 'Is there Life on Mars?' Apparently not.

Chelsea, London SW10
Sunday 28 November 1976

Dear David

So, how's life in Berlin? It must be so different living there after being in Los Angeles for so long. I've only been to Germany once: when I was 9 or 10, my school took a party of us to Cologne. All I can remember is being amazed that a city that the history books told us was bombed into extinction was so clean and new, without a brick out of place – whereas London, which lived through the Blitz and rose again and so on, was still full of old bombsites and derelict buildings – still is, in fact. It does put an interesting new slant on war, though, doesn't it? To the winners, the glory; to the losers, a new town hall, a lovely sports stadium and a beautifully landscaped municipal park. Maybe countries should stop fighting altogether and go on *The Generation Game*.

Lifestyle-wise, it certainly seems to be pretty hectic for you, at least if the more irresponsible music mags are to be believed. Splashed across the cover of *National Rock Star*, 'BOWIE HEART SHOCKER!' Oh my God! Even at work (yes, I have a job – I'll tell you about it in a minute), people started talking about it when they saw the cover and, bearing in mind they're almost all 30- to 40-year-olds there, that shows what an impact the story made. Ah, but then you realise this is *National Rock Star*, which means it's the same paper that ran an 'ELVIS TO PLAY BRITAIN' story back in September, in their very first issue, and then had to retract it in their second. So, rather than panic, I decided to hang on and see what the story really was – and, of course, it turns out there's not really much of a story after all.[117]

Have you finished recording the new album? It's interesting that you're working with Eno, of all people... He's one of those characters who seems to operate in such a different musical area from you (from anyone, in fact) that the end result is going to

---

117 According to a spokesman for the Berlin British Military Hospital, Bowie had 'overdone things, and was suffering from too much drink. He hadn't had a coronary'.

be either absolutely brilliant or absolutely bizarre. There is no middle ground! And is there any news on when the Iggy album might be out?[118] I've done my best not to get excited about it, because part of me still thinks Iggy's better off being a shadowy legend than a functioning performer. At the same time, though, if the new album is even half as good as his reputation demands, every other band might as well go home now. There'll be nothing to touch it.

What a contrast it must have been for you, though, going from the Iggy sessions to working with Eno with barely a pause for breath. Just don't get the master tapes muddled up! There was an interview with Ricky Gardiner[119] in *National Rock Star* a few weeks back (it may even have been the Elvis issue, so I hope it wasn't another of their hoaxes!). He said the sessions were going really well, and that all the musicians have a lot more freedom than they were expecting. Apparently you're calling the album *New Music: Night And Day* – hmmm, *new* music? Another change in direction? I know, you're going punk rock! Or, as that's already being done right now, *post*-punk rock. Four chords and a bulldog clip.

My big news is, I managed to get a job! I'm working at a travel agent's in Enfield, which is a hell of a trek every morning and evening: bus to Sloane Square, Victoria Line to Tottenham Hale, bus to Enfield. It takes for ever! But it has inspired me to start looking for a flat of my own, and at least I'm earning money – the dole was giving me £8 a week, here I'm taking home nearly £16, plus £1 a week in luncheon vouchers.

The work is exactly what you'd expect, only less exciting. I'm not allowed to book anybody's holidays, or do any real travel-related things at all, so I spend my day selling Red Rover bus tickets to old ladies and schoolchildren, and booking the occasional cross-channel day-trip. The good part is, it's a family-run business and all the other staff (five of them) have kids, so the shop closes at 4:00pm, which means, if the buses work out right, I can be home a little after 6:00pm and back in the West

118 Bowie and Iggy Pop were working on Iggy's *The Idiot* album through autumn 1976.
119 Bowie's current guitarist.

End before 8:00pm. I'm not sure that I want to be a travel agent for ever, but it's as cushy a job as I'm going to find.

Oh, and after all my joking about the exam results being useless, it was the Geography O-level that landed me the job! I had to do a little test at the interview, and apparently I was the only applicant who knew things like the capital of Romania, the difference between Sweden and Switzerland, and which way round the North and South Poles are. The boss looked at my CV, saw the O-level and said, 'Ah, that explains it.' I didn't have the heart to tell him I'd known those things since junior school and, if he wanted to find out what the O-level involved, he should quiz me on arable farming in the Russian steppes or some such...

Of course, I'm the youngest person here, but the others aren't quite so old that they hate all music – in fact, one of the women confessed that before she met her husband five years ago you were her ideal man! Turns out she was a big fan of yours in 1969. She still has her copy of the Philips LP, and she even saw you open for Humble Pie at the Queen Elizabeth Hall.

I asked her what she thought about your more recent music, but I don't think she'd paid much attention to any of it. She was married with her first kid by the time *Ziggy* came out, and pretty much lost touch with the music scene. I'm going to tape *Hunky Dory*, *Ziggy* and the *Santa Monica* bootleg for her, and try to wean her back into the fold.

She started me thinking, though, about how bands and their audiences change as time passes. A couple of years ago, the Rollers were the biggest band in the world, but today you barely even hear them mentioned. Ask most people and they'll say it's because the band became too big for their little tartan booties and tried to pretend they were a real grown-up group, which alienated all the little Roller Girls. The thing is, the Roller Girls were getting older as well, meaning their tastes would have been changing at the same time – which put the band in a hopeless position. If they stayed the same, churning out endless variations on 'Shimmy Shammy Shong' for ever, the fans would have walked away because they'd have grown out of it; and if they tried to change, they were running the risk of taking the wrong turning and losing the fans anyway – which is precisely what happened.

Compare that to someone like you, who's managed to change constantly and keep the same fans as well. There was no way you could have known in advance that the same people who bought *Ziggy* and *Aladdin Sane* were going to like *Young Americans* and *Station To Station*, but you went ahead with them anyway, and your audience followed.

Part of it, I'm sure, has to come down to how you were marketed, compared with the Rollers (or any other teenybopper band). They were pushed as something to scream at, and you were pushed as someone to think about. But that only works to a point: although T Rex had screamers, they also had a 'serious' audience, and where is Marc Bolan today? Actually, he's making some great records again, although I'm the only person I know who cares.

It has to be down to blind luck, with a little bit of common sense thrown in – maybe knowing *when* to change is as important as knowing what to change into. You were lucky, because you had Mainman behind you, who painted everything so much bigger and more important than it was. I know it's probably not your favourite subject to reminisce about at the moment,[120] but thinking back on those days it really did seem like the company was some massive superstar factory, bursting at the seams with larger-than-life media monsters. So what if it was just one massive (and massively expensive) optical illusion? It did the trick and you wouldn't be where you are today without it.

I don't know if you've noticed but Malcolm McLaren is trying to do the same thing with The Sex Pistols. He's got one band that everybody's talking about, and behind the scenes there's this whole 'punk' movement supposedly bubbling up. I don't know how many of these bands he's involved with, and how many are being grouped together to give the scene a sense of cohesion, but

120 Bowie's 1975 break with Mainman was somewhat acrimonious.

it's working. You can't even open the music press these days without finding something about one or other of the bands, and the Pistols tour next month is selling out everywhere.

It doesn't even matter whether it's genuine word of mouth or simply media hype. The fact is, for the first time since 1972 something is happening that is new(ish), exciting and dangerous enough to already be annoying 'serious' music fans. I can't tell you how many people I know are bitching that none of the bands can play their instruments – as if being the next Rick Wakeman was an automatic passport to international success. As far as I'm concerned, virtuosity has never been that important; I'd rather play The Monkees than The Moody Blues, and Gary Glitter's 'Rock And Roll' still fills me with more excitement than an ELP bolero. Music is about attitude first, instrumentation a very poor second. *Metal Machine Music* versus *Wish You Were Here* – no contest. *Metallic KO* or Barclay James Harvest? Have you heard Patti Smith yet? All I have is the 'Gloria' single, but that version of 'My Generation' on the B-side wipes the floor with everything.

And that's before we even start on about the Pistols and The Damned.[121] To be honest, I'm not sure whether it's a good idea for most of these bands to be making records yet, because I don't think there's that much going on in the music that you need to listen to at home. Right now it's more like a live, communal experience. There was a kind of two-day punk festival at the 100 Club a couple of months back; a bunch of bands who we'll probably never hear of again, up there making whatever noises came into their heads, and it was really exciting. The idea of hearing a Siouxsie And The Banshees record, though, is pretty scary – musically they were a shambles. But the attitude was there, plus the girl singer turned out wearing a swastika and, boy, did she piss people off – which is exactly what I was saying to you in my last letter.

A couple of the bands were OK – I enjoyed The Buzzcocks, and The Vibrators are always fun. But, having seen them live, do

121 Respectively, 'Anarchy In The UK' and 'New Rose'.

I need to hear them at home? Probably not, which is why Soul Boy and I spend most of our time hanging out at a couple of soul clubs he knows, like Louise's, and Shaggers[122] in Covent Garden. They're pretty neat places, if a little strange the first few times. You go to Louise's, and any minute you expect Michael York and Liza Minnelli to walk in and start acting out scenes from *Cabaret,* which might be why I like the place so much. I finally got to see the film and it's far and away my new all-time favourite. The club is very cliquey, but you start to recognise people after the first few times, and Soul Boy knows the woman who DJs there, so it's not too bad. The crowd's really interesting as well, and a lot of the more outlandishly dressed characters you see at punk gigs hang out there – the first time I heard 'Anarchy In The UK' played there, the punk crowd went mad!

Don't get me wrong, it *is* a good record. But it's nothing like their live sound. The Damned's one[123] is a bit closer – a lot rougher, not so well produced (the Pistols' sounds like Phil Spector producing Eddie And The Hot Rods), but they still don't capture the chaos and energy of the show. They'll probably figure it out eventually, but it struck me that this is the first generation of bands who've started making records and getting press attention as soon as they form, rather than slogging around the clubs and colleges for a few years 'paying their dues'. Which is all very nice for them, in terms of not having to live in a transit van for half their life, but it also means that they're going to be making all their mistakes in full view of the public – and every new band makes mistakes. If the Pistols' next single is a turkey, that's probably going to be the end of them, whereas if they'd trundled around in total obscurity for five years, built up a repertoire and an underground following, when their big break did come they'd be equipped to deal with it.

If punk does survive (and a few journalists are saying it'll be dead by Christmas), it's going to be interesting to see whether any of the groups can keep going after the first few singles. I'm talking about the British bands, by the way. The press keeps

122 Chaguarama's, on the site of the future Roxy Club.
123 'New Rose'.

trying to lump all those New York groups like The Ramones and Patti Smith into punk, but I really don't see it. The Ramones sound like The Searchers on speed, and Patti is a cross between Jim Morrison and Keith Richard, which is fair enough in its own way, but has absolutely nothing to do with what's happening in London right now. Unless you like The Stranglers, of course.

Meanwhile, have you noticed that the only people from the glam and glitter period who are still scoring hits – you, Bolan, Gary Glitter, Slade, Mud, The Sweet – are the ones who'd slogged around for a few years first? All the bands that appeared out of nowhere, though (like Slik, Sailor, The Rubettes and Kenny), have already vanished, because they didn't have the experience or the resilience to keep on going when things became tough.

The problem was, everyone started taking it all too seriously. Too many of the groups gave up on the sensibilities that endeared them to the glitter audience, and started looking for a way to win the admiration of other, more 'serious' crowds: the metalheads, the teds and so on. They looked at the bands who had crossed into glam from elsewhere – Alex Harvey, Stackridge, BeBop Deluxe, even Steeleye Span – and tried to take the traffic back the other way. But those groups crossed over on terms that the reformed popsters could never agree to. It's not enough simply to change horses in midstream, cos you have to wipe the slate clean altogether. SAHB could get away with recording 'School's Out' and 'Crazy Horses' because people expected them to do strange things like that (they recorded 'Cheek To Cheek' and 'Delilah' as well). But even when Ritchie Blackmore climbed on stage to jam with The Sweet, Deep Purple fans weren't impressed.

If you dig deep enough, there's still some worthwhile glam bubbling around, which means it might not be time to put away the mascara just yet. The Doctors Of Madness are on to their second album, which is almost as amazing as their first, and things are really moving for them. Their image is superb, a sophisticated malignancy aimed less at the people the band appeal to than at the people they're lampooning – picture spreads in the right-wing tabloids, the *Twiggy Show*, that kind of thing. The only danger is, the businessman in suspenders is simply society's way of dealing lightheartedly with the sickness that runs rampant every time the veneer of civilisation is cracked, and the Doctors' personification of that sickness might be a little too near the knuckle for both the neurotics and their neuroses – especially as the band don't seem to have any catchy singles with which to back it all up.

I also picked up an album by Metro, Duncan Browne's new group (remember 'Journey' a few years ago?). You ought to look out for it – the first track, 'Criminal World', has to be one of the sleaziest, dirtiest-sounding songs ever recorded, without overtly being either of those things. Everyone I've played it to goes, 'Oh my God, they'll never get played on the radio!' but they can't say why. But there's this aura of utter depravity hanging over it all – think 'Rebel Rebel' if her mother was a stripper. The rest of the album has the same mood, although it takes a bit of getting into – 'Criminal World' kneels down and bites your cock off. And there's not many records you can say that about!

Anyway, I'd better be away. I just wanted to check in and make sure you're OK. Good luck with the record!

Gary

Chelsea, London SW10
Thursday 2 December 1976

Dear David

Oh my God! I'm sure you must have heard about it by now, but I had to write to you. After everything I was saying in my last letter about punk not having any staying power, The Sex Pistols turned the whole thing around on telly last night. I'm sure you remember *Today*, the nice local-news show that comes on after the news? They were meant to have Queen on as the token musical guests last night, but when I arrived home it turned out that the Pistols were on instead. I've only ever seen my parents shocked into total silence by two rock groups – Alice and yourself. Well, the Pistols were the third.

Every truly legendary band has a reputation for doing something of spectacularly bad-boy proportions, whether it's The Beatles smoking dope in the loos at Buck House or the Stones piddling against a garage wall. But that's all it was – reputation. The general public read about it in the papers and heard about it on telly. But they were never able to see it in the flesh. Same with you and Alice – he never really cut up babies, and you never really went down on Ronno on stage. People heard that's what happened, and overreacted accordingly.

With the Pistols, there's no need for overreaction. They really did it. They went on live telly and swore their heads off. The papers today are completely insane – one guy called up the *Mirror* to tell them he'd kicked his screen in because he didn't think his little boy should be subjected to such foul language. But it's OK for the precious laddie to see daddy smash the telly – hmmm, interesting values at work there. Anyway, it suddenly doesn't matter what the Pistols' next record is like, cos they've made the leap to immortality regardless. And now let's sit back and watch all the little Pistols come chasing out behind them.

Of course, you do know that you're responsible for all this, don't you? Remember back in 1974, when the 'Rebel Rebel' film was meant to be on *Top Of The Pops* but didn't get to the studio for some reason? They put Queen on instead, and they landed their first ever hit as a result. Now it's Queen's turn to cancel, and on trot The Sick Pastilles. Bowie begets the Beast – now there's a headline to cherish!

Anyway, it was totally surreal going out last night. Soul Boy, a few other friends and I went to see this new group, The Tom Robinson Band, playing down the road in Fulham and, though the place was pretty full, it was like walking into a grave. Everyone was standing around looking completely shell-shocked – 'Oh my God, did you see the Pistols on telly?' It'd barely been a couple of hours, but already there was this real sense of paranoia going around. You'll remember from your mod days that theory that the government only tolerates youth fashions because they keep the kids from making serious trouble. The feeling now is that the Pistols have completely stepped over that boundary, and *are* making trouble.

Even before I left the house, I went upstairs and hid my copy of 'Anarchy', in case my stepfather decided to be a Model Citizen and sweep the filth out of his house. And every time a panda car passed the pub with its sirens on, you could feel the tension – and this wasn't even a punk gig! Robinson used to be in Café Society, who were on Ray Davies' label for a while, and some of the new band's songs still have a bit of that mid-1970s singy-songy angst to them. But that doesn't matter. Right now, punk is this wonderfully egalitarian thing, a musical movement that is defined by attitude rather than music. You could be a balladeer, a poet, a pianist, whatever – so long as your heart's in the right place. Robinson's is, although it was difficult to pay too much attention when you're expecting the flying squad to burst in any minute and throw everybody up against the wall on suspicion of being a secret Sex Pistols fan.

Nothing happened in the end, but I don't think people are being paranoid. I arrived at work this morning, and the first question Mr Richards (the boss) asked me was, 'You're not a punk rocker are you, Gary?' I told him if I was, he wouldn't have to keep suggesting I have a haircut – to which he responded, maybe I shouldn't get one after all, to reassure the customers! And so darkest Enfield has been deprived of its first punk rock travel agent.

Anyway, whatever you're up to right now you may want to take a quick spin over here and see what's happening. I don't know if, musically, it'll make much difference to you, but socially things look like they're going to get very interesting indeed. And this is only Day One. I can't wait to see what the Sunday papers make of it all!

All the best

Gary

Chelsea, London SW10
Tuesday 14 January 1977

Dear David

It seems hard to believe that only a month has passed since the Pistols were on *Today*. The punk movement has completely exploded, the authorities are doing their nut – I've never seen anything like it. Even the generation gap has gone insane. Once it was rock 'n' roll against the world, now it's punk against everything, and massive swaths of the average teenage record collection are being thrown away, in case they harbour a hint of Boring Old Fartiness.

It's the ideal time to go second-hand record shopping. Every time I go down to Cheapo Cheapos, another newly converted punk has traded in his entire record collection for a copy of *Live At CBGBs* (and he was probably back the next day, hoping to trade it back). Of course, a lot of what they're getting rid of is stuff you wouldn't want in the house in the first place: *Deep Purple In Rock*, *Led Zeppelin IV* (*Four Symbols*), the dreaded *Yessongs*. I know these records sold a lot of copies, but do they all have to sit in the same shop? There's some really good stuff turning up as well, though – I've picked up tons of old Stones and Kinks albums, a bunch of proggy stuff I never got round to at the time – guess who now has a complete collection of early Kraftwerk and Tangerine Dream albums? Oh, and while we wait for your new album, I found a copy of your first. In mono! It cost a bomb, but I was dead chuffed. I've never seen one before.

It'll be interesting to see how your new album gets on. A lot of the punk kids are old Bowie, Lou and Bolan fans, and I don't care how committed they are to the new bands: I can't imagine them giving up their old allegiances simply because you don't have a safety pin through your skull. In fact, if you want to get really boringly archeological about it, you can trace punk's roots back to the Velvets, Iggy, Ziggy (of course) – Johnny Rotten has the perfect mutant Ziggy hairdo, Eater are playing covers of 'Sweet Jane' and 'Queen Bitch', and every band on earth seems to be doing one Stooges cover or another.

Hey, remember that girl Kathy I used to go out with? I saw her last night, punked to the eyeballs, trendy as hell, swapping anti-beauty tips with a bunch of fellow punkettes…and looking absolutely horrified when I walked up with longish hair, jeans and an Alex Harvey Band T-shirt, asked her how she was and if she was still hanging around outside record company offices, hoping to see The Sweet. Mindless spitefulness, I know, but it felt good. Revenge!

In the meantime, the more the papers get uptight about punk, the more new bands are forming, to annoy them. What's more, Shaggers is reopening tomorrow as an exclusive punk-only club, called the Roxy. Soul Boy and I are going down for the opening. It should be a laugh – the main band is called Generation X. (Is that the best name in the world? Or the corniest?) We saw them a couple of months ago, playing in front of a stripper at some bizarre art exhibition at the ICA – different singer, different name and playing a set stuffed with old Stones covers.[124] Maybe I'll dig out my old Charlie Watts T-shirt for the occasion.

Do you have any plans to come back to England to see what's happening for yourself? Marc Bolan's been hanging around the clubs a lot, checking out bands and getting very excited by it all. He's even booked The Damned in as support on his next tour. That should be interesting, because I've only ever seen them at small venues.

You really should be here!

Gary

---

124 Generation X's Billy Idol, Tony James and John Towe were previously members of Gene October's Chelsea. The ICA show, their live debut, saw them opening for Throbbing Gristle.

Chelsea, London SW10
Wednesday 19 January 1977

Dear David

Either we've gone mad, or RCA has. How could they even dream of saying that _Low_[125] has no commercial potential? Side one is one massive hit single after another, and they haven't even issued one yet! Are all record companies this stupid, or did you just draw the short straw?

OK, so side two of the album is utterly unlistenable – 'a load of old wank' is how Soul Boy summed it up – but even that works to your advantage. Everybody was expecting an album of songs from which they would determine whether or not you were hip enough to be a punk hero, and you give them four bloody great slabs of echo and sound effects. What are you on about? I _avant garde_ a clue, ha ha. Even people who claim to have hated you their entire lives are now running around raving about _Low_. And now we know what you were on about when you wrote 'Five Years' – or, at least, what you'd like us to think you were on about. Five years until you strip away all the make-up and pizzazz and take everything – yourself, your image and your music – back to its bare concrete basics.

Of course, I don't believe you knew for a moment that you were going to do that. In fact, when you wrote that song you didn't know whether you'd even have a career in five years' time. But, over time, it must at least have crossed your mind that you were heading towards a date that you personally filled with as much symbolism (in rock terms) as Orwell did 1984, and that you needed to do something profound to mark it? The fact that punk came along at the same time, to give that profundity even more impact, was sheer blind luck but, in years to come, I can see _Low_ being regarded with at least as much respect as _Ziggy_ is now, and probably kick-starting a movement just as powerful. We're in for some interesting years.

125 Bowie's newly released LP.

We were on a club crawl last night, trying to find a half-decent band to watch, and virtually every place we went into seemed to be playing one side or other of *Low*, while people wandered around asking who it was...or, even, *what* it was. You couldn't have aligned yourself better with the punks if you'd planned it. And, if it's true that the Iggy album's going to be out in March, then you're laughing. It's strange: I went four years not knowing anybody else who'd even heard one of his records, and now everybody's walking around saying they were out buying Stooges albums even before *Raw Power* came out. I wonder what Iggy did with all the gold discs he must have been awarded. I finally found French import copies of the first two albums at the Virgin Megastore last week – £3.50 a pop. I could only afford to pick up the first one. Right now, my favourite track is 'We Will Fall', ten minutes of Iggy grunting, Cale's viola screeching and a lot more Doors influence than I was expecting. Seems like The Stranglers aren't as far off base as they initially appeared. I've seen a few bands covering 'No Fun' now, including the Pistols, of course; and The Damned do a raucous version of 'I Feel Alright'. But I bet no one's ever going to do 'We Will Fall'![126]

Looking back at the last few letters I've sent you, it sounds like all I do is go to gigs and buy records – got it in one! Actually, more gigs than records, simply because there are still not many new bands with records out yet (although they all seem to have deals!). I worked out the other night that I've been to more gigs in the six months since I left school than I went to the whole time I was in Bournemouth. OK, so most of them have been in crappy pubs, and involve groups you'd never want to see or hear again (if you ever get the urge to see something called Suburban Stud, *don't*), whereas before it was mainly 'chart acts' at the Winter Gardens or wherever, but you know what they say: if music be the food of life, live music is the meat and potatoes.

Plus, virtually everybody I hang out with now I've met at shows. I remember when I first left school and came up to London 'full time', I wondered how on earth I was ever going

---

126 It took a few years, but finally... Sky Cries Mary included a version on their 1993 LP *Return To The Inner Experience*.

to meet anyone new at all. Five years surrounded by pretty much the same people doesn't do much for your social skills, although you only find that out once you've left. It wasn't even a matter of being friends with them or not; you were stuck with them whatever you thought of them, and you grow used to them. Then, suddenly, there they weren't. And do I miss them? Not a bit.

Aside from Soul Boy, who I see pretty much all the time, the only contact I've had with anyone from school has been a phone call from Paul Banion before Christmas, and a 'I was just passing'-type visit from Michael Nish, of all people. He turned up at the house one day, then spent the entire evening asking if he could borrow things to show his friends, or borrow records to tape – 'I'll mail them back as soon as I'm done with them'. Yeah, of course you will. In the end, I dragged him out to see The Vibrators at some godforsaken college in Holloway Road somewhere. He stuck it for ten minutes, then remembered he had someone else to visit. And if that's what school reunions are going to be like, you can stuff them.

Everyone else, though, has completely vanished. It's so strange! I suppose with us all being from different parts of the country, hopeless letter writers and too broke to make long-distance phone calls, it was inevitable. And, to be honest, I really don't miss them that much – best friends one minute, forgotten the next. How fickle we are. Every so often I wonder what people like Jon James are up to, whether they've found a job or got into punk, but not so much that I feel the need to find out. We'd only end up reminiscing about the 'good old days', after all, and quite honestly school is still too recent a memory for me to get overly nostalgic about it. There's too much happening in real life.

Aside from that, I'm spending most of my time with this girl I met at Louise's before it closed. She's called Dawn and she shares my love of both your music AND The Doctors Of Madness. She saw them on the *Twiggy Show* about a year ago and has been following them around ever since. We're not going out together – I kind of get the feeling that she doesn't do things like that. But she's terrific fun anyway, and I'll have to keep trying.

Of the others, Noakes is the spitting image of the old *Blue Peter* host, right down to the pudding-bowl haircut; Alun is a desperately reformed hippy who works at one of those funny little record boutiques around Marble Arch, and literally lives in a sheepskin coat, which my stepfather is convinced is stuffed with drugs; and Kevin is a seriously brain-damaged Motörhead freak who only goes to punk gigs to complain that the band wasn't fast/loud/ugly enough. He's the only person I know who could give Johnny Rotten a run for his money in the miserable 'I hate everything' cynic stakes, especially since he found out that Rotten will be 21 in a couple of weeks and is thus, officially, a Boring Old Fart. Lemmy, on the other hand, is timeless, ageless and, therefore, beyond any such chronological failings.

None of them are especially big fans of yours, but I'm working hard to convert, and *Low* might do the trick – at least with Noakes and Alun. Kevin was over two nights ago. He sat through all 2'45"of 'Speed Of Life', then announced he had to leave because it was giving him an uncontrollable urge to take up modern art. Dawn and I ran into him a few hours later at the Roxy, haranguing Dave Vanian about how it was stupid to pretend to be a vampire, when he ought to die and then come back as a real one – and I thought, 'Jesus, it's Tom Major!' Remember I told you about that story I was writing, years ago? I can't even remember if I ever finished it, let alone what else it was about. But I'll have to see if I still have it.

Well, that's about all I have to write tonight. Congratulations again on making such a completely fucked-up album – the critics might hate it, but the boys and girls understand!

No Elvis, Beatles or The Rolling Stones…but plenty of Bowie in 1977!

Gary

Chelsea, London SW10
Tuesday 8 March 1977

Dear David

Thank you, thank you, thank you for bringing Iggy Pop back to life. Eight days ago, I'd never even seen him perform on the telly. Now I've seen him live four times, and every show was better than the last. It started at Aylesbury Friars last week, ended last night at the Rainbow, and I hope you won't be insulted when I say Iggy was so phenomenal that I didn't even look at the band – not even at the chain-smoking keyboard player six feet away from me at Friars!

It was one of those shows when you can't even say, 'Oh, I wish he'd played this' or 'I wish he'd done that'. Every night, there were moments when you could feel the entire audience hold its breath in case he was going to do 'something'. When any other performer climbs to the top of the speaker stack, you know half a dozen bearded roadies will rush out to help him down again. When Iggy does it, there's any number of distinctly possible outcomes, most of which involve head-first swan dives into the audience.

The only disappointment was that the album wasn't out in time for the tour, and won't be out for another couple of weeks, apparently. The new songs sounded amazing live, but reviews of the LP paint it as a virtual apocalypse: nothing like The Stooges, nothing like *Low*, nothing like anything. The excitement surrounding it is phenomenal. After all that Iggy's been through over the years, wouldn't it be classic if it got into the charts?[127]

How does it feel to be playing in a band once more? Especially somebody else's! I bet you never dreamed you'd be stuck on the sidelines again, playing piano while somebody else got sunburn from the flashbulbs? The Aylesbury gig was the strangest from that point of view, because everyone had heard you would be in the band, but nobody believed it.

---

127 In fact it did, peaking at No.30.

From what I heard around the place afterwards, some people went the entire show without knowing you were there – including one kid who'd obviously spent all day getting dressed up for the show, and even longer designing the most amazing outfit I've ever seen in my life. I do hope you saw him, half *Aladdin Sane*, half *Raw Power*, depending on whether you caught his left profile or his right. After the show, he was sitting on the ground outside Friars crying his eyes out, because he hadn't realised you were there. Ha! Call yourself a fan? His friends were doing their best to console him, telling him no one else knew either, but if there was ever a suicide waiting to happen it was him. There's a kind of happy ending, though – I saw him again at the Rainbow on Saturday, a few seats down in the row behind me and, by halfway through the gig, I was wishing he *had* killed himself, because he spent the entire show shouting out, 'David, I love you.' And I'm sure you're thrilled to know that he does.

Did you get the chance to go out to any other shows while you were in London? I'm off to see Bolan next week, feeling more confident about him than I have in years. The first single from *Dandy In The Underworld* is out, and it's a real return to form. Good for him!

Some of your other old friends are around as well, though, and doing really well. You probably know that Lee Black Childers[128] is managing Johnny Thunders And The Heartbreakers? Well, Sunday night, in between Iggy gigs, Cherry Vanilla played the Nash,[129] and Wayne County was at the Roxy. And both were amazing.

Cherry looks better than ever – red hair, tight clothes, wonderful voice, terrific songs, pure sex. You look at her and wonder what all the fuss is about Blondie. Cherry wipes the floor with her, musically and visually, but the most important thing is, it doesn't feel like she's putting on an act. She's not purring around like a sex kitten, she's not coming on like a cheap hooker. OK, so she was wearing a T-shirt with 'Lick Me' picked out in

<hr>

128 Mainman's official photographer – he took the photo adorning the inner gatefold of the *Diamond Dogs* album.
129 The Nashville, in West Kensington.

sequins and stars, and she must have spent half the show trying to stop the front row from trying to do that. But you watch her and nothing seems staged or forced: she's a naturally provocative performer and the sexiest thing on earth. She has the most amazing eye contact as well – every so often, you could see her eyes meet one of the audience's and, whoever he was, he'd melt. I know I did! Her material is really good as well. It's not at all punky in the sense of fast guitars and screaming, but it has a really crazy energy. With a decent band behind her (her current lot are faceless plodders[130]), she could rule the world. Dawn hated every minute of it, by the way.

Anyway, as soon as Cherry finished, Dawn and I jumped on a tube to Covent Garden to see Wayne at the Roxy. I can't believe the shows were on the same night – the opening band at Wayne's show, The Adverts, are phenomenal, and I really wanted Dawn to see them. As it was, Wayne was already on when we arrived, and you know what? I finally figured out why nothing ever happened for him when he was in London with Mainman – because he'd have stolen the show. Even if he'd not sold a single record (which is quite likely), he'd have been all over the papers every week anyway.

Watching the audience, it was almost like looking at my parents when the Pistols were on *Today*. Wayne was pulling out all the stops – dog food, sex toys, the lot. People didn't know what to do, where to look… Imagine the most insane, depraved drag show you've ever seen, with the most disgusting props. He had them all – forget the music, watch the show. Except the music is equal to the show. If you want to take things dreadfully seriously, you could probably sniff and say there's nothing clever about starting a song with the words 'I got fucked by the Devil last night'. But in terms of what punk is 'meant' to be – the destruction of taboos, the removal of barriers, the ultimate liberation of the spirit from the bullshit strictures of society (God, I can trot it out, can't I?!) – Wayne is so far ahead of the pack that for most of them it's not even worth trying to catch up.

130 Appropriately, the plodders turned out to be the then-unknown Police.

It was only towards the end of the show that people snapped out of their state of shock and began to react. A few people started getting into it, but there's always that bunch of morons who want to fight and throw things, and the problem with the Roxy is, they've not quite trained the bouncers yet. You'll see half a dozen punks thrown out for no reason, but the part-time football hooligans who are the real arseholes are left alone. So they're screaming abuse and throwing things and any other performer would have cut their set short and pissed off. Wayne, on the other hand, turned the full impact of the show – and some hilarious put-downs – on to them. By the end of the show, they were ready to kill him. We hung around after the show to say hi to him and Cherry (she came in a little after us), and there was still a bunch of thugs milling around the stage, kicking things and throwing plastic beer glasses at the roadies.

It was a fantastic gig, though – two fantastic gigs, in fact – and a reminder (much needed, if you ask me) that some of the British punk bands are taking themselves just a little too seriously. No one denies that a lot of punk's impact is political. But there's more to politics than speeches and rhetoric, and it's not enough simply to tell people to throw off their inhibitions. Sometimes you have to do it for them – which, of course, is something you know all about.

OK, I'm off to bed now – and I believe you're off to America. You probably won't receive this till after the tour, but I hope it goes really well. Oh, and congratulations on 'Sound And Vision'. If what your label regards as commercial suicide can get to No.2 on the chart, imagine what something they like could do!

All the best

Gary

Edmonton, London N18
Monday 30 May 1977

Dear David

Just a quick note to let you know my new address. I finally left
home last weekend, partly to be nearer work (hop on the 191
and I'm there in ten minutes!), but also because it was getting
unbearable there. The Rat Bastard has essentially turned into a
Guardian Of All Public Morality, and was banging on the walls
every time I played something that even remotely resembled
punk rock. Including *Aladdin Sane*, I might add. Seems those
loud guitars and screaming girls (it was during 'Panic In Detroit')
confused him.

I'm in a grotty (but tolerable) little bedsit – one room with a
bed in one corner, a Baby Belling in another, a sink beside the
window and enough room for the record collection, the music
centre and a little portable telly. Oh, and the most disgusting
wallpaper of all time: white with dark-red and gold diamonds at
irregular intervals across it and a thick yellow coating of
indeterminate origin over everything. I've smothered as much as
I can with posters, but there's still a few patches showing through.

The rent's £8 a week, which is apparently quite reasonable,
especially as I'm now on £25 a week at work. Plus, I figured out
that what I save on travel and aggravation *more* than equals the
extra I'm paying, so I'm feeling pretty flush at the moment.
Think of all the new albums I can buy!

It's a furnished room, so the only things I needed to bring
from home, aside from all my own junk, were a few pots, pans,
plates and stuff. And I made some fascinating discoveries while
I was packing for the move. I've always known I was a pack rat,
but I turned up the most amazing crap – relics of both my own
glam rock past and, I'm afraid, yours.

I found what must be the UGLIEST poster of you ever
published, from a fold-out magazine called *Popster*. It came out

around 1973, and I have no recollection of it whatsoever, although this is issue 14, so it was obviously around for a while. The poster is of you doing one of the mime routines in a ghastly hand-knitted jump suit, your eyes are half shut and you look like you're about to lay an egg. Then came the SECOND UGLIEST poster of all time, free with eight Curly Wurly wrappers and taken with a flash that turned your eyes as red as your hair. According to the back of it, the others in the series were Slade, Gary Glitter, Donny Osmond and David Cassidy. Where are they now?

What else... A cartoon strip from *Sounds* called 'The Man Who Dropped In For A Cuppa – Starring David Glowie', taking the pee out of the movie (obviously), tons of cuttings that I never got round to gluing into my scrapbooks... Oh, and, lovingly affixed to sugar paper and framed in cardboard, Wayne County's autograph, a couple of bus tickets and some café receipts from my trip to London for the 1980 Floor Show. Ah, memories.

My favourite discovery, though, was the exercise book where I listed the Top 20 every week, graphs showing my favourite records' journey up and down the chart cross-referenced with the Radio Luxembourg charts, lists of who was on *Top Of The Pops*, a log of every record I bought or swapped. I must have spent hours doing it every week, and the sick thing is, I don't remember any of it! The sheer enthusiasm astonishes me! These days, I can barely keep track of what month it is.

I've left a lot of the stuff at my parents' for the time being, simply because there's not that much storage space here – the record collection takes over most of it, and my books have swallowed the rest. But I'm pretty much settled in now. I even went and introduced myself to my 'neighbours' – two middle-aged navvy types with donkey jackets and DMs, who I don't think I'll have very much in common with, and a total hippy burnout who asked me into his room for a joint. Nobly, I declined – the place stank of feet and stale joss sticks.

There's also an old lady who has the whole of the downstairs, and seems nice enough in that faintly batty, lonely-old-girl kind of way. One of the navvies told me to watch out for my post – she opens everything that comes to the house in case it's from the landlord, plotting against her with the other tenants. I'm not sure what the arrangement is here, but apparently she used to own the whole house, then sold half of it off to be turned into flats, with the other half (where she now is) set to follow when she departs. She's now convinced that the landlord is planning to murder her, and has already called the police on him a couple of times: once for saying 'Good morning' in a sinister voice, and once for letting himself in the front door without telephoning first. He made the mistake of reminding her that he never telephones because he only lives across the road, so now she keeps her front curtains drawn all the time, to stop him from spying on her. God bless the aged English!

Finally, if you saw last week's *NME*, I had a letter published! I went to see Lou Reed at the New Vic and it was dreadful: he spent half the show sitting on the stage looking and sounding bored out of his skull, played a bunch of lifeless versions of dead songs, then pissed off after about an hour. It was especially disappointing after seeing John Cale at the Roundhouse a few weeks back, who was excellent. So, when I arrived home I wrote a letter... If you missed it, I've enclosed a copy for you.

Anyway, I'd better go, but if you're ever in Edmonton...

All the best

Gary

LETTER TO *NME*
I was going to write you a constructive letter denouncing The Stranglers, *Rock Follies* and the Eurovision Song Contest, but have just realised that all parties concerned are one and the same person. Did you see Lou Reed at the New Vic?
SWEET JANE, Edmonton

To Major Tom

RESPONSE
No. Did you?
   CSM [Charles Shaar Murray]

Edmonton, London N18
Saturday 16 July 1977

Dear David

Are you listening to this? Probably not, as you're not in London, but Johnny Rotten's on Capital Radio, and he's blowing the punk orthodoxy out of the water by playing the weirdest stuff: Tim Buckley, Nico, Gary Glitter, Neil Young ('Revolution Blues', of course – where would we be without Charles Manson?), Kevin Coyne... I wonder if anybody ever played 'Eastbourne Ladies' on the radio before?

'Rebel Rebel' was prefaced by some odd remark along the lines of it being about The New York Dolls... Really? We even got Peter Hammill, which was hilarious for me. I had a copy of *Silent Corner And The Empty Stage* at school, and convinced one of the first years that side two was a bootleg of unreleased outtakes from the *Diamond Dogs/Young Americans* period. As far as I'm concerned, Hammill was/is the only English songwriter who's in the same ball park as you, lyrically and musically – some of the stuff on *In Camera* and *Silent Corner* is so far out there!

What's going to be interesting to watch is how many people you'll suddenly be meeting who've been Hammill/Buckley/Nico fans for years, 'way before Rotten made them popular'. God, I can hear them now. The days when we had to hide our Nick Drake LPs behind *Radio Ethiopia* and *Ramones Leave Home* – in case the Punk Rock Taste Police came calling – are finally over. Liberation at last!

NME reprinted Iggy's Dinah Shore interview a few weeks back – a poor substitute for being able to watch it on telly, but better than nothing. I was surprised to see so little television coverage (ie zip) of the tour over here. You'd have thought that, with all the music shows pouring out of the box, one of them would have wanted the street-fighting cheetah. There again, apart from *So It Goes,* the only decent music show we've had on was *Supersonic,* which they killed off back in March, probably because there was no way Mike Mansfield could keep up his mad flamboyance in the face of the new influx of increasingly unflamboyant performers. I loved The Damned's appearance a while back. They did this totally snotty version of 'Neat Neat Neat', and Saturday kids' TV has never been the same since.

Talking of The Damned, the Bolan show was one of the best. I'm not completely crazy about the *Dandy* album, I must admit – the bits that are good are world-class, but there are a few duds on there as well. Live, though, he's still got it, and it was brilliant to hear him play 'Debora'! The encore was a bit draggy – The Damned came out and they did an endless version of 'Get It On'. But if you want to look at it from the point of view of Teacher Meets Pupil, it was fabulous.

Next time you tour, you may want to think along the same lines – relax a little, put together a really tight little band, get some punky upstarts to open for you (can I suggest The Adverts?) and let rip. Mix side one of *Low* with chunks of *TMWSTW*,[131] sprinkle with the best of every album, bar *Young Americans*, open the show with 'London Boys' – you'd kill 'em!

One thing's certain: you simply CANNOT go out and do the arenas again. That's fine for the creaking old dinosaurs who don't care what the punks think, because they know their audience comes from elsewhere (the grave, probably), but... I know it sounds corny, but the punk scene has given you its blessing, now you need to give something back to them. Iggy was a start – now show you *mean* it.

Oh, and you HAVE to revive 'Cygnet Committee'! Remember a couple of years back, how everyone was getting so excited about 'Life On Mars?', mentioning Lennon and 'Fame' in the same line? I was listening to 'Space Oddity' the other night, and you do it again... 'The Damned have no time to make amends', 'the silent Guns Of Love will blast the skies'. Guns = the Pistols, love = Sex. You clever bugger!

131 *The Man Who Sold The World.*

OK, so if you listen to what the song's saying, it's maybe a less-than-optimistic scenario – the Death Of The Dream and all that – but in a way it's already happening. It never felt that way at the time, but when I look back on last summer and autumn, punk had some kind of exclusivity to it, however many people who knew the bands, knew the clubs and so on. There were no rules, no dress codes, just this wondrous sense of absolute freedom from all the bullshit that normally associates itself with music.

That's finished now. Every time you turn around, there's a new 'punk' band playing around, and you can look at them and know that this time last year they had hair down to their buttocks and were voting for Lynyrd Skynyrd on *Whistle Test*'s Pick Of The Year. The papers are filled with punk fashion spreads – leather jackets, bondage strides and Dennis The Menace mohair jumpers – and the press has stopped writing about it, and started analysing it instead, as though we're caught up in some great philosophical cataclysm that cannot proceed till we know what it means. We know what it means already – or, at least, we know what it meant. It was meant to be an escape from everything it's become.

The record labels are signing up anything that even looks like it knows how to spit straight, the Pistols were on *Top Of The Pops* on Thursday and The Clash – everybody's Favourite Committed Revolutionaries – have just put out a single called 'Complete Control', all about how their record company is messing them around, and this is the only way they can hit back. Er, excuse me boys, but if the label was that evil they wouldn't have let you put the record out.

There's a little bit of reverse psychology going on here…along the same lines, maybe, as RCA telling us how much they hated *Low*? The more I think about that, the more it strikes me as a really well-considered marketing technique. They knew the way the wind was blowing, they knew that the punks were watching you carefully. What better way of cultivating a sympathetic response than by coming out and saying that they hated the record and didn't even want to release it? That way, everyone who buys it can feel they're cocking a snook at the establishment – instant street cred for one and all. Don't get me wrong – I'm not knocking it! It was a brilliant strategy and it worked phenomenally (shame they blew it by releasing 'Be My Wife' as a single; 'Speed Of Life' would have done far better). But I can't wait to see what they hatch for your new album![132]

So, did you celebrate Jubilee night in any kind of way? It was madness in London – street parties on every corner, flags and bunting, the works. It's funny, we hear how depressed and miserable Britain is, but give us an excuse for a party and we throw the wildest one in the world – and, in a funny sort of way, The Sex Pistols have a lot to do with it being so successful. Beforehand, I don't think a lot of people really cared about the Jubilee; there are a hell of a lot better things to spend that money on, after all, and there's a growing feeling that we don't especially need a royal family anyway. Then 'God Save The Queen' (the single, not the anthem) came along and drew such a thick line in the sand that a lot of people who might otherwise have ignored the event (or stayed at home complaining about it) suddenly felt they needed to participate, even if it was simply to show the punks who's boss.

Well, they certainly did that. There's a virtual war going on between punks and teds – even up here, it's taking your life in your hands to go around looking vaguely punky, unless you want a ton of teds to come tearing up from the Green to beat the crap out of you. But, from the point of view of sitting back and observing – a trick I learned from you, I think – it's been fascinating to see so many people joining together, determined to give the Queen a Jubilee to remember. Well, she certainly got that!

Dawn and I spent Jubilee night at The Ramones show at the Roundhouse and, even there, there was no escape – the DJ played the Pistols' 'God Save The Queen' during the interval, and it really was one of those hold-your-breath, lump-in-the-

132 *Heroes* was scheduled for release in September 1977.

throat moments, the entire place going absolutely crazy and there was that sense of community again. After the show, we drove out of London and up towards Harwich, sort of sightseeing, then slept in the car in a field some place. Even after midnight, parties were still going on in the streets, the whole sky was lit up with the bonfires and beacons, and it really was rather stirring, in an odd way. Whichever side of the Pistols versus the Palace debate you stand, on occasions like this you realise that it doesn't matter what the monarchy do or don't do, how much they cost, how much they're worth and all that. The fact is, they give the people something to believe in, and at a time when pretty much every other value has been destroyed. And that's worth more than every intellectual argument in the world.

God Save The Corgis!

Gary

Edmonton, London N18
Tuesday 2 August 1977

Dear David

You may want to reconsider living in Germany. Either that or get yourself a really powerful TV aerial. According to yesterday's *Sun* (the paper you can trust!), Marc Bolan's got his own teatime show beginning at the end of August. I can't wait. He's on such an up and up right now that it should be brilliant. There's talk of him wanting to get a bunch of punk bands on, which would be great. Aside from the handful who've been on *Top Of The Pops*, the only time we see any of them is on *So It Goes*, which is this sort of punk-rock version of *The Old Grey Whistling Kettle*. It's the best music show on by miles – Wreckless Eric's been on, The Jam, the Pistols (of course), The Buzzcocks... I love The Buzzcocks! If anyone ever wants to know what it's like to be a sex-starved teenager in 1977, take them to see The Buzzcocks. Every song is like a page out of the diary!

The other show you have to see is *The Fall And Rise Of Reginald Perrin*, with Leonard Rossiter. The second series starts next month and, I promise you, the first was so funny that you were in tears by the end of every episode. It reminds me a bit of *The Good Life*, in that it's another show about getting away from the rat race, but imagine Major Tom if he was a businessman working at a dessert manufacturers, instead of an astronaut. How would he escape from his current life? By stealing a lorry shaped like a blancmange mould, leaving his clothes on a beach in Dorset and faking his own death, of course! He even misses his wife and spends his free time writing letters to tell her how very much he loves her. Maybe you should think about reissuing 'Space Oddity' again. The show is one of the most popular things on at the moment, and – while there's probably a big difference between changing your name to Martin Wellbourne and attending your own memorial service, and drifting off into outer space in a command module – the message remains the same.

Summer is heaven in '77!

Gary

Edmonton, London N18
Friday 30 September 1977

Dear David

First, let me say how sorry I am about Marc Bolan.[133] Everybody knows how close the two of you were during the 1960s, hanging out together, gigging and recording,[134] and rumour has had the pair of you working together occasionally ever since. But it was only in the last couple of months that the true depth of your friendship really came out again – the news, back in March, that you were writing songs together...your appearance on *Marc* (it was finally shown here a couple of days ago)...the sight of you at the funeral...the foundation you've set up for Rolan.[135]

And little things, as well. Again, on the telly, the two of you messing around for that final song, the look on your face when he fell off the stage. That piece Marc wrote about you for *Melody Maker* back in March – 'Music Hall Humorist'. The affection was obvious even when it was published, but when I read it through again last night I found myself raging against all the years that passed, when you could and should have been working together, but other things – fame, success, careers – got in the way.

I remember you playing 'Lady Stardust' in the early days of *Ziggy*, and beaming Marc's face on to the screen behind you – and admitting, so many times, that he cleared the way for you to come through. But he never seemed to see it like that. As you rose, he fell, and in interviews there always seemed to be a bitterness and rivalry bubbling there, which came from some place far deeper than the usual inter-pop-star warfare (Beatles Slam Stones, Ferry Slams Harley).

I don't know. Maybe it was play-acting that the media – and, therefore, the fans – took more seriously than it was intended. But it always seemed such a sad end to a friendship. Whenever I read

---

133 Bolan died in a car accident in the early hours of September 16, 1977.
134 Bolan played guitar on Bowie's 1970 'Prettiest Star' single, Bowie supported Tyrannosaurus Rex on tour in early 1969.
135 Bowie established a trust fund for Bolan's infant son, Rolan.

that you were hanging out together again, I felt so pleased with even the possibility that the two of you had put the bitchiness all behind you. And, as soon as you confirm all the rumours and finally step out on a public stage together, this happens.

It seems so wrong, and it seems so stupid. The night it happened – the night before it happened – I'd started writing to you about how much I loved the new Iggy album,[136] wondering if you'd be touring with him again this month, looking forward to the release of the 'Heroes' single, all the usual stuff. The last bit I wrote before heading out for the evening was about 'Celebrate Summer';[137] how it had absorbed everything punk had to teach him, and reflected back everything he'd taught punk. A rebirth, a new dawn, his most important single since 'Ride A White Swan'...

Then I woke up the next morning and he was dead.

I can't imagine what it must be like for you at the moment. I never met him, I didn't particularly like a lot of what he'd been doing for the last few years, I only saw him play the one time. But when I look back at 1971 and early 1972, I cannot think of anything else that meant as much to me as his music. *Electric Warrior* was the first LP I ever bought. I saved up for it for three weeks, and I was so excited because it meant I wasn't a kid any more. Kids bought singles. Only grown-ups bought LPs. I spent as much time looking at the cover as I did listening to the record – I knew every word of the songs, I memorised every credit...and the first time I heard 'Monolith', with that funny little noise at the beginning, I wanted to take it back to the shop because I was convinced it was scratched. Oh, and I remember being so jealous of Burt Collins for being a flugelhorn player just when Marc was looking for one, and I didn't even know what a flugelhorn was. Next Music lesson, I asked the teacher what the most obscure musical instrument in the world was, so I could learn to play it and then offer my services to T Rex: 'Hey, I know you've got the flugelhorn under control, but what about...?'

136 *Lust For Life*, another Bowie/Pop collaboration.
137 Bolan's latest, final, single.

And then – what happened? You came along? That's too simple. He let me down, and when you're 12 and discovering the universe, that cannot be forgiven. I'd forgotten what a magnificent record 'Metal Guru' was until they showed a clip of his *Top Of The Pops* performance a few days after he died. But I didn't care for 'Children Of The Revolution', 'Solid Gold Easy Action', '20 Century Boy', 'The Groover'... It wasn't your rise that caused his downfall; it was his fall that permitted your rise.

Before then, there'd always been some kind of progression in his music, an unspoken 'And if you thought that one was good, wait till you hear the next one.' Now it was 'You've probably already heard the next one.' You were moving forward fast, whereas Marc (to paraphrase Mott The Hoople) was backsliding ferociously. Looking back, who can blame him for being pissed off at you? You were doing what *he* should have been, but (for whatever reason) chose not to.

And he did choose, because the records he was making once he'd hit the commercial bottom were as creative as anything he'd ever done in the past. They were creative in ways that maybe amused him, without a thought for the audience...or, at least, the audience that had grown up with him. Was he blinded by America? It certainly seemed that way sometimes. I remember bitching at you for touring America instead of coming back to Britain, because all it'd do was suck out your soul and turn you into Bachman-Turner Overdrive. I was wrong – or maybe I wasn't, because you certainly took a few wrong turns around then as well.

But you were still on a critical and creative roll. Marc didn't have that same luxury, and it wasn't until he admitted that the US is a black hole as far as musical taste and creative juices are concerned that he began the revival that ended...in exactly the place where it should have been beginning, with a fantastic new single, a TV show that was as brave as it was enjoyable (who else would have dared share the limelight with Gen X, Radio Stars, The Jam, The Hot Rods and the Rats[138] on the same

138 Bob Geldof's Boomtown Rats.

stage?) and the excitement bubbling up all over again. He was looking good – after all those years of bloat and puffiness, he'd lost weight, regained his enthusiasm. The Bolan Boogie was bang back on course.

And how does the Great British Public mourn him? When Presley died, every fart he ever expelled went sailing back up the chart. When Marc died, 'Celebrate Summer' went down, and it hadn't even entered the Top 75 yet! If ever a generation deserves to rot in hell, it's the one that watched their mums and dads (grandmas and grandads) send 40 stone of irrelevant fat to No.1, but couldn't pay the same respect to an Elvis of its own. And yes, I include some of my own friends as well.

A few of us saw him off as best we could. The night of the funeral (which we DIDN'T go to – there are some places where even devoted fans should not intrude), we piled round to Alun's place, played the records full blast and broke things. OK, it probably wasn't the most respectful response, or the most mature, but if Marc was watching he'd have got a kick out of it. In fact, it might even have been him who jogged the record player as 'Metal Guru' came on, and knocked the needle on to the next track. It's bad enough shedding a tear when I hear it on my own; I'd have hated it to happen in front of friends!

Anyway, I hope you're bearing up OK, and I promise, next time I write, it'll be happier thoughts.

God bless...

Gary

Edmonton, London N18
Wednesday 19 October 1977

Dear David

Where are you going to be the weekend of 14 January? I've been signed up for a trip to West Berlin, and it'd be wonderful if we could get together. Of course I wouldn't think of even trying to find my way to Hauptstrasse 152, Schoenberg, without an express invitation from you, but maybe we could meet up somewhere? I'm going to be there for three days, flying in on Friday 13th (hmmm, not sure if that's such a good idea!), and leaving again on the Monday morning.

It's a travel agent thing, of course. There's a new company started up, along the lines of Magic Bus, who are pushing 'alternative' destinations for hip little holiday-makers who want to see something more of the world than the Costa Del Sol and Disneyland. They're gearing it towards a younger market than most foreign packages – in fact, I was talking to their rep on the phone and he pretty much came out and admitted that one of the reasons West Berlin was chosen is because of the impact and popularity of your last couple of records. And I can't help wondering what the Russians are going to make of that, rows and rows of young English lovers kissing by the Wall, so they can come home and tell their friends that they are 'heroes', too?

I'm not sure what our itinerary is, or how much time we'll have for running around. The last time I went on one of these things – to the Channel Islands last January – most of our time was spent in seminars and meetings, and being conducted around Guernsey by the tour operatives. And I dread to find out what the others on the trip are going to be like. Sometimes I think I'm the only person under 30 in this entire business!

How are things with you? It's great to see *Heroes* doing so well – and the song itself has to be one of the most impressive you've ever written. You hear it on the radio and it's literally an anthem, a 'Stairway To Heaven' for the Blank Generation! Without the stuff about hedgerows and bustles. It's only when you listen to it carefully (headphones) that you realise how bizarre it really is. Fripp,[139] in particular, is all over the place, but the whole band sounds like it's on a crazed merry-go-round, which is spinning faster and faster, while you're standing in the middle calmly singing the song. In a really weird way, it reminds me of extremely early Roxy Music (Eno's influence?). I picked up a cassette bootleg of their first ever Peel sessions, and there's that same sensation of absolute dislocation between band and vocals. I love it!

The rest of the album – and you're probably as aware of this as anyone – has no alternative but to pale by comparison, and I wonder if I'd be too far off the mark if I suggested that you maybe pulled a few 'lesser' (by your standards) songs out of the cupboard, knowing that nothing stood a chance alongside 'Heroes'? I'm thinking of 'Joe The Lion', 'Secret Life Of Arabia' and the last couple of instrumentals. 'V2 Schneider's a goodie, *Trans-Europe Express* on a doodlebug to hell, and I really like 'Sense Of Doubt'. But the others could easily be outtakes from *Low*. I read somewhere that you and Eno have hours and hours more of this stuff in the can – take my advice and keep it there!

Anyway, I don't know if you're aware of it, but there's this whole new tribe of Bowie freaks wandering the streets. You see them in little gaggles in the corner at 'suitable' gigs...Ultravox, Japan, people like that. They're not complete clones – there's the occasional Ziggy or Aladdin, but for the most part they're more like tarty versions of the Thin White Duke...faggy fascists! It's a captivating look, but they're impossible to talk to. Dawn knows a few of them from Doctors Of Madness gigs (yes, they go to them as well), and I'm in the doghouse at the moment because I ended up having a huge row with one of them over (of all things) the meaning of 'Blackout'. He was holding forth along the lines of 'Yes, well, obviously it's about his heart attack last year' and quoting the line about 'Get me to the doctor.' So I said,

139 Lead guitarist Robert Fripp.

'Only if he'd been on the sake all night.' The next line, of course, is 'I'm under Japanese influence' – the hospital spokesman *did* say you'd simply been drinking too much.

Well, I thought that was a reasonable enough observation, but this kid went nuts, screaming about how sick he was of people who'd heard one Bowie record and now thought they knew it all, and how he'd been dressing like this since 1974 and listening to 'Dave Bowie' every day since then. Alright, I admit I was shit-stirring by now, but I remarked that I'd never, ever, heard you referred to as 'Dave', and I asked the others who were around if they had. 'Well, only by…whatever this kid's name was', they said, at which point the bastard clouted me round the back of the head and ran out of the club!

Of course, I ought to have leaped manfully to my feet and nailed his knees together. But, to be honest, I was so stunned that I sat there with a 'Did that really just happen?' expression on my face, while Dawn was simply blasting death glares at me. She barely spoke another word all evening, apart from to tell me it was my own fault and that's the last time she's ever going to introduce me to any of her friends. Naturally, I'm heartbroken.

What's funny is, the others in that crowd were alright – a bit pretentious and horribly self-obsessed – but we sat around talking about how great glam rock was. (My God, it's three years old and we're already getting nostalgic for it!) And you should've seen their jaws drop when I told them I'd been at the 1980 Floor Show.

One other classic moment that I know you'll appreciate. I asked what they thought about Iggy's *Lust For Life*, and one of them – and I swear, he could have stepped out of one of softy Walter's gang in the *Beano* when he said it – replied, 'We don't like him, and we don't understand why David should want to hang around with such a nasty, rough person.' Oh my God! I tried to tell them about The Stooges, what an influence on you they were in the early days, and how you were raving about Iggy even before you met him, but it didn't make any difference.

As far as they're concerned, Iggy is a dreadful influence on you and has to be stopped before you turn as dissolute as him. It was like being whisked back to 1972, when everyone was scared that anybody who came within three feet of you was going to be turned into a screaming homosexual. And I wonder – is there some kind of hysterical hierarchy of pop stars, each of whom is a little bit more evil and corrupting than the last? If so, who is at the end of it?

You'll turn Mott into fairies, Iggy will turn you into a thug…someone else will turn Iggy into a monster…and in a stinking black pit somewhere in an unimagined future, there is a fiend so foul that the world would rather self-destruct than utter his name. And the *Daily Express* is frightened of punk rock? Oh, don't they have a treat in store?

Lust For Life, meanwhile, is an absolute masterpiece, and quite possibly Iggy's best album ever. Did you hear that Eno quote about how listening to *The Idiot* is like being encased in concrete? *Lust For Life* is like having the concrete shatter while you're still standing in it. I love 'Fall In Love With Me' – it reminds me of some of the stuff Soul Boy and I used to play at school, the really heavy funk, only with a complete punk rock flavour. 'Turn Blue' is great as well. You were playing that on the last tour, weren't you?[140]

Did you go to any of the gigs on Iggy's last tour? Alun and I took the week off work and went to all six – we spent a fortune in coach fares and barely slept a wink all week, but it was worth it. Part of it was because The Adverts were opening; I like to think maybe you had something to do with that. I told you they were the best punk band of them all, didn't I? You must have heard their last single, 'Gary Gilmore's Eyes' – apparently it was as big a hit in Germany as it was over here. Well, the rest of their set is just as good, and if you didn't get to any of the UK shows then you missed a treat.

Iggy was phenomenal, of course. I was a little disappointed when I first heard you wouldn't be touring with him, but only

140 Yes.

until I found out Scott Thurston was on keyboards instead. He was bloody good. The only time we really heard your keyboards was during 'I Wanna Be Your Dog', and this time around they were everywhere. And the *Lust For Life* songs work fabulously live. Next time you see Iggy, tell him we need a live album. The last two tours were too perfect to disappear.

OK, I'd better wrap up now – Soul Boy, Alun and I are off to see Michael Chapman at the Marquee tonight, and you know what us old Ronno fans are like![141]

Don't forget to let me know about West Berlin in January.

All the best

Gary

PS I am not going to say a word about the death of Bing Crosby, apart from the inevitable gasp – the whole thing is too bizarre for words.[142] You didn't happen to be in Memphis sometime around the middle of August, I suppose?[143] Or on holiday in Italy?[144]

PPS I just arrived home and I have to tell you, you have a double! We were in a pub on Wardour Street, and there were a couple of guys at a table, one of whom could have been Tony Visconti and the other was the spitting image of you. None of us was sure, so we didn't really do anything, but if it was you – and if you heard half a dozen people talking loudly, and dropping random lines from your songs into their conversation – that was us![145]

---

141 Ronson was Chapman's lead guitarist before hooking up with Bowie.
142 Bing Crosby died on October 14, little more than a month after recording a Christmas special TV show with Bowie among his guests. Occurring just a month after Marc Bolan's death – itself following on from making a TV show with Bowie – the realms of coincidental credulity were becoming seriously distended.
143 A reference, of course, to Elvis Presley's death that month.
144 Opera singer Maria Callas died the same day as Presley.
145 Was it him? Bowie was in London that day, he did go out to Soho with Visconti and he did visit a pub for the first time in five years. But he later said how surprised he was not to be recognised. So maybe it wasn't him, after all.

Edmonton, London N18
Wednesday 18 January 1978

Dear David

Wow, what an amazing city! Returned from West Berlin Monday evening, and London has never looked so beautiful, or so clean! I don't know what I was expecting, but all I could think of, the whole time we were there, was something you said in relation to 'Art Decade': 'A city cut off from its world. Art and culture, dying with no hope of retribution.' And they want people to go there on holiday? Coming soon, a fortnight in the salt mines.

You always hear about how clean Germany is, so maybe the dustmen were on strike or something. But it was so grimy, and everybody looked so miserable. No, they didn't – they looked radiant, smiling and waving to each other, running around... But it wasn't *real*. You get the feeling that if you were able to stop somebody on the street, slow them down for a second and tell them to look around them, they'd cut their wrists on the spot. Is that what the city's really like? How can you bear it?

Sorry I was not able to meet with you, although to be honest there probably wouldn't have been time. We were shepherded everywhere – and there was me thinking it was East Berlin where that happened. We went to the Wall, but I'd swear it was a special tourist section, with grinning guards on Checkpoint Charlie, and a souvenir shop selling Soviet badges, East German coin and stamp sets... I was hoping I might find a glass snowstorm scene with a watchtower and a machine-gun nest in it, but they must have been sold out.

Not sure if we saw Hansa-By-The-Wall[146] – I asked the guide whether we'd be going anywhere near it, but he shrugged and said he'd never heard of it, in that awful way the Germans have of making everything you say seem utterly banal and insignificant. We were driven around in a minibus for two days;

146 The studio where Bowie recorded during his Berlin sojourn.

then, in the evenings, we had these strange 'meet-and-greet' parties, with the owners of various local hotels and B&Bs. You know that episode of *Fawlty Towers* where they have the German guests in? Imagine that in reverse – 'Don't mention the World Cup.'

I was at a table with this one old boy who was going on and on about how he'd been running one of Germany's most successful hotels before the war, but the Allies bombed it flat and now all he had was a little guesthouse... What can you say in those situations? 'Oh, that's so terrible' gets really repetitive after a while, and 'My aunt in Coventry feels the same way' seemed a tad inappropriate. I ended up nodding a lot, and playing with the cabbage on my plate.

For once, there were a few other people my age on the trip, and a handful who even had the same taste in music, so we pretty much spent the entire time together. Of course, they were from all over the country (I wish I'd known them for the Iggy tour!), but there was one couple, Nick and Mandy, who work at an agency in Bishop's Stortford and come down to London for gigs all the time. I'm not sure if they're going out together (I hope not, cos she's quite fanciable), but we're going to hook up sometime soon.

Anyway, I returned to London on Monday, dumped my stuff at home and then turned straight around to catch Wayne County at Dingwall's – a terrific show as usual, although he has certainly calmed the act down since the early days. It's a lot more straightforward, less insanely theatrical, but the songs are still fantastic and, even when he's playing it as straight and normal as he can, he's still 50 times more outrageous than anyone else around. Plus, the blond hair (a wig?) makes him look like an extraordinarily addled version of Debbie Harry, and the best thing is, he knows it. Remember what I was saying last time, about the Ultimate Rock 'n' Roll Animal? Maybe...

Did you hear the 'Fuck Off' single? It was hilarious... Three months before the Pistols came out with *Never Mind The Bollocks* and got everybody all hot around the collar with an eight-letter swear word, Wayne included a four-letter one twice in a single song title.[147] The album's out next month, and I can't wait.

What's next on your agenda? I've heard about the new film, *Gigolo*... Hope it goes well. And, of course, there's *Peter And The Wolf* – I wonder what we're meant to make of that, especially coming so hot on the wheels of the Bing Crosby thing. Another little gift for Zowie?[148]

And one last thing. I don't know whose idea it was to put 'Sense Of Doubt' on the B-side of the 'Beauty And The Beast' single, but I've not seen a song clear a pub like that since Roxy's 'Sultanesque'![149] An inspired choice.

Happy New Year (belatedly)

Gary

---

147 'If You Don't Want To Fuck Me, Baby, Fuck Off' was adjudged one of the Top 100 punk singles of all time by *Mojo* magazine in September 2001.
148 Bowie introduced the duet 'Peace On Earth'/'Little Drummer Boy' on the *Bing Crosby Christmas Special* as 'my son's favourite'. Though it was not released until March 1978, his narration of Prokofiev's *Peter And The Wolf* would, indeed, be described as a Christmas present for the boy.
149 The instrumental drone on the flip of 1975's 'Love Is The Drug'.

Edmonton, London N18
Thursday 2 March 1978

Dear David

Just a note to let you know I sent off for my tickets for Earl's Court, they've cashed the cheque and now all I have to do is wait. They'd better be good – I've never paid £4 for a gig in my life!

I was a little disappointed when the dates were announced and every show is in an aircraft hangar. I'd really convinced myself that you were going to go for the theatres this time around, and hit the same venues as Iggy did. But I suppose he can get away with a couple of nights at the Rainbow. You'd probably need to play there every night for a month, and *still* not fit in everyone who'd want to go; plus it's such a small stage there that it'd probably cramp your style. Do you have anything planned visually this time around? It'd be great to see the old Hunger City set[150] dug out – we've only ever seen clips on telly, remember!

As long as everything goes to plan, I'll be going with Dawn, Nick and Mandy, Soul Boy and a few others. We've all sent away for four tickets each, for all three nights. Wouldn't it be funny if they all came through? We'd end up with about 30 seats each evening, and it wouldn't be a matter of figuring out who could go, but who else can we get to go with us? Not that that's likely to be a problem.

Do you remember the tour company that took us all to West Berlin in January? They just went bust, but not before offering me a job, at almost twice the pay I'm getting here. Thank God I turned it down. They called me up at work and asked me to go in for an interview, so I took the next afternoon off and toddled down to their office in Marble Arch... My God, what a dump! It looked like one of those places you see getting exposed on *That's Life* – plastic seats, Formica table tops, a couple of phones and a nudey-girl calendar. The bloke I saw was going on about

150 The cityscape backdrop employed for the 1974 US tour.

how the business was expanding faster than they could cope with, and they needed to take on new staff, and because I'd booked so many people on to their trips (I'd only booked one, but from the look of the place that probably is a lot) I was exactly the kind of forward-looking chap they needed. And as soon as he used the word 'chap', I thought, these people don't have a clue.

I told them I'd let them know, which was hilarious! It was the first time I've ever gone for a job interview and told them, 'Don't call me, I'll call you'! I already knew I didn't want it, but I mentioned it to my boss the next day and was given the whole 'Ambitious young man... We can't stop you... You must do what you think is best... Sorry to see you go...' routine, before he finally said that, if I really did feel the need to move on, he could put me in touch with places that could offer far more security. In the end, I admitted I'd already decided to turn it down, then called and told them so. A lucky escape – plus, it's nice to know that this place cares.

So, what else is new? Not much. I did finally get a copy of that *Thin White Duke* bootleg that came out about 18 months ago, from your Nassau show. It was OK – not as good as I was expecting. That version of 'Station To Station' should be required listening for every would-be guitarist, and they put the Cher medley on side four, which was as surreal as I expected it to be. It was probably more fun to watch at the time than it is to listen to now, but I'm glad I finally got it.

I've also sort of started going out with Mandy. It's complicated, and I'm not quite sure of the relationship myself yet, but it turns out that she and Nick have known each other since they were kids and have always hung out together. As far as she's concerned, they're virtually brother and sister, and nothing's ever happened between them. Nick (who is now known as Pixie, because of these atrocious green velvety ankle boots he bought), however, seems to think they're as good as married. So they're in this really fucked-up relationship where he *won't* go out with anyone else, and she *can't*, because he keeps frightening all the guys off.

The obvious question, of course, was, 'Why do you put up with it?' She replied, 'For the same reason you and Dawn are always together', and that was without me (or, presumably, her) ever discussing our relationship (or lack of) in front of her. So the big plan is to try and pair the Pixie and Dawn off, while Mandy and I quietly extricate ourselves from them.

But that's enough of my troubles. You have a world tour to prepare for, so get on with it!

See you in June

Gary

Edmonton, London N18
Tuesday 13 June 1978

Dear David

A quick note to tell you not to even bother reading the UK reviews of *TV Eye*,[151] because they don't understand. As far as I'm concerned, it's the best document possible of the Iggy tours, both with and without you – superb track listing, uncompromising performances, totally disorientating (the 'ladies and gennulmen' welcome three songs in? Perfect!) and, up there alongside *Metallic KO* and Lou's *Rock 'N' Roll Animal*, among *the* greatest live albums of all time.

It's amazing – 18 months ago, you could barely buy an Iggy album with all the cash in the world. I was in Our Price at Leicester Square the other day and they had eight different ones, and a ton of singles as well. Make hay while the sun shines... I've been buying everything as soon as it comes out, because who knows when it'll start vanishing again.

Not any time soon, I don't think. Again, 18 months ago I couldn't imagine ever seeing him play live. I've now seen him 12 times, and each show is better than the one before. The last two nights at the Music Machine were amazing, even with that ridiculous stage they have there, ten feet high with a row of spikes on the edge. It started out with clouds of dry ice – literally tons of the stuff. (Or is it gallons? What do they measure dry ice in, do you think?) Suddenly Iggy reared up out of it, wearing a black leotard and fishnet stockings! There was an old German helmet involved somewhere, as well, but the best thing was, he seemed to be making up the set – and some of the songs – as he went along.

Great versions of 'Funtime' and 'Lust For Life', a surprisingly powerful 'Kill City' (I never really got into the album, as it always seems a little too *produced*), and a new song that was possibly called 'The Winter Of My Discontent', which rambled

151 A live album recorded on both of Iggy's 1977 tours.

on for hours and was completely spellbinding. Fantastic! If you're even half as good, it'll be money well spent. Yes, all my tickets came through! I cannot wait!

All the best

Gary

Picture Postcard - Greetings From London
Sunday 2 July 1978

Dear David

Can I be frank? (You can be anyone you like, dear. Just call me Dorothy.) The first night you were rusty. The second night you were tired. And the third night you were shit.

Yours disgustedly

A Former Admirer

Edmonton, London N18
Wednesday 27 September 1978

Dear David

I'm sorry, but I really need to know. What on earth is this *Stage* monstrosity that has just materialised? The shows were not the best you've played in your life but, hey, even gods are only human sometimes. But to balls it all up so royally, and then stick out a double album to remind us. Ground control to Major Tom – please switch your brain back on.

If I hadn't known it was you, I'd say sides one and two of *Stage*, at least, are the work of some particularly misguided impersonator. Not only does it not sound like David Bowie, but it doesn't sound like the performer knows any David Bowie songs. And it's not even a halfway faithful record of the gig!

Where do the problems start? Resequencing the songs into chronological order? Opening the album with 'Hang Onto Yourself' and 'Ziggy Stardust',[152] to kid us there's even an iota of the old Spiders magic on display? Removing the sound of the audience? (Why? Surely you could have silenced the yawns?) Missing out the one song in the set that we really *did* need to hear again (you really should record 'Alabama Song' for a single)?

You know I've never lied to you in my letters, and you know me well enough now to understand that I really do care, not only for you but also for everything that you represent – to me and to everyone who has grown up with your music. Yes, you're a pop star, and no, you never made anybody any promises. But in a way that's precisely why you've come to mean so much to so many people.

Look at everybody who broke through at the same time as you. Elton and Rod are the only ones who've truly survived, but it's not the loyalty of their original fans that has sustained them, but an ability to keep generating new ones as the years passed.

152 Those two songs opened Bowie's live show during 1972–73.

The people who bought 'Maggie May' wouldn't touch 'Hotlegs', the ones who bought 'Rocket Man' would rather explode in space than listen to 'Ego'. You're unique in that you've both retained the old fans and gathered new ones, and the reason for this is that we trust you and we trust your instincts.

You killed Ziggy, but we forgave you and bought *Pin-Ups* by the truckload. You went disco – we listened, and maybe gained a new appreciation of soul and funk in the process. You duetted with Bing Crosby, and we applauded your all-round talent. RCA called *Low* commercial suicide, but we bought it to prove them wrong and, if you were to descend from your ivory tower and look around, you'd hear the children of *Low* all over the place. People say Kraftwerk were the impetus behind all the synthi-punk bands floating around these days, and the bands themselves might agree. But it still took *Low* to get them off their arses and do something – which means that they can drone on all they like about *Ralf And Florian*, but it was 'Speed Of Life' and 'Sound And Vision' that really started it for them.

And how do you pay us back? With a show of such unadulterated vagueness that the only life on stage all night was the sound of you butchering another fond memory. 'Ziggy played guitar', you sang, but I don't think you even know who Ziggy was any more. The 1974 and 1976 tours both thrived on rearranging the old songs, keeping them fresh for yourself, but bringing them back to life for us. How can you even imagine that you did that this time around?

You've probably guessed – I really didn't enjoy the gigs. No spectacle, no sense of occasion, no interesting lights to take our minds off the bored-looking guy in the daft baggy pants. I knew it was bad when Mandy turned around and asked if that was the keyboard player from Fumble. 'Yes,' I said, 'and that's the violinist from Hawkwind.' David Bloody Bowie is on stage and we're playing Rock Family Trees. Good job you never had a support band.

The set list was interesting, I'll admit. 'Warszawa' was an exciting intro, 'Heroes', the ideal set opener, and so on. Forget the lifeless nightmare of the sing-along-a-cabaret section... I'm sorry, the 'Ziggy'-era oldies...and at least some thought went into the sequencing. But the live album doesn't even let us keep that happy memory, and what does that leave us with? I'm sorry, but even your trousers were better than *Stage*. At least, in years to come, you'll look back at them and laugh. I bet you'll never even listen to *Stage* again.

Can we have our old Bowie back, please? You know – the interesting one who respected his songs as much as we do?

Gary

PS I see Decca have finally reissued 'Liza Jane'.[153] Hurrah. At least you have one decent record on the shelves right now.

---

153 Bowie's first ever UK single, recorded with The King Bees in 1964.

Edmonton, London N18
Friday 16 February 1979

Dear David

You know how sometimes you're so upset over something that you rattle off a response without giving a second thought to any future ramifications it may have? Well, I'm guilty of exactly that and, last night, I paid the price. Mandy and I went to see The Human League at the Nash – we've been to a few of their shows, and they're one of the few new synthi-punk bands who truly acknowledge their glam rock heritage. And, of course, they were wonderful. But I'm really wishing we'd gone somewhere else entirely.

There we were, happily bopping away when, suddenly, Mandy virtually pulled my arm out of its socket and pointed to this guy at the back of the room. And we all know who it was, don't we? I know I've 'seen' you around town in the past, but this time there was no mistake. For a start, pretty much everyone else in the place had recognised you as well, and there was a buzz going round that was as loud as the band. Plus, we saw you sign a few autographs, talk to a few people... Did I ever tell you about the punk girl I met last year, who saw you at some club the night you played Boston with Iggy? She ran up the stairs to get your autograph and your bodyguard promptly threw her back down again. Obviously things have changed since then, because you seemed to be loving every moment of it.

But did I dare even walk over? After that last letter I wrote to you? It's not even as if I thought you'd recognise me. I could have asked for your autograph, got a 'Gary, Best Wishes', and you'd never have known me from Adam. I don't know how I felt – embarrassed, ashamed, horrified? My last letter to you may have been honest (at least, honest about my opinion), but it was rude as well, and that's completely unforgivable.

It's completely up to me whether I like something or not, I know. But to accuse you of not giving a damn for your fans wasn't only wrong, it was unfair as well. And the idea of walking over (knowing I'd just called you a fraud), then coming the big fan, 'Gee, David, I love you', felt so hypocritical that I couldn't move.

Mandy was still trying to pull me over ('Come on, it's him!') and I was pulling away ('Nah, it might not be', or 'Let's respect his privacy'). So, she let go of me, I tumbled backwards into our table (yes, the crash that I know you heard – because you looked over – that was me), and I was sitting there in a puddle of fag ends, while she had you sign the back of an old train ticket. I noticed your writing went over the edge, and one day I'll probably laugh at her for only getting two-thirds of your autograph. Right now, though, I feel sick about the whole thing.

After you'd gone, we talked quickly to the band. They said you were asking them about their slide show – it *was* bloody good, wasn't it? And I did get *their* autographs, for whatever consolation it might become. But even now I can't believe what happened and that I was so stupid to send that last letter to you. Again, please accept my apologies and, for my part, I promise to always think before I mail.

All the best

Gary

PS If you are into catching new bands, whatever you do, DON'T MISS THE PSYCHEDELIC FURS! They're playing all over north London at the moment, and they're excellent. Think early Roxy crossed with the Velvets, with 'Station To Station' running all the way through.

Edmonton, London N18
Wednesday 14 March 1979

Dear David

Next time you're in London, you wouldn't do me a favour, would you? Put on your most tattered jeans, battered jacket and dirtiest shoes, then go down to Billy's. You can't miss it. It's the hole in the ground off Dean Street with a long line of clothes horses parked outside. Don't worry. They won't recognise you, and they certainly won't let you in, which is when you take off your hat and sunglasses, announce that you're sick of listening to your old records anyway, then fly away in a waiting limo.

In fact, don't even do it for me. Do it for everyone who believes music is for everyone, and not just an elite handful of pampered pillocks whose only stylistic advantage over the rest of the world is that they know a passing bandwagon when they see one.

What killed punk? It wasn't the music, it wasn't the record companies, it wasn't the media finding new things to write about. It was the part-time poseurs who saw a picture of Sid Vicious in the *News Of The World* and decided that his look was the *only* look a well-dressed punk could ponce around in. Punk was the first fashion to come along whose stated goal was to destroy the traditional stereotypes of the English as a staid, reserved, conservative race. How ironically inevitable that it would promptly become a stereotype itself. Uniforms beget dress codes, dress codes beget elitism and, before you know it, the land is in the thrall of a self-appointed fashion police, and if you're caught in last week's bondage trousers you're dead.

For most of the last year, Billy's was pretty much the only place in the West End you could go to where you knew you weren't going to be battered into submission by a nonstop diet of dodgy disco or dodgier umpteenth-generation punk. Kraftwerk, the Velvets, Roxy... And Tuesday nights are nonstop you.

But try to get in the place if you're not suitably swathed in Mum's best tea towel. Do you remember the Rocky Thighs cartoons in the *NME*, the ultimate glam star with the pierced everythings, luminous bat wings and a talking codpiece? He is alive and well and walking the streets of London with a brat pack of precocious teenage fashion victims hanging on his every gyration. Yes, maybe I am pissed off because I turned up there without dying my hair 17 different colours and putting on Mandy's best frock and combat boots. But we'd just come from a Radio Stars gig, and who can possibly look their best after something like that? I've been turned away from clubs because they're sold out, and that's fine. But never because *I* haven't sold out. Scumbags.

It's a shame, because Billy's *is* a fun place and, like I said, they do have the best music in town. But, to quote D H Lawrence out of Mott The Hoople,[154] 'If you make a revolution, make it for fun.' The scene around Billy's has all the makings of a *real* musical revolution, one that could learn from the mistakes of punk and change what currently looks like an extremely dire new decade. There's already a ton of bands around whose music clearly comes out of the same kind of corners as yourself. Kraftwerk, Roxy, early Eno...Human League are in there, of course, Ultravox and Japan, and that's just the bands everyone knows. Simple Minds, Nicky And The Dots, Orchestral Manoeuvres In The Dark, Human League, Joy Division, Tubeway Army, The Psychedelic Furs, Siouxsie And The Banshees, and that's before you even start looking at the avant-garde stuff. Between them, they could send the music scene off on its most fascinating tangent in a decade.

There's a really interesting sexuality to it as well, which may be a re-creation of the old glam affectations, but has a lot more confidence to it – a kind of cross between Johnny Rotten's remark about sex being nothing more than a couple of minutes of squelchy noises and The Tom Robinson Band's 'Glad To Be Gay'. Androgynous homosexuality meets the drag queens from hell.

---

154 Lawrence's *A Sane Revolution* was reprinted in the sleeve design of Mott's *Mott* LP in 1973.

Bind all this together, give it a catchy name for the media to hang something on, and you could make punk look like a simple dress rehearsal. Instead, that's all this new lot are concerned with – their dress. It's a bit like the mods, in that the music is virtually irrelevant. As long as it's quirky enough for them to do that bloody stupid robot dance to, they're happy as pigs in shit. But, whereas the mods had the rockers to act as a kind of balance, and to take their minds off preening in the mirror, this lot don't seem to have any natural enemies at all.

Well, maybe they should, and who better to lead the assault than their idol? Remember Lou Reed talking about making an anti-glam album called *Get Back In The Closet, You Queers*? Ask him if you can borrow it. Better still, maybe you could make it with him. Book a listening party at Billy's with oodles of advance publicity, get every little scenester in the country down to preen and then slice the tops of their heads off with *Metal Machine* meets *The Man Who Sold The World*. And employ Iggy as a bouncer for the night. That'd really terrify them.

Anyway, forget the club, but I do recommend that you see all the bands I've mentioned. The Furs are the best – I've probably caught them half a dozen times now, including a show at the Pegasus where they brought a Hoover on stage and played it as though it was another instrument. It was one of the best things I've ever seen or heard, just this relentless roaring behind the band, with the lights so low that if you moved even a few feet back from the stage (I was standing by the PA – I had no choice but to move!) you couldn't even see what was making the noise.

The singer, Butler Rep,[155] reminds me a bit of you, in that he looks great, has a terrific voice and knows how to move around. Most of their set is melodic and atmospheric, but they really understand how to build the tension and a mood. Every song is a little bit more psychotic than the last one, until they close with 'Chaos', which is exactly what it says. They explode into it, a fully fledged freak-out with everything turned up full blast, while Rep rants and raves into the mic. They're completely amazing,

155 Richard Butler's original stagename.

and they're the most original band around by miles. Let me know if you're going to be in London any time soon, and I can tell you where they're playing next.

All the best

Gary

PS I've enclosed my entry for Capital Radio's 'Bowie The Traveller' contest.[156] As you're picking out the winners, I figured it wouldn't hurt to get a head start.

BOWIE THE TRAVELLER
by Gary Weightman
When the cameras flash on the stage dark as night
His eyes gleam bright like traffic lights
Red for danger, green for go
But he heeds not the traffic code
The world has no borders for there are no limits to song
From Gloucester Road to Detroit, from the Thames to the Mekong
The restless pen takes flight with the wings
(Which are feathered by the words he sings)
And soars across earth's mountains and planes
London, LA, Berlin, then home again
But that word has no meaning, or if it does it's unravelling
For the Thin White Zig will never stop travelling

---

156 The London radio station ran a contest inviting listeners to submit a short story or poem entitled *Bowie The Traveller*. Twelve winners would be personally selected by Bowie himself.

Edmonton, London N18
Saturday 26 May 1979

Dear David

Traitor! No sooner do I tell you to do everything in your power to destroy Billy's, than you rush down there to film your new promo film![157]

Well, that's what I reckoned when I first heard the news, but now I've had a chance to think about it I realise that you're even sneakier than I am. What better way of killing an elitist cult than by telling the world it should join? My friend Pete and I walked past there on Tuesday, the place was mobbed, the doorman was going nuts, and it was all down to 'Boys Keep Swinging'!

I thought it was the perfect single the moment I heard it, and that was an amazing performance on *The Kenny Everett Show*. I couldn't believe it when it started dropping down the charts after just a couple of weeks, but then you put out that fantastic film[158] and suddenly you're back in the Top 10![159] Next stop, No.1.

I've seen more and more bands making these little films – it's a good idea, but I do wonder what the point really is, especially as hardly anyone gets to see them after their one or two airings on *Top Of The Pops*. I know you did a film for 'Be My Wife', but was it ever even shown anywhere? Same with 'John I'm Only Dancing' and 'Rebel Rebel' – that's the one with the eye patch and the red guitar, isn't it? I've seen stills, but I don't think the actual film has been on over here.

OK, I hate to ask, but what the hell is 'Boys Keep Swinging' about? It has a really convincing glammy feel to it, kind of an updated 'Rebel Rebel' crossed with a real punk energy, and I've heard a few people describe it as a tribute to the resilience of youth culture or some such. But that's way too simplistic, especially in the light of the film. So, spill the beans and I promise not to ask you about another song again! Meanwhile, I love the story about how you made all the band members

157 In modern parlance, a video.
158 Bowie's first with video director David Mallett.
159 Having apparently peaked at No.15, 'Boys Keep Swinging' dropped to No.19, then rebounded to No.9 on the May 22 chart.

swap instruments for the session, regardless of whether they'd played them before or not. The guitar solo at the end is fantastic, by the way.

So, how did you enjoy doing 'Bowie The Traveller'? I was rather glad I didn't get selected in the end – I heard it was madness, with thousands of fans trying to see you, and the Q&A part of the show was too stupid for words. How ironic you saying you wanted to talk to fans – because you were tired of being asked the same questions by journalists – only to be asked all the same questions anyway! I'm not sure what I would have asked if I had been chosen. There can't be many questions left that you haven't endured over the years. In fact, that's what I would have asked: 'What is the one question you really wish someone would ask you?'

As for *Lodger*, 'Yassassin' is my favourite track at the moment, and I was wondering how much influence did Simon House have on that? There was a similar-sounding track on Hawkwind's *Quark Strangeness And Charm* album a couple of years ago,[160] and he was all over that. I also liked 'DJ' – you know that's going to be a massive hit if RCA are smart enough to release it, cos disc jockeys can't resist any record that has the words 'DJ' or 'radio' in the title, no matter what the rest of the words are. I loved it when Costello brought out 'Radio Radio': the record slagged the radio to death, but the idiot DJs played it all the time. 'I am what I play' – what a fantastic put-down. The only tracks I'm not sure about are 'Repetition', which sounds a little forced, and 'Red Money', but that's probably because I love the original so much.[161]

I'm not quite sure how *Lodger* completes the *Low/Heroes* trilogy, though. It's a very different-sounding record, and a lot more conventional, at least in as much as it's all songs rather than a mix of songs and instrumentals. In fact, if there's any companion piece for it, I'd have to say it's Roxy Music's *Manifesto*; songs like 'Trash' and 'Manifesto' itself are certainly cut from the same kind of cloth, and the idea of naming the two

160 'Hassan I Sabha'.
161 'Red Money' employed the same backing track as Iggy Pop's 'Sister Midnight'.

sides 'east' (for the darker stuff) and 'west' (for the more Americanised music) is something I could certainly have seen you doing. I always think of *Low* as a kind of musical enema, flushing out all your past influences and leaving you with just the bare bones, which you built on with *Heroes*. But *Lodger* reaches back to earlier ideas, sounds and voices. 'Boys Keep Swinging' and 'Red Money' are the obvious examples, but 'African Night Flight' has a hint of 'Panic In Detroit' about it, as well as a bit of The Walker Brothers!

You must have heard their *Nite Flites* album by now? Most of it's the usual big ballad stuff, but Scott's four songs are so completely round the bend that it's hard to believe this is the same guy who was groaning 'No Regrets' a few years ago. I was sort of expecting to hear something by him when you were on *Star Special* last weekend.[162] Wow, what an amazing desert island you'd have, with that lot to keep you company. I taped the show, then made another copy without the talking in between songs, and it makes a great compilation! I own a lot of the records you played – the Doors, Iggy, Lennon, the Velvets, The Mekons, King Crimson, Beck, T Rex, the Stones (and, yes, even Blondie!) – and I'm going to hunt down a few of the others.

I can't believe you like Talking Heads, though. I saw them the first time they came over here, opening for The Ramones at the Roundhouse, and they were alright – quirky but with loads of energy and sharp edges. They reminded me of a wasp trapped inside a glass jar, buzzing angrily around and looking for something to sting. But their last couple of albums have been appalling, the sound of a band that reads too much of its own press, and feels compelled not only to prove they're still as clever as everyone says they are but that they're even cleverer. They've already stopped writing tunes in favour of obscure chemical formulae, and David Byrne has all the vocal soul of a man reciting algebraic equations. You can imagine their on-stage introductions – 'Here's one about the cosine of the number 834.975'.

---

162 Bowie played DJ on a BBC Radio One special, playing a riveting selection of 27 tracks sprawling across the musical spectrum.

I'm having the same problem with Devo. Those early singles that Stiff released over here were terrific, really fresh and intriguing. But that whole 'are we not men' business really grew boring after a while – it was an intriguing idea for one record, but they're whipping it to death. If you own the first ever Sparks album, listen to 'Biology 2'. Everything Devo will ever create is captured right there. I'm not sure whether Eno was the right person to produce them, either. He's at his best working with people who are coming from a very different musical place than him, which is why you made such a perfect partner for him... I liked what he did with the first Ultravox album, because their excitement and naivety still shone through. But put him with people who share his ideas, or at least like to think they do, and it vanishes up its own bum. And now he's working with Talking Heads! Oh dear.

Finally, I read that piece in *Melody Maker* about you and Lou Reed having a big bust-up at the Chelsea Rendezvous a few weeks back.[163] Don't tell me – you asked if you could have the *Get Back In The Closet* title for your next album, didn't you?

All the best

Gary

---

163 *Melody Maker*'s Alan Jones reported on the fracas in the April 21 issue.

Edinburgh, Scotland
Friday 31 August 1979

Dear David

THAT WAS AMAZING! I just returned from the premier of *Bowie '73* (Pete, his sister and I drove up specially to see it) and all I can say is, you've made the best rock concert film of all time! It brought the whole lot back to me – the *Clockwork Orange* intro, the restlessness of the crowd, the sheer adrenalin rush of the opening 'Hang Onto Yourself'... 'My Death' was magical, the medley was perfection and, as for Ronno's solo during 'Moonage Daydream'...

I still play the *His Master's Voice* bootleg fairly regularly, but seeing the entire show made me realise how spectacular it really was. When you've had a record for a long time, you lose some of the excitement you felt when you first heard it. Well, *Bowie '73* brought it all back, and then some. And the retirement speech was heartbreaking all over again, even with the benefit of hindsight. How long till the film gets out on general release? And will there be a soundtrack album of the entire show?

I heard a few people complaining that the sound quality wasn't as good as they'd have liked, but what do they expect from a live show? As you proved with *David Live*, and as (I hope) you learned with *Stage*, you cannot fuck around with live sound, no matter how honourable your intentions may be. What happened on the night is what should happen on the record, mistakes and all. Besides, imagine if you did decide to redo bits. You'd have everybody wanting to change things – you might decide you didn't like your vocal, Woody may want to do a different drum part, Ronno might want to change his solos and, before you know where you are, you're back with the original studio versions, and dubbing applause all over them, like that Stones live album from the 1960s.[164] *Bowie '73* is history as it happened.

---

164 1966's *Got Live If You Want It*, famously cut in the studio and then, indeed, overlaid with crowd noise.

Talking of bootlegs, did you hear about all the busts a couple of weeks ago? The BPI[165] bootlegged a boot[166] of your 1976 Wembley shows, then went out in search of shops selling them! Isn't that sort of thing illegal? Giving someone something, then busting them for owning it? Plus, I do wonder how an album can be considered a bootleg when it was made by a legitimate company, with the support of the artist's own record company? What really infuriated me, though, were the news stories saying there were tens of thousands of copies of the original floating around out there. Anyone who knows anything about bootlegs knows that *Don't Touch That Dial* is impossible to find. Nobody I know has a copy, and I heard there were only a couple of thousand made, most of them being sold in Japan, where it was a legitimate release![167]

Besides, it's not as though that's even the best of the bootlegs from that tour – *Thin White Duke* is the one that everyone should own (why don't you release that officially?).[168] The Wembley recordings just don't have the same excitement. But I suppose taste and quality weren't really the point of the exercise, were they? All I know is, of the three shops where I did most of my shopping, two threw away their stock as soon as they heard about the raids and the third has closed down altogether.

The whole affair sounds really dodgy to me, and I do hope that you didn't have any personal involvement in it. I must admit, I'd be surprised if you did. I know you love music as much as I do, and I'm sure you've bought a few bootlegs in your time, even if they're Velvet Underground ones! That's what the BPI doesn't seem to understand – the people who buy bootlegs are the real fans, who'll buy pretty much anything with their favourite artist's name on them, particularly during those periods when the artist himself doesn't have anything new in the shops.

It always makes me laugh when I read about the music industry losing money because of bootlegs. What's more to the

165 The British Phonographic Industry Ltd.
166 The original *Don't Touch That Dial* boot was retitled *The Wembley Wizard Touches That Dial*.
167 According to contemporary Japanese copyright law, live recordings of foreign artists made before 1978 were considered public domain.
168 Two tracks from the show did, in fact, appear as bonus tracks on the 1991 Rykodisc reissue of *Station To Station*.

point is that they haven't figured out a way to make money from them yet. I buy two or three LPs a week, and a lot of them, I'll admit, are – sorry, *were* – bootlegs. But if I can't buy bootlegs, I'm not going to go out and buy official LPs instead. I'll spend my money on something else entirely. In fact, right now I'm saving up for the New Year, and a mighty transatlantic shopping binge. Look out America, here I come! There's a big travel agents convention in New York, we leave on 3 January and come back on the 9th. Six whole days of record shops!!

I'm really excited about it. The boss and his wife were originally going to go, but they have family staying with them for Christmas and New Year, so, rather than have to rush, they're sending me and the new girl in the office, Kaye. She's a couple of years older than me (22), and came here from some firm in your old stomping ground of south London. Very pretty, single and free... Well, you can't blame a boy for trying, can you?

The only part I'm dreading is, if I run into Mandy and the Pixie. Did I tell you we broke up (she dumped me) during the summer? She decided that she was meant to be with Nick after all, and within a month of us breaking up they were engaged and married! So, a Pixie nicked my girlfriend from beneath my nose, and now they're in the toadstool field where every pixie goes... Maybe I should write a song; it sounds like a hit single to me. Then I could give it to Gary Numan – or Gary Old-Bowie, as a lot of people prefer to call him – although I'm not sure I quite understand why everyone says he's ripping you off. If anyone should be getting pissed off, it's Kraftwerk. And, probably, The Bay City Rollers. Weren't they all clones as well?

It's funny. I saw Tubeway Army opening for The Adverts back in 1978, and they were just another tinny little punk band, all mach ten guitars and ranting vocals – they encored with one of the worst versions of 'White Light, White Heat' I've ever heard. And now look at them. 'Are "Friends" Electric?' was a great record, I must admit, dead atmospheric and very haunting. But I played the album and wasn't overly impressed, and I've been driven quite insane by the new single ('Cars') and it's only been out a few days! Quite honestly, I'd rather hear them do 'White Light, White Heat' again. At least that has a bit of a tune.

All the best

Gary

Somewhere over the Atlantic, probably
Wednesday 9 January 1980

Dear David

So, that's America? It'll be lovely when they've finished it.

No, I had a fantastic time – and if this plane is flying a little slower and lower than it's supposed to, it's cos of all the records I've got packed in the hold. Second day in, I asked the bellboy at the hotel where the best record shops were. He sent me down to Greenwich Village – drew me a map and everything. Oh my God, have you ever travelled on the tube over there? It's terrifying! For a start, all the stations are like the Angel, Islington, with an island in the middle and the tracks on either side of you. Every time someone walked past, I was convinced they were a psycho who was going to push me one way or the other.

Got down to Washington Square and, the first street I walked down, bingo. And the second, and the third... You could barely put one foot in front of the other without tripping over another record shop. I had to get a taxi back to the hotel, because no way was I going to stand around on the underground with $100 worth of records (of *all* descriptions, if you know what I mean) under my arm.

I got a whole pile of your records, from 45s I'd never seen to bootlegs I'd never heard of, and one thing that... I don't know if it even is you, because I've certainly never seen it mentioned in any discography or biography, but... You know that band you were in back before The King Bees, called The Konrads? Did you ever make a record? I found one on American Decca, 'I Don't Know How Much'. The label says it was recorded in England, and the writing credits are Neville Wills/Tony Edwards.[169] I had the guy in the shop play it and it certainly isn't you singing. There doesn't seem to be a sax, either, so maybe it's another one to file alongside David John And The Mood, in the pantheon of Bowie Records That Never Were. But it's a nice little curio. I also

169 Decca 32060, The Konrads' 'I Don't Know How Much', was composed by Bowie's then bandmates Tony Edwards and Neville Wills, although Bowie's own involvement remains unknown.

picked up Billy Fury's cover of 'Silly Boy Blue'. I've never seen a UK pressing of it, and I reckon the US one must be even rarer, so that was quite a find.

I picked up a ton of other singles. At 25 cents each, who could resist? Albums for a buck – gimme dozens! Found some really weird American pressings of familiar British albums. My favourite is Roxy's *Country Life* with the Fraüleins excised – the guy in the shop told me the regular cover was banned, so the record company did a close-up of the bushes instead, figuring that Roxy fans would get the joke. I got the first Sparks album, from when they were still called Halfnelson, and a quadraphonic version of Mott's *The Hoople*. They played me a bit of it and, even on a regular stereo, it's a completely different and totally fucked-up mix. Why didn't you ever go for a quad album? I know the system never took off at home, but apparently it was quite the hit here for a while, right around the time of *Diamond Dogs/Young Americans*. If nothing else, you could have had fun doing the remix!

As usual with these trips, most of our time was spent in seminars, or being dragged around the city meeting hotel people, caterers, other travel agents... I'm happy to report that the vast majority of American travel agents are as exciting as their British counterparts, which means not at all. I do wonder why a profession that, in theory, should attract the most adventurous and curious people around, instead ends up with wall-to-wall gumbies. Or maybe I don't wonder at all.

I couldn't get over the difference between American hotels and European ones. I remember reading exactly that same thing in Ian Hunter's *Diary Of A Rock And Roll Star*, but that was written eight years ago... Surely things must have changed since then? Yes, they have. American hotels have become even better, British ones have become even worse.

Single rooms with double beds! Telephones that work! Minibars with alcohol in them and room service that's available all night. OK, I still found a copy of *Gideon's Bible* in the bedside table, but I found a *TV Guide* as well and I seriously considered barricading myself into the room and watching telly for the rest of the trip. Fortunately, and contrary to absolutely everything we're brought up to believe, American television is just as bad as ours, but there's a hell of a lot more of it. I mean, I love *M*A*S*H*, but not three times a day, every day, and not with canned laughter, either.

As for music, I looked everywhere for something even remotely resembling *Top Of The Pops* or *Whistle Test*, and they have nothing like either of them. It's funny – we sit at home and read about Iggy on *Dinah Shore*, and you on *Johnny Carson*, and the impression is that this sort of stuff is on all the time. Then you get here and discover that they're all hour-long chat shows with the 'musical guest' crammed in between the commercials. And, again, they're on every night. Imagine that – a TV schedule ruled by Russell Harty and Parkinson. It's terrifying! And the commercials are insane; just a succession of madmen screaming about how you have to buy this revolutionary new product or all your hair will fall out and your children will grow up to be lepers. No wonder Americans are so loud, with that kind of barrage going on all the time.

One show I didn't miss, though, was your appearance on *Saturday Night Live*. I can't believe I was here to see it, especially as one of the last things I watched before leaving the UK was *Kenny Everett's New Year's Eve* show. Loved the new version/film of 'Space Oddity', but the *SNL* performance was even better. Where on earth did you find those backing singers? Was one of them named Klaus Nomi? The bellboy said he sees him playing around fairly often, and that he's a baker. Weird!

What on earth do you think America made of the performance, though? People here thought Ziggy was bizarre... That version of 'TVC 15' was so screwed up that even I was taken by surprise. Great versions of 'Boys' and 'The Man Who Sold The World' as well – complete reinventions. You really ought to put them out on an EP, maybe with the new 'Space Oddity'.

As for the rest of the show, I can't say I was too impressed. A few bits were amusing, and Martin Sheen[170] was pretty good. Have you seen *Apocalypse Now* yet? It's an excellent film. But the whole programme reminded me a bit of amateur night at a hard-up Butlin's. The jokes and sketches were very hit-and-miss and the impressions were so sub-Mike Yarwood that half the time I didn't even know who it was meant to be until someone in the sketch said, 'Mr President', or whatever. No wonder the imported sitcoms we get aren't any good. If this is what they consider to be radical humour, imagine what makes the average American laugh.

You'll be pleased to hear that my fears of running into Mandy and the Pixie were unfounded. Someone who knows them said he quit to become an assistant manager at a branch of Freeman Hardy Willis (all the better for buying more green velvet booties, no doubt), while she's only working part time now, because she's pregnant! What a future their child has in store – half human, half woodland sprite. Maybe they should name it Puck.

My fiendish designs on the lovely Kaye came to nought as well, so I did most of my running around on my own. There was a whole bunch of Broadway shows laid on for us to go to if we wanted, so I went to see Philip Anglim in *The Elephant Man*. I'd wanted to see it when it was on in Hampstead a couple of years ago and never did, but there's something deliciously decadent about travelling 3,000 miles to see a play that was once on three miles from my house. It was really good. I remember reading the John Merrick story years ago when I was a kid, in one of those trashy Freaks and Monsters paperbacks. I loved it, because it was one of the few genuinely authenticated British cases in the book. The rest were all Americans. Has any other country on earth spawned so many half-boy/half-spider dancing-chicken-mutant geeks? They really ought to test the water or something, cos it can't be healthy.

170 The show's guest host that evening.

The biggest surprise in the play was the complete lack of make-up. I was expecting Anglim to come out wearing something like those Slipperman costumes Peter Gabriel had for his last Genesis tour.[171] Instead, he pulled it all off with nothing more than facial expressions, body movements and vocal effects, and it was spectacular. When he first comes on stage, you're thinking, 'Yeah, right', and within half an hour you're completely sucked into the role and it doesn't matter what he looks like. You see the lumps and bumps anyway. It really is one of the greatest performances I've ever seen, and one of the best plays as well. If you do get the chance, you have to go see it.[172]

As for any of the places I intended going to – Max's, CBGBs, Hurrah! and so on – I didn't get to any of them. I went all the way through the gig guide in the *Village Voice* and it was dreadful. Any bands I'd heard of seemed to be playing in clubs in the arse end of nowhere, and vice versa. The only gig I ended up going to was one evening when I was roped into bar-hopping with a bunch of guys from Blackpool (of all places), and wound up in this disgusting little bar off Canal Street, watching some terrible band whose name I never did catch but who made the worst punk band in Britain sound like the height of proficiency. Hey boys, it's not all about playing at 500 miles per hour, you know. If it was, we could all have stayed in 1974 and listened to Focus records.

So, being as the hotel was all-expenses-paid, I spent most of my time either in the restaurant or the bar, with one entire evening devoted to fighting off the advances of the Klaus Nomi-fan bellboy. Finally, after three hours of dropping increasingly unsubtle hints, he asked me outright if I was gay. I told him no, at which point he apologised and said he'd assumed I was, because I seemed to be such a big Bowie fan. I assured him that your reputation (and your following) in England is presumably a little different from what it is in America.

As for New York itself, it's fun to visit, but I could never imagine living there. One of the trips we took was out to see the

171 Performing 1974's *Lamb Lies Down On Broadway* album.
172 In fact, Bowie had already attended the play during his New York visit the previous month.

Statue of Liberty, and you look back at the city and it's one of those classic 'Bugger me!' moments. It's so huge! Walking around is like being at the bottom of some massive steel and glass cavern. Before you get here, you already know that the skyscrapers are absolutely enormous, but it's not until you're standing on the pavement looking up that you truly understand how absurdly high everything is. I had the chance to go up the World Trade Center but turned it down. I used to get vertigo on top of Rochester Castle, so that place would do me in completely!

And the crowds! You know what it's like on Oxford Street on the Saturday before Christmas, when they're doing roadworks on the pavement outside Selfridges. New York's like that all the time. I ran out to buy some ciggies in the middle of the night and the place was still seething. One embarrassing moment on that outing... I was looking round the biscuits aisle (sorry, cookies!) and came across a box of Pop-Tarts. Of course I burst out laughing – I still treasure my copy of Cherry Vanilla's photo book,[173] but I can't imagine what it tastes like. Or why they'd stack it alongside the Captain Crunch. Oh well, two cultures divided by a common language and all that...

The noise is amazing, as well. The hotel had double glazing at least, but all night long there were sirens and lorries tearing around, huge trucks washing the streets down at some ungodly hour of the morning. I will *never* complain about the pace of life in London again! You've been there a lot, haven't you? How do you stand it?

I'm sure I have plenty more to write, but the stewardesses are moving around again, handing out all this paperwork we have to fill in before Britannia will welcome us back to sanity, so I'll finish now.

Happy New Year, Happy New Decade...

Gary

---

173 Vanilla's sexually charged photo collection, published in 1974, shared its title with the popular American pastry.

Edmonton, London N18
Thursday 7 August 1980

Dear David

You're the Elephant Man! I couldn't believe it when I heard the
news! I told you it was the best show ever, didn't I? I would kill
to see you in the role – you have to bring it to London once you're
done with the American run. Either that, or I need to get back
over to New York. I hope it goes really well for you – the reviews
have been fabulous so far – but I suppose it also means that we
won't be getting a tour this year to back up the new album?

Had you already decided to call the album *Scary Monsters
And Super Creeps* when you took the role in the play? If not,
that's an amazing coincidence, although I wonder who the 'super
creeps' are. Love the new single, and the promo film is your best
yet. Just the way it's filmed is so spooky, but the bulldozer was
the finishing touch. My only question is: Why a clown? It's a bit
Leo Sayer, isn't it?

'Ashes To Ashes' is a magnificent song, and one of your best
in years. I had some reservations when I first heard you were
writing a sequel to 'Space Oddity' – the original only narrowly
falls short of being a novelty song in many ways (countdown,
moon landing, Stylophone), and the idea of a follow-up raised
some very parlous fears. Did Benny Hill write a sequel to 'Ernie'?
Did Rolf Harris create a *third* little boy? Did Typically Tropical
go anywhere other than Barbados?

Not only did you pull it off, but now we know why you
rerecorded 'Space Oddity' itself earlier this year[174] – however,
not why you put it on the B-side. I loved 'Alabama Song', and
have done since the Earl's Court gig. But a lot of people found
it too harsh for a single and passed it over completely. If they'd
known 'Space Oddity' was also part of the deal, it'd probably
have done a lot better – and, of course, would have been a
perfect herald for 'Ashes To Ashes'.

174 Following its airing on *The Kenny Everett Show* in December, the rerecorded 'Space Oddity' resurfaced as the
B-side to spring 1980's 'Alabama Song' single.

I read somewhere that there's a 12" single coming out in the US segueing the original version of 'Space Oddity' and 'Ashes To Ashes' as *The Continuing Story Of Major Tom*. Any chance of them releasing that over here? 'Ashes' on its own is powerful enough but, with that sort of push behind it, it could be massive. Especially if you're not going to be around to help with the promotion.

Meanwhile, I'm curious. We all know now what happened to Major Tom, but what about his wife? Did she remain faithful to a husband who's bouncing around in outer space? Or did she say 'Fuck him', file for divorce and marry somebody with a more down-to-earth job? I must say, everyone is treating the major like some kind of isolationist icon but, from the wife's point of view, he's a bit of a bastard, isn't he? There she is, stuck with all the bills and everything, and the only time she hears from him is when he calls up ground control: 'Tell my wife I love her… But I'd rather be up here on my tod, than sitting around at home with her.'

If the world is that distasteful to him, he'd have been a lot kinder to do a Reggie Perrin – clothes neatly folded on the launch pad, 'Missing Presumed Exploded In Space'. The rejection would be a lot less cruel that way, at least in the long run. Knowing someone is dead must be preferable to knowing they're staying away deliberately, because at least you can get on with your life. At the same time, though, if they're staying away, then you can hope they'll come back. If they're dead, you know they won't. I wonder if it'd be possible to find a middle ground, a sort of Major Reggie? Or is that what joining a band and going on tour is all about?

According to *NME*, we went to two of the same gigs last month, and I didn't even know you were in London! There was The Roches at the Venue. I'd never heard them before, but I heard Robert Fripp was a fan so I figured I'd give it a go. It was OK, but not really my cup of tea. What did you think?

Then there was Iggy at the Music Machine and, to be honest, it wasn't the best gig I've seen him do, which is a shame because I'm really enjoying *Soldier*. It's a real return to form after *New Values*, which was so slick and slight. 'Loco Mosquito' just kicks things off with such mad energy, and it really doesn't let up. Your track, 'Play It Safe', is hysterically funny: I met Ivan Kral, Iggy's guitarist, after the show and he was telling me there's another version that's even wilder and funnier...and something about the Queen?

It was a real thrill to meet him. I loved his stuff with Patti,[175] and it's gratifying to see him bounce straight from her band to Iggy's. You know he used to be in Blondie as well, *and* he made the *Blank Generation* film about the New York punk scene in 1975–76. How long ago that all seems now! Five years... Isn't it strange how prophetic that song became? Five years between glam and punk, five years from then till now... But can you even begin to compare what was happening in New York and London in 1975 with what's happening today? I saw *Blank Generation* at the Essential[176] a while back, and it was really entertaining, a real trip down memory lane. But it was really sad as well, in a way. There's Television, Patti, Blondie, The Ramones, Talking Heads, The Heartbreakers, Wayne...and, of them all, Wayne's the only one who's stayed the course without losing everything that made him special to begin with. Well, almost everything – I think he's officially Jayne now.

Of all the others, though, it's a full-scale wipeout. Television and The Heartbreakers have split. (What did you think of Tom Verlaine's solo album? A couple of decent songs but, once past 'Yonki Time', nothing that even begins to recapture *Marquee Moon*), Patti's retired, The Ramones are a cliché and Talking Heads have been completely eaten by Eno. I'm sorry – I know he's a friend of yours – but that last album sounded like a bunch of Chemistry students seeing who could stick the most test tubes up their arse without breaking one.

Do you think anybody is going to come out of the last few years and make a lasting career for themselves? Even in the early days of glam, you could look around and know there were some

---

175 Kral was lead guitarist and sometimes co-writer for all four Patti Smith Group LPs.
176 A specialist cinema in Wardour Street, London.

genuine superstars coming through, people who would be in it for the long haul, rather than getting buried by the machine – yourself, Elton, Marc (to an extent). David Essex surprised me, I must admit, but he seems to have some staying power as well.

This time around, Rotten may remain, by virtue of personality and reputation alone, and I like to think The Banshees will survive in some form, if only because they managed to kick punk out of their system pretty quickly, and are now into this really fucked-up Voodoo Dolly/Edgar Allan Poe kick, Hammer Horror films with a Gavin Bryars soundtrack. We're probably stuck with The Jam as well, although they've become so mainstream that it's not even fun to take the piss out of them any more. Plus, Paul Weller is rapidly turning into the new Roger Waters – the bigger he gets, the more he complains. Grumpy bastards are fine in their place, but only when they have something to be grumpy *about*. If you're selling a million every time you open your mouth, life's probably feeling pretty good, don't you think? Hey, Roger, don't hide behind a wall – jump off the top of it.

One person who is worth watching is TV Smith, the old singer with The Adverts. I think of him as part of that succession of very English songwriters that includes people like Peter Hammill, Kevin Ayers, Bryan Ferry and yourself (of course), and some of his stuff with The Adverts came closer to touching the soul of punk than anyone outside the Pistols. Listen to 'The Great British Mistake' or 'Cast Of Thousands' – very lyrical, very visual and pretty disturbing as well. His new band, The Explorers, have just played their first few gigs and, so far, so excellent. (Plus, they have the bassist from The Doctors Of Madness, and you remember how much I used to love them.)

Have you heard The Psychedelic Furs' album yet? I heard you'd been to see them – brilliant, aren't they? The album was a bit of a disappointment at first, simply because it didn't have the same dark, visceral drone to it that the live show does. But give it a few spins and it's even stronger: the songs stand out, and you have to love a band who can take an in-concert freak-out ('Blacks'/'Radio') and pull it off in the studio. It's not often that that works. The B-side of the single, '****', is amazing as well – it makes 'Sense Of Doubt' sound toe-tapping and I can't wait for it to start turning up on jukeboxes. Now all they need to do is reinstate the Hoover.

What do you think of The Cuddly Toys? I assume you've heard their version of 'Madman'[177] by now. I saw them a few times back when they were still called Raped, and always had a good time. They were total trashy glam with a punky edge back then – seems they've not changed an ounce. The single's pretty good, isn't it? I've got a rather bad cassette copy of the demo you recorded with Marc, although I'll be honest and say I've never been 100 per cent convinced that it really was genuine.

The songwriting credits on the single seem to make it official, but there's a lot of stuff floating around that claims to be the two of you together – tracks like 'Exalted Companions', 'Casual Bop' and 'Skunk City'. The quality's so poor, though, and the songs are so unfinished – who knows? I've got a couple of things that are meant to be you and John Cale as well, but a plinking piano and a yowling vocal could be anyone.[178] Recording equipment has become so easily accessible that anyone with half an idea and a sense of sick humour could be creating these things. Have you heard that tape going round of Syd Barrett's last recording session, from Abbey Road in 1975? If it's really him, it's at least interesting from a historical point of view. But all you get are a few instrumental guitar sequences and, really, it could be anyone.

Anyway, I'd better get off. Work has been really hectic lately with all the cheap airfares coming in. God bless Freddie Laker! I'll write again when I've heard *Scary Monsters*.

Gary

PS If Major Tom *is* a junkie, where does he get the stuff from? It's hardly standard NASA rations, is it? Maybe there is life on Mars after all!

177 A Bowie/Bolan demo dating from September 1977, recorded when the pair met up prior to Bowie appearing on the Marc Bolan TV show. The Cuddly Toys' cover version was released in 1980.
178 Cale confirmed in 1985 that 'Velvet Couch' and 'piano-la' were indeed unused collaborations with Bowie.

```
Picture Postcard - A Souvenir Of London
Tuesday 19 August 1980
```

David!

You're No.1! Here's hoping you stay there for ever![179]

Congratulations!

Gary

Edmonton, London N18
Friday 19 September 1980

Dear David

Well, you said you wanted to make an album of commercial music and you've done that alright. I've had *Scary Monsters* for a week now, and even when I'm not playing it the songs are stuck in my head: get one out and another one marches straight in to replace it. It's not complete songs, either; just odd lyrics and phrases. Right now it's 'Up The Hill Backwards' – 'I'm OK, you're so-so'. I love that line.

Is there anything on the album that wouldn't make a killer single? Especially on side one. 'Scream Like A Baby' and 'Because You're Young' let side two down a little, not because they're bad songs but because they're not as earth-shattering as everything around them. And I can't believe you found another decent song on the Tom Verlaine album. I went back and replayed the LP and you're right – I'm not sure how I missed 'Kingdom Come' first time around.

'It's No Game' (either part) is a masterpiece – your next 12" single should bang the two together into one massive opus; 'Fashion' is bound to be your next No.1 ('beep beep'!) and 'Teenage Wildlife' reminds me of 'Heroes', with added histrionics. Your best album since... when? Definitely since *Low*, and maybe since *Diamond Dogs*. Neat sleeve as well – very distinctive. I bet Edward Bell's phone is ringing off the hook right now![180]

I have this theory that very few bands are capable of making more than four truly killer, all-time classic albums in their career, but you might have just become the exception to prove the rule: *Hunky Dory*, *Ziggy Stardust*, *Aladdin Sane* and *Diamond Dogs* were already up there; *Scary Monsters* is moving up fast. But try to think of anyone else who's done it. Even The Beatles and the Stones released as many comparative clinkers as unadulterated

---

180 The artist responsible for the *Scary Monsters* cover would subsequently design similar sleeves for Hazel O'Connor, TV Smith's Explorers and Rikki Sylvan, among others.

masterpieces, while nobody from the 1970s came close to their overall standards. Even Roxy only did a couple that were nonstop amazing from start to finish. So, congratulations – it's not the most widely recognised accolade you've ever snatched, but it is one of the most important!

Aside from the album, the other big talking point over here has been the excerpts from Angie's book in the *Sun*.[181] I was pleasantly surprised by what I read; the teasers set it up as some kind of monstrous kiss and tell that would leave you looking like some kind of sex-depraved vampire monster, whereas she seemed more interested in simply telling the story, and maybe spreading the credit around a bit more than most people normally do. In fact, my biggest complaint was that she's occasionally vague on the facts – such as, what was the song Cherry wrote on a theme of 'Space Oddity', and which band performed it?

I really liked the bit where she's talking about all the kids who used to write to you with their sex questions, though. 'Suddenly I found myself playing "Dear Marge".' That must have been really strange, although I suppose you set yourself up for it in a way. Let's face it, for a lot of kids growing up in the early 1970s sex was the half-naked tribesmen with giraffe necks in *National Geographic*, and dog-eared copies of *H&E*, beach balls strategically placed in every picture. You weren't simply the only bisexual they were even aware of, you were probably the first one they'd ever *heard* of, and certainly the only one who seemed at all approachable. It's not the sort of subject you can broach with your parents, is it? And the other kids at school would probably kick your head in if they knew you were wondering which way you swung.

At the same time, I do wonder what possible response you could make to that sort of letter. 'Dear David and Angie, I keep having funny dreams about my best friend's willy. Does this mean I'm a homo?' 'Stop dreaming and just do it – that's the only way to find out for sure.' And then the kid'll

181 Ex-wife Angie Bowie's *Free Spirit* memoir was serialised in the newspaper beginning 12 September, fortuitously coinciding with the release of *Scary Monsters*. The book itself was published the following month.

show the letter to his mum, and you'll be on the front page the next day – 'David Bowie Bent My Baby'.

However you responded, you certainly made a difference – to individuals, of course, but to people's attitudes in general. One of the most amazing sights I've ever seen was at a Tom Robinson gig at the Marquee a few years ago. It was a Saturday night, a bunch of football supporters were in, and everyone was watching them very warily, convinced they were simply there to crack a few queer skulls. Instead, the band went into 'Glad To Be Gay' and this army of thugs was singing along as loudly as everyone else. Which goes to show (as the old cliché goes) that you can't judge a book by its cover. Even if it does look illiterate.

Now, of course, being (or appearing to be) gay is virtually an essential fashion accessory, and even the tabloids have accepted it as a fact of life – at least among the more flamboyant elements of society. The new romantic movement is all but queer by association, regardless of the individual bands' affiliations, and there are a few people on the fringe – the singers with Dead Or Alive and Culture Club, for instance – who seem as open about it as you used to. Whether or not they go all the way, as they say, is a matter for them and their publicist to sort out, but right now such associations are doing them no harm at all.

It'll be interesting, of course, to see what would happen if someone in a more traditionally 'manly' profession came out and admitted they were gay, like a rugby player or a weatherman. Or the singer with a heavy-metal band that isn't Queen. Pop music and theatre can get away with it because they already have a certain glamour attached to them. I'm not sure, however, whether Morally Outraged of Chipping Sodomy would be happy watching the ten o'clock news if he suspected that the newscaster was wearing suspenders under his suit. Unless, of course, it was Selena Scott.

Anyway, I'd love to know what you thought of *Free Spirit*, forgetting it was written by your ex-wife, forgetting all the stuff about affairs and the divorce, and reading it simply as a chronicle of the Mainman years? I really think she captured the magic of that whole period, at least as we, the fans, understood it. There's a bit in *Diary Of A Rock And Roll Star* where Ian Hunter talks about your lighting crew wanting to work with Mott, on what should have been a night off, because it helped make Mainman seem more like a family – and Angie confirms that impression. No matter how badly things ended (who ripped off who or whatever), for the two or three years when Mainman was at its peak it really was a united front, everybody working for one another, looking out for each other and making (or planning to make) some of the greatest music of the 1970s. I do wonder if you ever miss that sense of community, and of being at the centre of such a brightly coloured and wildly creative maelstrom?

I wish someone would write a book that focuses purely on that period and just on the people who were at the centre of it – yourself, Wayne, Cherry, Dana, Angie, Ronno, Scott Richardson, Simon Turner, Ava Cherry, Mott, Lou and Iggy. All the little side-projects that were going on, the guest appearances and, above all, the actual mechanics that went into creating the illusion of Mainman as this towering edifice overflowing with superstars. Forget the business stuff, the money and all that. Give us the Hollywood flash.

Enough about the past; what of the future? Any plans for *The Elephant Man* to come over to London yet? You're going to be opening on Broadway in a few days. Good luck! Are you nervous? I liked that bit in the *NME* interview[182] where the journalist pointed out that you're playing to an intimate audience for the first time since the Ziggy days. That has to be strange – I'd not even thought of it like that, although when I remember the theatre where I saw the play it's tiny. I imagine you're used to places like that now, after the runs in Denver and Chicago... Probably, the real problem is going to be adjusting back to the aircraft hangars next time you tour on your own!

Well, that's all for now, so congratulations on a magnificent album, good luck on Broadway and have you decided what the

182 With Angus Mackinnon, 13 September 1980.

next single will be? (Subliminal whisper – 'Fashion', 'Fashion', 'Fashion', 'Fashion', 'Fashion', 'Fashion', 'Fashion'.)

All the best (BEEP BEEP!)

Gary

Edmonton, London N18
Friday 19 December 1980

Dear David

I wanted to write and wish you a happy Christmas – or, at least as happy as it's possible to have, after what happened to John Lennon.[183] Remembering your own fears about a major rock star being assassinated by a lone loony fan, it must have been like having all your worst nightmares come true.

Please look after yourself – and maybe, when *The Elephant Man* is over, come home?

All the best

Gary

---

183 The ex-Beatle and co-writer of Bowie's 'Fame' single was murdered outside his New York hotel on 8 December.

Edmonton, London N18
Wednesday 22 July 1981

Dear David

Is it really seven months since I last wrote to you? And, it dawned on me a few days ago, nine years since I first wrote to you! Every year seems to race past faster and faster – maybe Pink Floyd did know what they were on about in 'Time'. Scary thought...but not as scary as realising that suddenly I'm 21, assistant manager of the same travel agency I've been with since I left school... Bloody hell, I'm more or less a grown-up! And Zowie's what, ten years old now? Where does the time go?

You'll see from the address that I've moved house at last. Four years in the same single-room bedsit finally grew too much for me when I realised the rent had almost doubled in that time. It was £8 when I moved in, with a few small increases that I didn't really think about. But when I received the letter telling me it was about to go up to £15, that was enough. So now I have the entire upstairs half of a house right by Silver Street Station – still in Edmonton but a lot closer to the night bus.

It was really bizarre going from one room to five. Looking around, I cannot imagine how I crammed all this stuff into that tiny little space. Plus, I have half a garden now. The couple downstairs seem nice enough. They both work at the hospital down the road and keep fairly strange hours, so I never see them. He's a doctor and she works in the pharmacy, so if I'm ever feeling dicky I can probably run downstairs and get seen to there! The only downside is, with the train station so close, the house tends to rattle a bit when the trains go through. But apparently you get used to that sort of thing.

Had a wild flat-warming party, which ended up with me drinking way too much and, from all accounts, spending most of the evening trying to get off with Pete's sister, Sylvia. From what Pete told me a few days later, she finally agreed to go out with me simply to shut me up, convinced that I'd have forgotten about it the next morning. But I fooled her cos I didn't, so she was stuck coming with me to see The Birthday Party (noisy Australians – an acquired taste, if you're lucky) at the Moonlight Club, and since then we've been more or less inseparable.

She works in the personnel office at a big factory up the road in Tottenham, so she's in the same kind of boat as I am – having to dress dead smart and respectable for work, then running home to find something utterly inappropriate to go out in. We've been to bucketloads of gigs, although it's the same handful of bands virtually all the time. TV Smith's Explorers are playing around London all the time now. They just headlined and (I think) sold out the Venue, which was one of the best shows I've seen all year... Coincidentally, their latest album sleeve was designed by Edward Bell.

Caught Richard Strange a few times as well. He was the singer with the Doctors, but he's solo now, doing a one-man show called *The Phenomenal Rise Of Richard Strange*, which you'd enjoy – it's the story of a rock star (also named Richard Strange) who is made the head of a dictatorship, because they (the architects of the revolution) think he'll be a silent figurehead. It turns out he has ideas of his own, though, and starts ushering through all sorts of reforms and changes, so they bump him off. He (the real Strange, not the fictional one) runs a club on Wardour Street called the Cabaret Futura. It's worth popping in next time you're in London – Strange doesn't play every week, but he does consistently book interesting people.

I assume you've been keeping tabs on the new romantic scene? I'm not its biggest fan – that night at Billy's scarred me irreparably. Soft Cell look they might turn into something worth watching. The singer has a certain sleazy charm to him, and their version of 'Tainted Love' has a grimy and only half-heartedly hidden dirty-sex subtext that reminds me a bit of that band Metro from a few years ago. 'I'm sorry, I don't pray that way' – what sort of an insinuation is that?

A couple of Duran's singles have been OK, and I liked the first few Spandau Ballet, when they were doing the mutant-funk thing. Or Culture Club while they were a white transvestite reggae group. But that's about it. I never got into Adam Ant at all, and too many of the other bands seem to be simply flogging off some decidedly dodgy wares from behind a momentarily saleable mask of make-up and fancy dress. Which sounds awfully familiar...the difference being, at least last time around there were some classy songwriters hiding behind the clothes horses. Even Chinn and Chapman had some future classics in their bag of tricks. This time around, everything seems so shallow, although maybe I'd feel different if I was still 12 or 13. Or maybe not.

Who do I like, then? The Cure, of course. *17 Seconds* was one of the best albums of last year, but *Faith* is even better – imagine you're sitting in a burned-out cathedral while a thousand years of past ritual and history echo off the walls. I saw Soul Boy the other day for the first time in a couple of years (he got married a while back, and the missus spirited him off into a world of domesticity and DIY), and he was complaining that it's simply depressing for depression's sake, and that might be true. But it's also a beautiful record – sort of a Mozart's *Requiem* for rock 'n' roll.

I'm also really getting into the whole goth thing that is swirling around, not so much that I'd start dressing in black and smoking clove cigarettes, but I am paying attention to the music at least. It's interesting, in that it's the first movement in rock to blend popular movies, literature and culture with the music, rather than shooting off on arty tangents... *The Pan Book Of Horror* series, Hammer films, glam rock, *Doctor Who* – they're all in there somewhere. OK, Bauhaus can be a touch pretentious, but deep down there's still more *Carry On Cabbie* than *Cabinet of Dr Caligari* about them. You may have heard their version of 'Telegram Sam' a while back? Or 'Bela Lugosi's Dead', which was the most amazingly creepy record, about ten minutes' worth of clicks and creaks. You could imagine it as the soundtrack to pretty much every Dracula film ever made. The first few times I saw them, a couple of years ago, they were playing places like the Nash, the Rock Garden, Billy's and the Moonlight. The last time I caught them, they were headlining the Lyceum.

My long-forgotten dalliance with The Bay City Rollers has come back to haunt me, as well. Sylvia was a rabid fan in the day, and was telling me about this new band Ian Mitchell (the youngblood they brought in after one of the Longmuirs was pensioned off) has teamed up with (of all people) John Towe, the old drummer with The Adverts and Generation X. So we toddled down to the Bridgehouse in Canning Town and, believe it nor not, it was a great show! Really tight power-pop, with a bunch of Rollers songs glam-punked up for variety. They played an amazing version of 'Shang-A-Lang' as an encore, as well, with Mitchell all tarted up in a schoolgirl outfit. Been to see them a few times since, they're so much fun! Oh, and this'll make you laugh, Syl has a whole pile of old Rollers and associated records. And around the same time as the band was recording the most god-awful version of 'Rebel Rebel', Ian Mitchell's new band, Rosetta Stone, was down on Haddon Street, posing for a pic sleeve[184] by the old K West sign!

What are you up to now that *The Elephant Man*'s finished?[185] I heard a tape of you being interviewed on some New York radio station,[186] talking about your video projects and, of course, I've been picking up all the new records that seem to be flying around these days, even though I probably have a thousand versions of each one already. 'Oh goody – the umpteenth reissue of the old Pye stuff.' 'Excellent – I needed another copy of the "London Boys".'

I did like the K-Tel album,[187] though, if only because that weird alternate version of 'John I'm Only Dancing' turned up on it – someone said it was also on early pressings of

184 The Japanese 'Sunshine Of Your Love' single.
185 Bowie left the production on January 3.
186 *David Bowie Plus Five* in February 1981.
187 1980's *The Best Of Bowie*.

Changesonebowie,[188] but I missed that. But whose idea was it to release *four* singles off *Scary Monsters*?[189] I know I said that every track *could* be a monster hit, but I didn't think you'd take me at my word. I'm assuming 'Up The Hill Backwards' will be the last one? And it was typical that 'Crystal Japan' would turn up on the B-side, a couple of weeks after I put out £5 for the Japanese import.[190]

Oh, and of course there's the BBC play.[191] That should be really interesting – and it follows on so nicely from 'Alabama Song'. (I assume now that you're not going to be doing the *Threepenny Opera* movie that was mentioned a while back?) Are you going to be doing the soundtrack in the same style as the single? That's what it needs. The play is marvellous; I read it a few years ago (we all go through a Brecht phase, it's a vital part of growing up), and Baal himself is virtually a prototype rock star…the *first* rock star! It'd be intriguing to see you portray him that way – a disreputable cross between Brecht's original vision and Turner in *Performance*, foul and fey in equal doses. Then, with 'Alabama Song' as the template for the music, you'd capture it perfectly – apocalyptic Teutonic folk rock. Adam and his Ants, top that!

All the best

Gary

188 It was removed following the first pressing, to be replaced by the original 1972 single version.
189 'Ashes To Ashes' was followed by 'Fashion', 'Scary Monsters' and 'Up The Hill Backwards'.
190 An instrumental recorded for a Japanese TV commercial in early 1980, and released as a Japan-only single that March.
191 The BBC's new schedule included plans for Bowie to take the title role in an adaptation of Brecht's *Baal*.

Edmonton, London N18
Wednesday 3 March 1982

Dear David

Baal was on the box last night, and the good news is that I loved it. The bad news is, I'm the only person I know who did. Syl fell asleep, and everyone else I know switched it off halfway through. Philistines!

The EP[192] put a lot of people's backs up, I think. So stark, so bare-bones, it made 'Alabama Song' sound like 'Suffragette City'! And someone was obviously listening when I told you Baal himself should be based on Jagger in *Performance*! There was one priceless echo, when Baal is asked what his relationship is to music, and he admits he doesn't really care for it. Couldn't you just see Ol' Rubber Lips standing there in his dressing gown sniffing, 'I don't like music.' Comical little geezer, indeed.

Baal, on the other hand, isn't comical at all – or rather, he is, but in such a dark way that the humour of his situations and reactions is so subtle as to be invisible. People sat there expecting some sort of Ziggy meets *Cabaret* sex show, with a proto-rock 'n' roll dementoid swaggering around singing dirty songs. Instead, they received this very bare and absurdly exaggerated drama, half-narrated by a wretch, I swear, who looked like a red-haired version of Lonely from the old *Callan* shows. I don't think I've ever seen you embrace a character so fully, at least in a film (I can't speak for *The Elephant Man*, of course). Watching it, I could only imagine what you must have been like during rehearsals. I can picture you lying under an easy chair, refusing to speak with anybody else and, if they did dare disturb you, simply snapping, 'Fuck off, I'm playing Baal.'

The *Radio Times* interview was interesting, by the way. Have you really spent all your time painting (and presumably acting), instead of writing songs? I suppose from the point of view of recharging your batteries that's not a bad idea. I was thinking the

192 A five-song soundtrack EP was released the week before the broadcast.

other night, you were extremely prolific during the 1970s, almost alarmingly so. An album a year was the norm, two albums a year was not unusual. You did it in 1973 and again in 1974, while 1977 as good as brought four, if you count the Iggy albums. Plus there were the one-off singles, the odd collaborations… At a time when we really were getting used to other 'superstars' settling into the comfy routine of a new album every millennium or so, you were charging ahead all the time. That's why people are beginning to worry about your recent silence – by other artists' standards, your lack of albums for the last couple of years would be business as usual. By your standards, the silence is deafening!

I'm wondering how much of this can be traced back to John Lennon's murder? Looking back, that really does seem to have been the watershed – you were out of *The Elephant Man* within a month, and have you even been back to the US since then? And now that you're living in Switzerland, you've probably cut yourself off as far from the rock 'mainstream' as it's possible to go. Even people you want to see have to tunnel in under the Alps to get to you and, when you want them to leave, you can set all the cuckoo clocks chiming and break out the triangular chocolate.

It's kind of funny, though, that no sooner do you settle there than you run into Queen and end up scoring your biggest hit yet (or, at least, your longest-running No.1)! I'm still completely in love with 'Under Pressure'. Every time I listen to it, I seem to hear something else I'd not noticed before. You probably remember how much I hated Queen when they first came out, although I did warm to side two of *Queen II*. Remove the guitar solo songs and the next few albums weren't bad, either… In fact, I still dig out *Sheer Heart Attack* when I have the house to myself. There's something about the album that screams 'Remember 1974!' at me – because so many of the other kids at school had it, it was completely inescapable for a while. But I completely lost touch with them after that. Once past the hits that batter their way into your brain whatever you do, I don't think I paid any attention for five years. And then 'Under Pressure' came along, and I've been playing catch-up furiously!

What impresses the most is, it really is a joint effort. I love the way you and Freddie bring out all the best vocal tricks you've developed over the years – the Mockney operatics you introduced for 'Heroes', the paralysing, soaring shrieks that Freddie honed on 'Bohemian Rhapsody'. But it works! And, with the band locked into that loose funky overload, it's no surprise at all it was such a huge record.

'Cat People' is excellent as well, and I can't wait for it to come out – the record *and* the film. I've loved Malcolm McDowell since *If...* (of course – which boarding school boy's fantasies weren't set on fire by that?), Nastassja Kinski is sensational, and I've always had a soft spot for the original film. The record sounds exactly the way the movie should look, and your vocals rank among your most honestly impassioned ever, up there with 'Heroes' (and, yes, 'Under Pressure'). Giorgio Moroder's own sound is all over it as well, of course – another winning combination! You don't half pick them...

It's about time you finally got around to recording with Moroder, because it feels like the two of you have been circling one another's territory for years now – you with *Low* and *The Idiot*, him with 'I Feel Love' and the Sparks albums... Did you hear *Number One In Heaven*? Sparks are probably the only people on earth who can rival you for regularly changing direction for no reason whatsoever and, if a few of their swerves aren't necessarily successful, at least they're never boring. The only albums of theirs that I haven't enjoyed were the *Big Beat* and *Introducing* albums, which came along at the end of their hit-single phase, although it's interesting that they almost made *Big Beat* with Ronno!

I can't remember where I read that, but apparently they rehearsed it together in someone's garage, and it was only because Ronno was already committed to do the Dylan tour that it didn't happen. I wonder which would have worked out better for him. It's odd to read about him popping up in different musical circles, running off a few guitar lines and then disappearing again. He should be firmly entrenched as the superstar sideman of the age, but all he wants to do is drift. Some of his stuff with Hunter has been so amazing (the *Schizophrenic* album and tour were unbeatable), but even that partnership never seems able to make up its mind where it wants to go next. It's such a waste. I just hope that he's happy.

Anyway, what's next for you? I know you're doing *The Hunger* with Catherine Deneuve – I hear Bauhaus are going to be in it as well. I told you they were worth it, didn't I? I also read somewhere that you might be playing Blackbushe this summer. Don't! That girl Mandy dragged me to see Dylan there a few years back, and I can honestly say that if there's one place worse for seeing gigs than an aircraft hangar, it's an aerodrome. From where I was (third stinking puddle from the left), it was a dreadful show. Stick with the arenas – at least they have roofs.

Anyway, I'm off (I bet you wondered why this letter smelled, didn't you, ha ha). Have fun with *The Hunger*. I'm sure you will!

All the best

Gary

Aerogramme - Paris, France
Saturday 14 August 1982

Bonjour Monsieur David

Syl and I decided to take a romantic weekend in Paris – which hasn't turned out to be too romantic, as we had a blazing row the moment we got here, about whether we should go shopping or see the sights. We finally agreed to differ, so she went off to do one, I went off to do the other and, voilà, here I am in a petit sidewalk café (sorry, Frog was never one of my strongest points), having spent the entire afternoon in the most amazing little record shop off Montmartre. I steered clear of British and American artists (as I can find their records anywhere) but, of course, I checked the David Bowie section and what do you think I found? Only an Italian 'Space Oddity' single! In Italian! It didn't have its piccy sleeve, but who cares?

Got a whole bunch of Jacques Brel records as well, mainly EPs from the early 1960s, and a few others that looked good – Françoise Hardy, Serge Gainsbourg, Johnny Hallyday, all the people we've heard of but never hear at home. They'll probably all be bog-awful (French rock 'n' roll – a contradiction in terms), but they'll make interesting conversation pieces. Probably.

I visited the New Rose shop as well. I've heard so much about the place over the years, but ended up not buying anything – you can find exactly the same records at Rough Trade in London, and they're cheaper. So tomorrow I'll do the sights. I am curious about the Eiffel Tower and Notre-Dame, and I had a quick wander around Montmartre this afternoon. Went past the Pigalle as well – transvestite heaven, even in mid-afternoon. I've never had so many offers from so many creatures of indeterminate sex in my life. Thank goodness I couldn't comprend a *mot* they *dit*; I'd probably have died of shame.

This place is really fun, though. It's one of those long, dingy little places with a jukebox at the far end, and there's a bunch of hip young student types clustered around one table, singing along with it... And you wouldn't believe what 'I Eat Cannibals' sounds like in heavily French-accented English! Presumably, a lot like these Brel records will, should I ever try singing along with them. There is a reason different countries have different languages. It's to stop people singing things they do not understand.

Must go – 'Come On Eileen' has come on for the third time, and I really don't think I can stand it again. I'll write again when I get home.

Au revoir

Gary

Edmonton, London N18
Wednesday 15 December 1982

Dear David

Season's greetings – and a quick chorus of 'Little Drummer Boy', perhaps?

So, it looks like all those rumours about you leaving RCA are true. It's going to be strange buying a new David Bowie record and not seeing that familiar label spinning around... You know, when I first started my scrapbook, I spent days trying to soak the label off one of your records so I could stick it in there. I ended up faking it with tracing paper and an orange felt-tip pen, with one of those lovely green and white sleeves around it. Today, I'd take a pair of scissors and cut it out of the vinyl. The last couple of months, every time I turn around you have something else in the stores – and it's all either old or horrible.

I passed on the picture-disc package,[193] I'm afraid, simply because I hate picture discs – you can't play them and this lot are quite spectacularly ugly. And, though I did buy it, I'm refusing to play the Bing single,[194] not because I doubt the sincerity of your performance, nor because I find the whole affair of load of old humbug. I don't think a five-year-old skeleton from anybody's closet is an especially appropriate way of celebrating the season.

Bowie Rare[195] turned out to be a disappointment as well. I've often sat around making cassettes in readiness for the day when somebody tied me to the train tracks and said, 'Compile a decent Bowie rarities album or else,' and *Bowie Rare* bears only the mildest resemblance to even my blandest creation. As far as I can see, it's three different albums compressed into one – one of B-sides and non-LP singles, one of unreleased tracks and other odds and sods, and one of collaborations, all of which we do need to have. The trouble is, with only 11 tracks, it ends up

193 A set of ten past 45s were repressed as the limited edition (25,000) *Fashions* picture-disc collection.
194 Bowie's appearance on the 1977 *Bing Crosby Christmas Special* finally made it out on 45.
195 Officially released only in Italy, this B-sides/rarities collection was heavily imported into the UK.

falling flat on its face in every direction. Where are the Mercury 45s? Where's 'All The Young Dudes'? Where's the sense in any of it? Ho hum.

I must admit that I'm surprised to have all this activity now. Assuming you really are leaving/have left RCA, you'd think they'd wait until we know what your plans are for next year before digging into the vault. There are rumours flying everywhere that you're recording with the guys from Chic. Hmmm, *More Young Americans*? And I know you're setting up a world tour for next year, because… Well, let's just say that when a sparrow flaps its wings, a travel agent plans its route.

You know, in all the years I've been doing this (six… oh my God, that's longer than I was at boarding school!), it never dawned on me that when people like you want to go on tour it's people like me who help make it happen. Then, back in the summer, I received a call from the manager of a local left-over New Wave Of British Heavy Metal bands – Conqueror Worm or some such – saying they were putting together a short European tour and could I help make sense of their itinerary?

So I took down the details. It was one of those typical 'If it's Tuesday, it must be a hellhole in Belgium' excursions that makes absolutely no sense to anyone, then I called around a few of the West End companies where I know people, to see if anyone could give me pointers. To cut a very long and not especially interesting story short, I ended up on the phone with this guy who books tours for a living, who talked me though the whole thing and worked out the entire route for me. It was rather funny, because we were talking about general things as well, and he revealed that his hobbies include crossword puzzles and solving complicated mathematics problems. It seems booking tours allows him to combine both pastimes *and* get paid for it.

He's been doing this for years, and has some incredible stories, which were really funny…but would probably make you cover your ears and start screaming, 'Don't remind me!'

Imagine trying to negotiate a British tour by train, immediately after the Beeching cuts, when nobody was sure which lines were still open and which had been closed! Or the time another group walked into his shop with a road map, trying to figure out how they were meant to get around when, as far as they could see, all the roads ran north–south, and all their shows were in the east or west. Hell, and I think I have problems with idiots who think a week in Florida will be a suitably central base for them to visit the Statue of Liberty, Mount Rushmore, Hollywood and the Grand Canyon.

Anyway we've kept in touch, and last week he was telling me how a friend of a friend is currently involved with your people, putting together what sounds like an absolutely enormous (six months long?) world tour. Which would suggest that the album rumours are correct? Will the movies still be coming out while you're on the road? I was surprised to hear about *Merry Christmas Mr Lawrence*. You've never struck me as being into war films. Repeat after me – 'Eat lead, sushi sucker.' Ah, a childhood buried in *Commando* comics... Good to see *The Hunger* has a release date as well. It seems centuries since you made it. Any idea why it was held back so long?

I've heard that Bauhaus's performance, while short, was really good – and I suppose you've heard their current single, a spot-on version of 'Ziggy Stardust'? Apparently, they were so sick of having people slag them off for sounding like you that they decided to really sound like you. And now, you watch, people will slag them off because they don't.

There's a heart-stopping version of 'Third Uncle' on the B-side, by the way... I was in Paris the first time I heard it (oh, hark the little jetsetter!). It came on the radio and, of course, you cannot understand a word their DJs say, so I was listening to this, knowing it wasn't the Eno original but baffled as to who could possibly be doing it so well. It drove me nuts!

And on that note I'll wish you a very happy Christmas, a wonderful New Year, and I think I'll sing you a rousing chorus of 'Little Drummer Boy' after all. I mean, if I can't escape from it, why should you?

All the best

Gary

Edmonton, London N18
Monday 18 April 1983

Dear David

To paraphrase what Tony Visconti said about 'Space Oddity', I don't particularly like it. But it's going to be enormous.

I suppose congratulations *are* in order for the birth of your latest bouncing baby LP and, maybe, I should even feel flattered – a cover of one of my favourite ever records, and a new version of one of your best recent songs. But...I'm trying to look at *Let's Dance* from your point of view, and accept that this time you had to get away from the dramatic experimentation, masks and make-up, if only because that's what everyone was expecting. You know from experience that your core audience will stick with you through weird and weirder, but it's been three years since *Scary Monsters*, and that's a long time. A whole new generation has grown up, to whom 'David Bowie' is simply some old geezer that Gary Numan used to like, who used to dress up funny and be a different character every time. *And where's Gary Numan today?* Hanging out with Zaine Griff, probably, and wondering where it all went pear-shaped.

The fact that little of what that entire new romantic movement accomplished did anything more than embellish your own original creations does not lessen that fact. Besides, if we want to get really deep and meaningful, the 1980s are probably more alien to you than you ever could be to us. I know that one of punk's big political aims was to dispose of the dreadful Labour government that was grinding the country into the dirt through the 1970s, but whoever imagined we'd end up with Thatcher? Or maybe it was inevitable – what alternative was there? That's the one consequence that nobody seemed to think through. Overthrow one lot and you have to have the others.

You've got to admire Thatcher's style, though. In 1978, 'youth' was complaining that there were no jobs, no money, no future... She walks in and suggests a return to National Service. Suddenly, the dole doesn't seem so bad after all. People complained that the country had lost its stomach, so she went out and beat up the Argies. The woman has an answer for everything, even if she doesn't always get the question right, and the fact that she antagonises so many people only proves how good she is at her job. No matter how evil we think she is at home, imagine how the rest of the world feels. They won't be fucking with us for a long time to come.

Did I ever tell you there was a kid at school who fancied Margaret Thatcher, back when she was Minister of Education and the most evil thing she'd done was take away the kiddiwinks' free milk? He always leched after older women anyway – he thought Esther Rantzen was the sexiest beast on six legs. But Thatcher really got him going... So, I ran into him at the Gary Glitter show at the Lyceum last month, and couldn't help reminding him of his childhood fantasies. It turns out that he's a member of the Young Conservatives and has a signed picture of her.

Oh my God! From glam fan to fascist pig in under ten years. It makes some of your transformations look positively restrained, and that, I reckon, is exactly what you were aiming for. There's no way you could out-freak the sheer freak show that this decade has become, so you unfreaked everything. A nice straight album from a nice straight dude. Or maybe I've got it completely wrong, and this whole Italian restaurateur look is your most cunning image yet. After all, even aliens need someone to wait tables for them.

The other side of *Let's Dance*, of course, is also the other side of the Atlantic. There's a couple of tracks ('Ricochet', for one) that probably have nothing to do with anything. But I doubt whether you could have constructed an album that is more likely to fire off half a dozen American hits and MTV videos, if you'd changed your name to Johnny Cougar (or 'Who?' as we call him over here) and brought Chic in to polish all the rough spots away… Oh, that's right, you *did* bring Chic in to polish all the rough spots away. And a jolly good job they did, as well. Who's next – Abba?

Don't get me wrong, cos there are some great songs on there. OK, so 'Modern Love' reminds me of Mike Oldfield's 'On Horseback' (play them side by side and you'll see what I mean). But I love the sax honks, and the chorus is so idiot joyful that you'd have to be real grump to dislike it. Hell, David, you even sound like you're enjoying yourself!

I threw a 'listening party' for some friends on Saturday, but instead of playing the full LP I put on a cassette I'd made, with Iggy's 'China Girl', Metro's 'Criminal World' and the original 'Cat People' instead of the new ones. And, not only did nobody notice(!), but those were the tracks everyone picked out as their favourites – plus 'Let's Dance', of course, which you literally can't avoid right now. Good to see the 12" version on the album as well. Some of my favourite singles of the last few years have been 12" mixes but, unless you buy the buggers the moment they come out, you'll never see them again! Did I congratulate you on getting to No.1, by the way? Probably not – foregone conclusions can be so dull sometimes!

Which is probably what you're thinking right now, reading me ranting on about how I prefer the originals of all the 'covers'. Of course I do – I remember hearing how much you loathed The Sex Pistols' 'No Fun' because you loved the original so much. Same here, and it probably merits the same response. You didn't remake those records for me (and people like me). You did them for the vast majority of people who've never heard any of them, and I'm sure Iggy[196] and Duncan Browne[197] are grateful for that! I don't know how many copies the Metro record sold, but the only copies of 'Criminal World' I've ever seen, apart from mine, were in a box full of the things at a little junk shop in Shepherd's Bush a few years ago. And that's always a bad sign!

At the same time, though, I'm not certain this is how I'd like the world to discover that song. The brooding menace, the black

196 Co-author, with Bowie, of 'China Girl'.
197 Co-author, with Peter Godwin and Sean Lyons, of 'Criminal World'.

sexuality, the sinister arrangement that lifted the original 'Criminal World' so far into the realm of the psychomodo are simply swept away. Pete hit it on the head when he called you the slum landlord of rock 'n' roll, converting even the stateliest mansion into a row of dilapidated tenements: 'Squalid urban strip bar for sale, one careful owner...', 'Tear it down and build a nice big pile of bedsits...'.

Having said that, the rest of *Let's Dance* isn't exactly *Hunky Dory*, is it? I simply cannot imagine you rushing down to the rehearsal room armed with 'Shake It' and announcing, 'Hey guys, I've written a super new song!' And, as for 'Ricochet' – what the hell were you thinking? If you'd done it on *Heroes* with Eno and Fripp, it could have been one of the best tracks on the album. But did it ever cross your mind that a New York disco band and a Texas blues guitarist[198] might not be the best musicians with which to try something like that? My advice – put it out as a single, but get Godley And Creme to mess around with it first. It probably wouldn't sell a bean, but I bet it'd sound amazing.

Lyrically, you really seem to be holding back. What's the matter – you don't want to waste fine words on the plebs? The songs aren't quite catchphrases, but they're not exactly overflowing with vision, are they? 'Let's Dance' itself is the worst offender. I was watching the video and you're using some extremely powerful (and very condemnatory) imagery. But what we're seeing on the screen has absolutely nothing to do with what you're singing in the song. Even the red shoes, which are pretty much the only element that is common to both, appear within an entirely different frame of reference.

'Let's Dance' itself is a perfect dance record, a good teenage love strut ('Rebel Rebel' without a bad bone in her body). But that's all it is. Watch the video, though, and only half listen to the song, and you get completely sucked in. The pictures become the words, the medium becomes the message and – Hey presto! – you've reinvented protest rock. I can't help wondering if that's wise, though. In the past, you made videos that either

198 Stevie Ray Vaughan.

complemented the song or simply provided a moving picture to accompany it. You never let the video detract from the song. 'Let's Dance', though, is almost a case of the song not detracting from the video, which would have been a neat idea if it wasn't for the fact that there's a few hundred other bands who've made the same moves already. Duran Duran didn't need to go to Sri Lanka and ride elephants to make whichever record that was come to life, but it certainly detracted from how dull the actual song was. Now you've gone and done the same thing...which, I suppose, was the intention. Everything else about this album is a complete reversal of what we expect from you, so why shouldn't the video follow suit?

Rock 'n' roll should be a two-way street. What you get out of a record depends upon what you put into it. Half an ear? Or all of your soul? Too many videos short-circuit this process, bypassing the listener's emotions completely. Once, you'd hear a song and make pictures in your head. Now you see a lava lamp and go, 'Wow, psychedelic!' There's an upside-down cross and it's, 'Ooh, heavy metal.' There's no thought process involved whatsoever, unless you habitually think about flash cards. That's why Bananarama are considered pop trash and Bonnie Tyler is meaningful, spooky angst balladry. It could easily be the other way round, but one made the right video and the other didn't. Right now, you're in the Culturally Concerned/Socially Aware box, which isn't a bad thing. But it has nothing to do with your music, and that *is* wrong.

I know you've often said that few of your songs can really be said to be about something specific, but even your instrumentals are packed with imagery that the audience is quick to pick up on (maybe with a bit of help from a perceptive review or one of your own remarks). All 'Let's Dance' says is...'Let's dance.' I wonder what you're going to do for a 'China Girl' video – scenes from an old-time doll-making factory?

After all that, I must admit I'm really looking forward to hearing the new material live. Yes, I've already received my

Wembley tickets (only two nights – the bastards sold out the rest), and this time I'm not even going to suggest you should have done a theatre tour. It's a big album, so it needs big venues.

Are you looking forward to the tour? It's probably going to be strange for the first few shows – your first gigs in five years! How are you getting on picking the live set? Presumably you'll be wrapping the greatest hits around the new record, but I wouldn't mind betting there won't be room for too many tracks from *Low* and *Heroes*?[199] Can I just say to be careful with the older material? You can take normalcy too far. You stripped a bunch of those songs of their mystery on the last tour. Don't strip them of their dignity as well!

But there I go again, trying to tell you what to do – knowing that whatever you end up doing you'll be doing it for a reason. And we, the fans, have to trust your instincts, like we always have.

Good luck – and enjoy the shows! I know I will.

Gary

---

199 In fact there were just three – 'Heroes', 'What In The World' and 'Joe The Lion', with the latter dropped from the set after just two shows. Bowie later admitted he wished he'd drawn far more from those albums.

Edmonton, London N18
Monday 4 July 1983

Dear David

They were the best of times, they were the worst of times. I'll be honest, I had a lousy time at Wembley – and I don't think it was even your fault really. I hate that venue. Milton Keynes was better, but the best show of all had to be Hammersmith, which was – if you'll pardon my French – fucking amazing!

I still can't believe it happened. There were rumours you were going to do it, there were more rumours about who you'd be doing it with and there were even rumours about what you'd be wearing while you did it. All that was certain was, who you were doing it for.[200] Local lad makes good, indeed, and it only cost £50 a ticket. (Believe it or not, the touts were buying for almost £100. God knows what they were selling for.) And was it worth every penny? Does the Pope poop in the woods?

I never fell for the story that you were going to reform the Spiders for the night, if only because you wouldn't have had time to rehearse them. Plus, it wasn't quite the anniversary of the final Ziggy show and, just as you never get to open your presents four days before Christmas, so you don't get to resurrect Ziggy four days before he dies. But I'll admit that the very expectation and uncertainty raised the whole show so far above the standard 'Tonight we're going to a gig' feeling that, if I hadn't already picked up tickets for the Bowl gigs, I'd happily have missed the lot of them for the thrill of going to the Odeon.

Of course you can't please everyone. I heard a few people complaining afterwards that all you did was scale down the stadium show and play the basic Serious Moonlight live set. In a way, though, that's what made the gig so memorable, experiencing those songs within the most intimate setting you've played since the Marquee. I hope you recorded the show! Remember that double live album the Stones put out a few years ago,[201] with three

200 The 30 June 1983 gig was a benefit for the Brixton Neighbourhood Community Association.
201 1976's *Love You Live*.

sides from a stadium gig, but the best tracks from a little club in Canada? At the very least, yours[202] should follow suit.

Anyway, after seeing so many of the shows I will say that the biggest pity is that you didn't play the new songs live a few times before recording *Let's Dance*. All four[203] are sounding so powerful now. Plus, I really prefer Slick's playing to Stevie Ray's.[204]

Why doesn't anyone play unreleased material live these days? It's always album first, gigs later... Someone suggested it's so they can foil the bootleggers, who'll be rushing out 'new' LPs before you know where you are (it happened to Pink Floyd). But I really don't see what difference it makes. If a band's big enough to merit a bestselling bootleg, the thing's going to sell no matter how many new songs are on it. And, they're also big enough to make sure the bootleg won't make any difference to their 'official' record sales. You know from your own experiences with the *Ziggy*/*Aladdin Sane* material that a song needs to be lived in before it really takes its final form. Compare the first versions of 'Drive-In Saturday' you played in late 1972 (preserved via the wonder of bootlegs, of course) with what it ultimately became. How many hours of studio time would it have taken to render it so perfect if there had been no gigs to knock it into shape? Now compare the LP version of 'Modern Love' with the ones you're playing every night. No competition... *Let's Dance* is what it is. The live album could be incredible.

And so to Milton Keynes. Just like Wembley, I only wound up with tickets for two of the shows – the first and last. I enjoyed them but, after Hammersmith, I was probably a little bit jaded. In fact, you *could* have reformed the Spiders for the night and I'd still have been thinking about the Odeon show. Maybe Syl's right and outdoor gigs really aren't any fun.

She only came to the first one with me, then took revenge by dragging me to see Nick Heywood at the Dominion. I fought against going like a true hero, but wound up having fun anyway... Tim Renwick turned out to be playing guitar for

---

202 A live album from the 1983 tour was planned, but was ultimately superceded by an in-concert video.
203 Only 'Modern Love', 'Let's Dance', 'Cat People' and 'China Girl' made the live set from the *Let's Dance* album.
204 Vaughan was sacked shortly before the tour began, and replaced by *Young Americans*/*Station To Station* veteran Earl Slick.

him, so in between the teenies screaming out for old Haircut 100 hits I got in a couple of yells for 'Conversation Piece' and 'Cygnet Committee'.

Anyway, I'm going to try to catch you later in the tour. I'm going to be in LA in early September, so I'm aiming to grab a few extra days and get to the Anaheim Stadium show. I'll let you know.

All the best

Gary

Edmonton, London N18
Wednesday 19 October 1983

Dear David

Oh well, I never made it to LA. My trip ended up being postponed, although from the sound of it the show I really needed to be at was Toronto. Did you even know Ronno was going to be there? It must have been a complete shock when he turned up backstage, and a real thrill when he agreed to come out and play – for you and for the audience. The first time on stage together since the Marquee! OK, it'd have been better if it could have happened at Hammersmith, but no matter. The door has been opened, the chemistry is still there. Let this be the first of many more reunions! Did you really only do 'The Jean Genie' together, though? I'm surprised – if I'd been you, I'd have had him on stage the whole time. Even if he wasn't playing, the sight of him standing there would have made it the gig of the year.

Talking of 'The Jean Genie', I bought the *Ziggy Stardust* live album[205] last weekend – and where was it? Where was Jeff Beck? And what the hell did you do to the guitar solos in 'Moonage Daydream'? Was it even the same show? Where's the preamble to the farewell speech – the thankyou and whatever that might seem irrelevant to you, but that make what came next so much more dramatic? I'm not going to accuse you of butchering it, cos it's your party and it'll fry if you want it to. But really, you couldn't have done a better job chopping the balls out of the show if you'd simply dumped the soundtrack altogether and replaced it with outtakes from *Stage*.

The film itself was as good as I remembered it from last time (editorial scissors notwithstanding). But it could have been so much better, and you *have* to be aware of that, don't you? Or are fans really the only people who get precious about the minute details? In which case, maybe more artists need to listen to them.

205 Previously known as *Bowie 73*, the retitled soundtrack (and film) was last sighted at the Edinburgh Festival in 1979.

Well, that's that off my chest. Let's talk about some happier triumphs. I've finally seen *The Hunger* and *Merry Christmas Mr Lawrence,* and I have to say you make a far better actor than you do film editor. They're two such completely different films that it's impossible to say which I preferred. *The Hunger* completely wiped the floor with the book.[206] I've never found vampires particularly sexy, and even Anne Rice bores me. But *The Hunger* worked on every level it aimed at.

An observation that may or may not be completely out on a limb, though…it was very interesting that you didn't contribute to either soundtrack, but left the glory to performers who are, shall we say, more than a little indebted to you? And both have admitted it – Bauhaus, with 'Ziggy Stardust', and David Sylvian, every time you listen to 'Drive-In Saturday'.[207]

My first thought was that, after what happened with *The Man Who Fell To Earth*, you simply didn't want to be rejected in favour of The Mamas And The Papas once again. But it also struck me that, as you shot both films towards the end of your RCA contract, you held yourself back to annoy the label, then suggested a few entertaining replicas to annoy them even more. And somehow, I hope that is the reason. Anyway, I think it's safe to remark that the pupils have learned much from their teacher. 'Bela Lugosi' is timeless and I doubt whether even you could have done 'Forbidden Colors' greater justice than Sylvian. It's one of those songs, like 'Cat People' (the original, of course), that it's impossible to hear without immediately wanting to watch the film again.

The big news at this end is, I'm finally moving up in the world. Or so I've been told – I'm not so sure. Richards has been bought out by a big travel agency in the West End and, after a few weeks of hellish uncertainty, when we didn't even know if we still had jobs, the new owners finally told us that the shop will be staying open, we're all being kept on and the only internal change is, I'm being moved up to manager!

Are congratulations in order? I dunno. I'm running this branch, but now I have to answer to a towering hierarchy of

206 By Whitley Streiber.
207 Sylvian took his surname from a line in that song.

area managers. In fact, if you trace the chain of command, I end up in much the same position as I was when I first started here, except with a bucketload more responsibilities and half a dozen people below me. We had the first 'forward-planning' meeting a fortnight ago and any decision that I used to be able to make for myself now has to be cleared through head office – and that's everything from taking a customer's deposit for a world cruise to ordering a fresh stock of Red Rovers.

We can even say goodbye to the days of running round to the stationers for a new box of Biros. Absolutely everything has to be filled out on special requisition forms and mailed through to head office. It's a complete waste of time, a total waste of energy and, to give you an idea of how inconceivably labyrinthine the whole setup is, when I somewhat facetiously suggested that we hire a school leaver to handle the new paperwork, I was told that I might want to consider looking for somebody with proper secretarial training so we wouldn't waste time having to train them up.

The contradictions inherent in that conversation are so baffling that I didn't even want to set the wheels in motion. But just as I was closing up on Friday, in came a call asking me to check the wording of the Positions Vacant ad. Fast work? Well, yes and no – ask for a totally redundant new employee and you get one in a week. Ask for a new supply of one-day tube passes, and Christmas looks like arriving faster than they will. Oh, and you'll love this bit. The company's TELEX number is MINITRAV – as in Orwell's Miniluv, Minipax, Minitrue and Miniplenty. And there I was thinking that 1984 was still ten weeks away.

Do you have anything special planned for that momentous year? An official video release for the 1980 Floor Show might be nice – I finally caved in and bought a video player a few months ago, but there's so little of interest out at the moment that it was hardly worth figuring out how to operate it. Which, says Sylvia, is why she hasn't. Smart girl!

Finally, have you heard Soft Cell's 'Soul Inside' yet? An amazing record – a complete emotional meltdown, the sort of thing you (or, at least, I) want to crank up to full volume in the middle of the night, when you're reaching the very edge and you don't even know how you're still managing to breath. I don't know if you've been paying attention to the group's career, but for a Top 20 pop group they've got some remarkably depraved little notions bubbling under the surface, which they don't even try to drape with innocence or coyness.

It's total decadent glam rock, on synths and drum machines – and you should hear what Almond does to Brel. I swear, his versions of 'If You Go Away' and 'The Bulls' are among the best I've ever heard – certainly up there with SAHB's 'Next' and your 'Amsterdam'. Something I've noticed with Brel, especially since I've started listening to his original recordings, is that too many people simply narrate the translations; Almond lives the lyric, and the meanings behind it, which is the difference between a classy songwriter interpreting someone else's songs and a simple singer singing along. It doesn't matter how perfect a voice you've got, you have to understand what a song is before you can get inside it. That's why Alex Harvey could cover 'Delilah' and make it sound like he really has just slaughtered his girlfriend, while Tom Jones – whose voice, of course, is a thousand times better – sounds like he's reading the same words off a cue card. Almond, needless to say, is a great writer – 'Say Hello, Wave Goodbye' and 'Black Heart' are absolute works of art and, right now, 'Soul Inside' is the soundtrack of my life. I'd love to hear him cover one of your songs (he's already done Lou Reed and Syd Barrett) but, better still, I'd love to hear you cover one of his. Try 'Catch A Falling Star'. I think you'll get quite a kick out of the bile.

Enjoy the rest of the tour

Gary

```
Tottenham, London N15
Tuesday 29 May 1984
```

Dear David

I can't believe six months have passed since I last wrote – it's frightening. Back when I was at school, six months seemed like for ever, and more or less was. These days, it's barely enough time to get dressed and ready for work in the morning. Add the fun of moving house to the equation, and I've not had time to lick a stamp, let alone sit down and write a letter.

The move was on the cards back when I last wrote to you, in October; the difference was, this time I was buying not renting, and I'm sure you know what a nightmare that can be. It wasn't even as if anything went wrong. Everybody I complained to rolled their eyes and did the Monty Python Yorkshireman routine – 'It only took six months and the estate agent fees cost almost as much as the house? Luxury!' Add the interest rates, which seem to treble every time I open the paper, and I did have a few moments of serious doubt. But I'm in now, and I still have another week before I go back to work – at a new company! Maybe I will get those shelves put up in the kitchen, after all.

As you probably gathered from my last letter, life under new management got off to a bad start and became worse. I quit when they started computerising the whole business. Nothing against computers – like New York, they'll be great when they're finished. But right now, it takes longer for the machine to start up than it does to do whatever it was you wanted. The things are full of gremlins, the 'experts' at head office are as clueless as the rest of us, and have you ever tried lining a document up in the printer and getting it to write on anything remotely resembling the correct line?

The whole system was impossible, and head office was completely unsympathetic, probably because they don't have to work with the things. Someone read somewhere that computers are more reliable than people, and the fact that we were too stupid to figure them out just proved that fact. The moment I knew I'd got this job, I announced that, if computers were so clever, they should get one in to replace me. My old assistant is now running the shop, and she's already called up asking if we have any more jobs going!

So now I'm back in a small office. In fact, it's tiny – me, the boss and a secretary/receptionist in three rooms above a junk shop halfway up Tottenham High Road. Every Saturday morning, we have to help the old boy downstairs drag out these huge iron railings, which he puts over the windows to stop the football hooligans breaking the glass. They come right past here on their way from the Hale to White Hart Lane. But it's worth it, because I've half furnished the house from his shop, some wonderful antiquey bookcases, a 1930s radio cabinet... Right now I have my eye on a 1950s television cabinet, which I'm going to gut then install a new TV into. It's phenomenal – it has doors so you can shut off the screen and pretend it's a radio. *The Tube* will be vastly improved if we don't have to look at Jools Holland.

Meanwhile, you should see the records I've been finding in there. There are crates and crates of old 45s scattered all over the place. It's one of those troves you dream about finding your whole life, knowing that you could spend the rest of your days simply sorting through them all. I haven't turned up anything super-rare yet – no forgotten caches of John's Children 45s or Mercury 'Holy Holy's – but I've built up the glam-and-thereabouts collection that I was too broke (or too embarrassed) to have at the time, and suddenly records that I loathed a decade ago sound like the greatest things on earth. The Rubettes, the Rollers, Kenny, Buster, Slik, Rainbow Cottage, all subhuman life is there! Thunderthighs, Twiggy, Peter Noone – those three are about the nearest I've come to anything of yours, but I'm having more fun than I've had from any new music in years.

Everyone's going on about how Orwell got the whole *1984* prediction wrong (as though he ever even claimed he'd get it right), but one thing that he did hit on the head was the sheer mindlessness of the music. How many machine operatives does it take to fill the Top 40 with pap? None – it does it all by itself. The Flying Pickets' assault on 'Space Oddity' is entertaining enough, Bananarama have now proven the longest-running One-Hit Wonders in history (and they keep on getting better) and The Cure are always reliably out to lunch. But, even as I confess to completely revising my attitude to the crap we endured ten years ago, I cannot imagine the early to mid-1980s ever being subject to a nostalgia boom. The Thompson Twits' 'You Take Me Up' – yeah, there's a forgotten classic in the making. Nena's '99 Red Baboons' – that'll bring a tear to the eye, won't it? And dear Grandad, please, please, tell us about the day you bought Depeche Mode's 'People Are Stupid' on the day of release?

What do you think of the Frankie Goes To Hollywood business? I'm convinced it's the most amazing hype ever – the whole thing with the DJ publicly banning it on air, then persuading the rest of the BBC to follow suit, was too convenient and too public. Everyone knows that a radio ban increase sales. Look at Judge Dread, if you need any convincing on that score. But if a record really is a danger to public morality, surely the only moral thing to do is to pretend it doesn't exist. They never played The Anti-Nowhere League's 'So What', but I never heard of anyone actually banning it. They just ignored it and watched it go away. Same with Wayne County's 'Fuck Off'. But 'Relax' didn't simply get banned; it got banned so loudly that the fact it *wasn't* being played was worth 100 spins a day.

I can't believe that anyone was genuinely taken in by the ban, because it was obviously all a publicity stunt. But people were willing to play along with it anyway, especially once they realised 'Relax' is probably one of the best white dance/funk records of all time. And it was all done with machines. Game, set and match to Winston Smith.

Anyway, if you really need an indication of how atrocious things have got, I picked up a boxful of those old *Top Of The*

Pops albums... Yes, the very ones that I used to despise so much, and that, if I remember correctly, I dumped off at that second-hand shop near the school, in exchange for a scratched copy of *Kimono My House*. They're still vile, they're still utterly unlistenable, and it's probably a sick mutant attempt to recapture my childhood that makes me even want to give the things houseroom. But right now I'm having a ball.

Did you ever hear what they did with 'Life On Mars?' Absolutely amazing – completely rearranged, a totally over-the-top monster orchestral version that, if you forget the fact that the guy who's singing it forgot to bring his voice to the studio, makes yours look underproduced. There's also a killer version of 'The Man Who Sold The World', dementoid Lulu style, and a 'Space Oddity' that is so bizarre that you can almost forgive them for what they did to 'The Jean Genie' and 'Love Me Tender'. I'll make you a tape – it'll give you something to scare the band with while you're making the new album.

How's that going, by the way? That's one thing I love about the way you work – you don't let any advance information sneak out of the sessions. I only found out which studio you're in by accident, and I'm not sure I have the full address, so I hope this package arrives in one piece.

All the best

Gary

PS Off to see The Psychedelic Furs at Hammy Odeon tonight... Another rare oasis of sanity in the desert of modern mediocrity. Betcha they won't be playing the Hoover, though.

Tottenham, London N15
Saturday 27 October 1984

Dear David

I'm sorry, didn't I make myself clear? I sent you that tape of *Top Of The Pops* covers of your songs for a laugh, something to amuse yourself with while you worked on your latest opus. You weren't meant to employ it as the template for half your new record.

'Loving The Alien' – terrific song, even if I am still struggling to find the Major Tom links people are talking about. Surely it's more Erich Von Daniken, although I'm sure Peter Schilling[208] would probably find something to add. 'Blue Jean' – brilliant single, amazing video. Channel 4 premiered it at midnight a few weeks ago, and I was phoning people up, telling them to get up and get themselves in front of the telly to watch it. Christ, I even convinced myself that you'd put the masks back on, and we were going to get an entire album of Screaming Lord Byron songs... Eddie Cochran meets Alice Cooper... Winston Smith meets *Pin-Ups*, and five Iggy Pop songs to keep everything on the edge.

And then I played *Tonight*. No, first I bought it. Then I played it. And then I took it back to the shop and exchanged it for *The Unforgettable Fire*[209] and wondered what Eno must be thinking about the records you're making these days. I'm sure there's an Oblique Stategy[210] for it. I drew one – it says, 'Turn it upside down'.

It's not like it's even a good album that I don't happen to like, which is where *Let's Dance* resides. It's genuinely, and unquestionably, a horrible, horrible record. The production is weak, the playing is lacklustre and I don't think it even matters that covering so many old Iggy songs might at least introduce new listeners to his own records. Anybody who genuinely enjoys

208 German-born Schilling scored a minor hit in mid-1984 with his own conclusion to the 'Space Oddity'/'Ashes To Ashes' saga, 'Major Tom (Coming Home)'.
209 The latest U2 album, produced by Eno.
210 A reference to a set of cards designed by Eno, each of which contains a one- or two-sentence proverb to be applied to any decision-making process.

your versions of 'Tonight' and 'Neighbourhood Threat' is going to run a mile from the originals. That's if they're not caught and taken back to the asylum first.

I was curious to hear 'God Only Knows', if only because it's one of the songs that's been bandied around from the old Astronettes album. Sorry I spoke. You can take it off now. If that's what The Astronettes' version sounds like, no wonder you never released it. 'Heroes' meets Kermit the Frog, and we thought Bryan Ferry was the only person who could pull that off.

What happened? I keep flashing back to a remark you made a while back, when you said you hadn't written any new songs in a year. Two years later, you've still only written eight, which, taken together and sensibly whittled down ('Modern Love', 'Let's Dance', 'Blue Jean', 'Loving The Alien' and a Fripp-and-Eno-style 'Ricochet'), would make up one side of an interesting album. You've spread them over two complete LPs, and it doesn't work.

You pulled it off last time, and that's fine. Old fans were simply so thrilled to have you back that they were willing to forgive the clinkers, while new fans knew no better and thought you always sung songs like 'Without You' and 'Shake It'. This time around, though, there's no safety net. Old fans want a return to form, and new fans want *Let's Dance Again*. And you've not given them either.

Theories... You had a big hit with an album that even your biggest fans are calling a sellout, so now you're trying to rehabilitate it with a disc that makes *Let's Dance* sound like it's oozing sincerity. But why did you even bother? *Let's Dance* was big enough that you didn't need to start worrying about a new album for at least a couple of years and, even if the label did demand something new, a live album would have filled the void quite nicely.

I read the *NME* interview where you said you wanted to keep your hand in, so you cranked out a load of covers because you didn't have enough new songs to fill out an album. What a load of old tosh that was! Surely you remember the guy who cranked out almost the whole of *Aladdin Sane* while travelling around the USA? And, as for that crack about not wanting to put out original songs that would merely tread water, I've yet to see a single review that doesn't think that would've been a far better option. History will record *Tonight* as entering the chart at No.1. But that was before anyone heard it. Three weeks later, there are as many copies in Record And Tape Exchange as there are in the HMV shop. And if you don't believe me, just go and count them.

With one ill-considered album, you've managed to undo 12 years of loyalty, forbearance and forgiveness. And, knowing you as well as I think I do, I can't help wondering whether this whole debacle was deliberate, and that you consciously set out to make an album that wouldn't simply horrify your old fans but would make the new ones lose interest as well. *Low*, to the power of several thousand. Back then, after all, you were simply stripping away all the razzmatazz and taking your own work back to basics. This time, there's something deeper going on, and maybe something a little more desperate as well.

Bear with me for a moment, please. When you build your career on a certain unconventionality, whether it's illustrated by image, attitude or music, you are either bound to maintain it every time out, or risk losing a lot of what you worked for in the first place. You realised that in the run-up to *Let's Dance* – you'd spent ten years pleasing yourself and had been fortunate enough to find a huge audience that enjoyed watching you do it.

Now, however, it was time to step out into an even wider, broader universe and find out if you could cut it out there as well. That's what people meant when they talked about *Let's Dance* being your breakthrough – in commercial and cultural terms, it really wasn't. In terms of proving you could hack it alongside the day's top pop darlings, however, it was a major step forward. You'd always been a very big fish in a fairly large pond. *Let's Dance* let you become a monster whale in the ocean.

Unfortunately, at the very moment when you should have been at your sharpest, looking round at the competition and figuring out how to stay one step ahead – which is what kept you going through the 1970s – you suddenly lost interest and stopped looking around at all. It's a bit like that so-called ancient Chinese proverb (which I recently read somewhere isn't as ancient or as Chinese as people think it is), 'Be careful what you wish for, because it might just come true.' You'd spent a decade working towards the top of the tree and, for the first time in a decade, your business affairs were in a place where you alone would benefit from all your efforts.[211] Once you were there, though, you realised that it wasn't simply the goalposts that had moved, but the entire playing surface.

Before, you'd looked around at the underground for your rivals and the art-rock community for inspiration. *Top Of The Pops* was as close as you came to the general public, and you only appeared on that show twice all decade. Now you were standing before the same drip-fed jury as Michael Jackson, Duran Duran, Lionel Richie and Rod Stewart, and suddenly it wasn't enough simply to be smarter than everyone else. Now you had to be flashier, crasser and more showbiz than them – and *Tonight* was the sound of you throwing up your hands in horror and admitting, not that you *couldn't* do it, but that you didn't want to. Filling the album with covers was your way of distancing yourself from the monster you'd become (as opposed, as you once said about Ziggy, to the one you'd created). Filling it with Iggy songs was a way of spreading the largesse – the blood money, if you like – around the people you felt could use it, without you having to soil your hands with it (we're speaking metaphorically here, by the way).

You need to get back to what you're good at. Glam was special because it tore up the 1960s, it broke all the rules, it blurred the distinctions between black and white, right and wrong, pop and rock. It set the stage for punk rock and a lot more besides. But, in assimilating that, the 1980s have rendered

211 Under the terms of Bowie's mid-1970s break with Mainman, his former mentor continued to receive 16 per cent of all Bowie's earnings until September 1982. Cannily, Bowie began work on *Let's Dance* that November.

it impotent. Steve Priest turning out on *Top Of The Pops* in gay-bar leather and swastika armband outraged more sensibilities than Holly Johnson's game-show potty-mouth ever could. When you said you were gay, Britain was horrified, the Yanks were alienated. When Boy George hinted at much the same thing, they yawned and threw another faggot on the fire. Pete Burns once said, 'You used to hear bricklayers say they'd like to give David Bowie one,' but when Boy George asked if he could be Burns' friend, 'I told him to fuck off. I don't talk to men in dresses.' You made such an impact that you're still around today. But George – where is George?

Pop music, that most gloriously subversive of all 20th-century art forms, has completely lost what was essentially its only reason for being – the power to shock. Once it was said that this year's revolutionary is next year's Young Conservative. The principle remains the same, but the process has gone into overdrive. The Stones were shocking because they were dirty, you were because you were gay, Alice was because he was frightful and the Pistols were because they had potty-mouths.

But who is taking their places as the 1980s yawn their way into oblivion? Frankie Goes To Hollywood? The Beastie Boys? Marilyn? Rock 'n' roll's meant to be music your mother wouldn't like, a roar of defiance that not only repels but outrages. Instead, it's turned into a packed lunch and a peck on the cheek before you head off to the office for the day. Inviting royalty to their concerts, and supermarkets regaling us with orchestral Muzak in the chart, are the opposite ends of a garage wall of respectability that previous generations would simply have pissed against. Bereft of its urge to outrage, what is rock but a toothless hag, warbling feebly against a backdrop of cocktail lunches and presidential garden parties, and for every kid whose parents still listen to their scratchy old Beatles records there's another dozen who've to fight Dad for possession of the latest Cult album. Or the latest David Bowie.

Maybe this is all a load of old bollocks. Maybe you truly believe *Tonight* is a worthy successor to whichever past album any listener chooses to name. Maybe you're still patting yourself on the back for finally making the LP you've always dreamed of. Somehow, though, I doubt it. You know what a pile of shit it is as well as the next man. And I won't be sending you any more tapes of my *Top Of The Pops* albums. You can buy them for yourself.

All the best

Gary

```
Tottenham, London N15
Sunday 28 April 1985
```

Dear David

What are you doing on 13 July? Well, if you're passing by Edmonton Town Hall at 3pm you could always come to my wedding (I would have sent you a formal invitation, but the printers screwed up and we only ended up with about half of what we ordered).

Yes, it's taken four years, but Sylvia and I are finally getting married. We wanted to do it on the 22nd, which is the anniversary of when we started going out, but with family and friends coming from all over the country we figured a Saturday would be better. And as the 20th was, mysteriously, all booked up, we backed up a week, because apparently not many people want to marry on the 13th. I went for 3 o'clock because if it's good enough for a football match it's good enough for me. Or so I told the registrar. You should have seen the look on her face!

I must say, there's not been much news from your end these last few months. Still hiding out after *Tonight*? I heard you went down well at the Tina Turner gig a few weeks back[212] – someone I know who was at the show said 'Tonight' worked a lot better live than it did on record, which must have been gratifying. I still think it was rubbish, though.

The only 'big' shows I've been to this year were Nico at Dingwall's, just after Christmas, and Leonard Cohen at Hammersmith Odeon in February. That was an odd show – very smooth, very slick and very, very long. He played for something like three and a half hours and, to be honest, it grew a little grating after a while. Then, just as you're giving up hope and wishing you'd stayed at home, he kicks everyone off stage and does a short acoustic performance, and all the doubts and horrors float away. I don't know if you're a fan (somehow,

212 Bowie guested at Turner's Birmingham NEC show on 23 March.

I think you must be), but if you're planning going to see him be prepared for the long haul.

A couple of other interesting gigs are coming up. There's Nick Cave at the Palais tonight, which could be entertaining. The new album might not be as strong as it should be, and he's one of the most unpredictable live performers I've ever seen – dreadful some nights, brilliant on others. We will see. Gary Glitter's coming up next month as well, and you know in advance what that's going to be like.

It's almost uncanny the way so many of his old singles now sound so appropriate for his current situation? Listen to them, and almost every one of them is about how his fans stuck by him through thick and thin, and how much he loves them for doing so. And things that were corny back in the day – 'Always Yours', 'You Belong To Me', 'I Love You Love' – are valedictory anthems now. The only thing I can compare it to is if you were to go out and play an entire set of 'Dudes', 'Rebel Rebel' and 'Rock And Roll Suicide', topped off with a completely over-the-top 'Heroes'.

Of course, the only show that anyone else is talking about is the festival Geldof's arranging for the Band Aid/Ethiopia fund. I do wonder if it's going to happen… The Band Aid single was a success, but even from an organisational point of view it was fairly straightforward. Be at the studio at such and such a time, such and such a day and bring your famous friends. In and out in a morning. And, if you can't make it down to sing, leave a message on the answerphone – we'll use that instead. Brilliant!

A day-long festival, on the other hand, sounds like a disaster waiting to happen, and you only have to look at the American video,[213] with everyone turning up in their best stage costumes and hamming it up like showbiz superstuds, to see that. At Band Aid, everybody looked like they'd been dragged out of bed, the song was rushed, the production was scratchy, the video was loose. But the American version was so *produced*, it left you feeling that they spent longer on the camera angles than they did

213 USA For Africa's 'We Are The World'.

writing the song. Can you imagine unleashing all those egos on one stage? With their managers and accountants and PR people all hanging around backstage to make sure nobody gets more camera time than anyone else? What a nightmare!

Have you been approached to play the festival? It probably wouldn't be the worst decision you've ever made – however it goes down, the publicity is going to be enormous, and that on its own will generate a bucketload more money for the charity. Plus, the whole affair is turning into the most stupendous indictment of our so-called 'leaders'. On the one hand you have the Ronnies and the Maggies and co sitting around watching while an entire country starves to death; on the other, you have a bunch of pop stars – the same long-haired layabout drug addicts and sex fiends who exert such an appalling influence on impressionable kids – going out and doing something about it.

I hope it does happen. I've always liked Geldof, and his heart is certainly in the right place. But I do wonder what its long-term effects will be? Woodstock – half a million hippies in a utopia made of mud – proved that rock 'n' roll could sustain the semblance of a society, at least for one weekend. But once the festival closed so did the utopia, and Woodstock's only legacy today is the amount of money people have made off it. This is different, if only because the money is already spoken for. But if Band Aid works, what'll be next? Every charity on the planet will start organising its own 'Aids'. Followed by every religion, every political party... By the end of the 1980s, rock 'n' roll itself could be utterly crushed beneath several tons of good intentions and naive ideals, and no one will be able to turn the clock back and insult the Queen for fun, because to do so would seem uncharitable.

Plus, if God had intended rock 'n' rollers to cooperate with one another, He wouldn't have created the music press. 'Beatles Slam Stones', 'Bolan Bashes Bowie', 'George Handbags Marilyn'... The music industry doesn't simply thrive on rivalries, it needs them to sustain itself. Turn rock 'n' roll into one giant, soft-hearted love-in and we might as well all go off and become stamp collectors.

Anyway, we'll see what happens soon enough. And right now, I'm betting that nothing will.

All the best (and please do try to make it to the wedding)

Gary

Tottenham, London N15
Tuesday 30 July 1985

Dear David

Well, at least now I know why no one else was getting married on 13 July! I didn't believe it when the date for Live Aid was announced, and all I can say is, thank heavens for VCRs! Enough people I know were taping it that, with a bit of synchronised timing and a helluva lot of frantic phone calls, I was able to get the whole event recorded – all 16 gruelling hours of it – to watch when we returned from the honeymoon. And no, I didn't try to postpone the ceremony. Syl would have killed me if I had.

I caught a bit of your segment. There was a TV in the hotel lounge and I slipped out during the reception in time to watch a couple of the songs. Nice band you had behind you, and I was really impressed with 'TVC 15'. What an odd choice for your opening song! In fact, your whole set seemed somehow pointedly anti-recent years – no 'Let's Dance', no 'Blue Jean', and such a raw version of 'Modern Love' that it took me a moment to reconcile it with any other version I've heard.

But would I be wrong in thinking the most pertinent moment was not that you volunteered to cut your set short by one song, so they could show the newsreel, but that the song you dropped was 'Five Years'? Hardly a crowd-pleaser, certainly not a stadium filler, and not even a hit single. Obviously you intended to convey some sort of message with that one and, come 1990, we'll probably find out it what it was. In the meantime, a few hints wouldn't hurt.

Can we expect 'Dancing In The Street'[214] as a single? Even in the last couple of days, opinion seems to have shifted from a definite 'No' to an equally definite 'Maybe'. I figure you might as well just do it and get it over with – this way, at least it'll raise more money for the cause. (Yes, even with that atrocious video!

214 Bowie's duet with Mick Jagger, recorded exclusively for the Live Aid event.

Were they your own pyjamas, or did you hire them for the occasion?) Keep it in the archive and the bootleggers will be in like a shot.

I won't bore you with tales from the honeymoon. We had ten days in Turkey, and I only went record shopping once. Found nothing of any real significance – I was hoping to come across some of your fabled oldies, preferably 'Yassassin',[215] but the only one of your records (cassettes) I found was *Tonight* – as a UK import. Oh well.

Finally, how's filming for *Absolute Beginners* going? As far as I can tell, it's either going to be one of the greatest movies ever made or one of the worst. The book,[216] of course, is so sainted that a lot of people have already persuaded themselves that the movie is going to stink. But the fact that everyone concerned[217] has the courage even to contemplate tackling such a sacred cow suggests that they must have something more up their sleeves than a simple musical re-enactment of the novel.

Your involvement is interesting, of course, because it kind of points you back in the direction of the 'fascist dictator' controversy of a few years back (seven, in fact – unbelievable!). What I've read hasn't been too explicit about what your role entails, or on which side of the battle lines your character falls, but we can take it as read that you're not one of the kids! In terms of your own career history, it'd have been hysterically funny to cast you in the Oswald Mosley-type role, but maybe that comes a little too close to reopening old wounds. Anyway, I hope it works out as well as your last few films. It might even give you something to keep busy with while you're writing a decent album's worth of new songs!

All the best

Gary

---

215 *The Lodger* track was issued as a Turkish single in 1979.
216 By Colin McInnes.
217 Goldcrest films and director Julien Temple.

Tottenham, London N15
Friday 16 August 1985

Dear David

You'll never guess who I saw last night! Mick Ronson *and* Tony DeFries! There was a story in *Melody Maker* about Ronno being back in London, working with a singer named Sandy Dillon and playing Dingwall's. Of course I had to go – with fingers crossed that it was going to be more interesting than Mr DeFries' last 'discovery'.[218]

It was. Sandy has an amazing voice, one of those super-smoky croaks – think Annette Peacock if she didn't have the jazz thing going. She started the set on her own, running through three or four songs at the piano, before Ronno came out, blasted out an amazing solo guitar number and then played along with Sandy for the rest of the show. He looks great and sounds even better and, while you could probably argue that his presence has more to do with promoting Sandy than contributing to the music (most of the people at the crowd were obviously only there for him), it still works really well. I don't think she's ever going to be an *enormous* success (a little too edgy, a bit too unconventional), but who'd have thought Kate Bush would make it? I don't know what your relations are with DeFries these days – probably not too good, from what I've read elsewhere. But if you can find a way of seeing a show you really should.

The other band that you really *have* to catch is Sexagisma. My friend Dave dragged me down to Greenwich to see them – opening for The Glitter Band, of all people! It was the same night as the Sandy Dillon show, so I really wasn't that keen on going: mad dashes across London aren't easy at the best of times, and who the hell knows their way around Greenwich? But Dave was so persuasive that I finally gave in, even though he refused to tell me anything at all apart from a very mysterious 'You won't be disappointed.'

218 DeFries launched John Mellencamp, as John Cougar, in the late 1970s, saying Bowie was his Eddy Arnold, Cougar was his Elvis.

I wasn't. Imagine that the current glam revival was taking place somewhere outside of the oldies circuit...that Gary Glitter and Slade were able to sustain their recent comebacks with records as immortal as their old ones used to be...and Ziggy was back with Weird and Gilly. Sexagisma are all that, *and more*!

They look amazing: feather boas, glitter trousers, platform boots, the lot. Their set is half glam covers (including 'Cracked Actor' – never one of my all-time favourites, but no matter) and half originals that sound like glam covers, and the encore was completely out of this world, starting out as the *David Live* arrangement of 'The Jean Genie', turning from that into 'Blockbuster', from there to 'School's Out' and then back to 'The Jean Genie' for the finale. Oh, and an Alice Cooper-style execution, involving buckets of blood and the death of one of their dancers!

The most amazing part is, words like 'revival' don't fit what they're doing. I've only seen/heard them the once, but they inject a really 'contemporary' sound into the music (damn, I hate that phrase) – big drums, flashy guitars, the lot. I really don't know what you'd make of it. But, assuming you could go in disguise and not feel self-conscious about their obvious devotion to your old records and image, I do think you'd get a kick out of it.

Meanwhile, it looks like we're on for 'Dancing In The Street' – which means you can probably already start celebrating another No.1. It's amazing, isn't it? You went through the 1970s making some of the greatest records of all time, and the only chart-topper you had came from 1969. The 1980s, however, have already brought you three No.1s,[219] and would anyone dare compare your last couple of albums with even the worst of your old ones? Apart from your accountant, that is...

I've mentioned this before, but there's some real historical revision going on right now surrounding your career. People are behaving (journalists, especially) as though you've been an unknown cult for the last 20 years, and only broke through to the mainstream with 'Let's Dance'. Excuse me, but aren't you the

---

219 'Ashes To Ashes', 'Under Pressure' and 'Let's Dance'.

guy who sold out Earl's Court, Wembley Arena, Madison Square Garden and pretty much every other major venue you wanted to play? The one who had two No.1 singles in 1975 alone? The one who spent nearly two years in the chart with *Ziggy Stardust*, and had three successive album chart-toppers during 1973–74? Hell, if that's a cult, I'd love to see what *success* would have been like.

I know *Let's Dance* probably outsold all your other albums put together, and an eight-month tour of worldwide sports arenas is nothing to sneeze at. But to say that you never became a 'superstar' until you'd done all that is pretty damned imbecilic, like saying The Beatles never meant anything until Paul put out *Band On The Run*. Superstardom isn't only a matter of making lots of money, it's about becoming part of the cultural furniture, which is what you spent the entire 1970s doing. Maybe you weren't as huge in America as you are now, but that was their problem, not yours.

The odd thing is, this new way of thinking is even being picked up by the fans. I was talking to some people at the Sandy Dillon gig, and they were complaining that you've gone completely downhill since you became 'popular'. I told them to lighten up a bit, that you'd done quite a lot of good things since the days of 'Rubber Band' and 'She's Got Medals'.

Yes, I know it was an easy target, but it did confuse them for a minute. But only for a minute, because one of them had brought a copy of the *Love You Till Tuesday*[220] album down for Ronno to autograph – and the fact that Ronno isn't on it didn't phase either of them for a moment. He's probably signed a lot weirder things than that over the years, after all.

An odd album, that, wasn't it? I must admit I haven't played it too often – I'm afraid of 'When I'm Five'. But it was good to get the King Bees single on there, and 'Ching-A-Ling Song' is one of those understated little masterpieces that really deserves more attention than it received. The fact that you reused parts of the melody for 'Saviour Machine' adds to its appeal. Have you ever thought about collaborating with Deram for a proper retrospective of your late

220 The recently released 'soundtrack' to a short promo film Bowie made in 1969.

1960s stuff? And all of it this time, not dribs and drabs. There's so much stuff that's come out on bootleg, things like 'Little Toy Soldier', which really should see the light of day. And maybe you could even clear up some of the little mysteries – like, are you playing on that American Konrads single?[221]

They've released so much else of that material in so many different forms over the years, usually with the most inappropriately up-to-date cover photos, that it's time for them to draw everything together like they almost did with *Images*, throw in some more unreleased stuff and do a proper box set of it, along the lines of that Dylan *Biograph* collection. Now that it looks like compact discs are here to stay, and people are already predicting a day when we'll have to replace our entire record collections, it would be nice to think they might make it worth our while.

I picked up a few of the RCA CDs (*Ziggy*, *Aladdin Sane*, *Diamond Dogs*) and I must admit I felt a bit cheated by them. There's meant to be so much room on these discs for music, so there's no excuse at all for not sticking on something extra, even if it's just a few odd singles and B-sides. The packaging is appalling, as well. No lyrics, none of the gatefold or inner sleeve information we were given with the records... I know CDs sound better than vinyl (well, some of them do... I'm not so sure about these ones, though), but they're only worthwhile if they replace the old LPs in every way. As it is, we have to keep the records as well, to have all the little extras. Do I smell a major con going on? Or am I just a grumpy old Luddite, rotting away in a tar pit full of scratchy vinyl and temperamental typewriters, fighting furiously against the super-shiny digital age? Answers on a postcard please...

All the best

Gary

PS Don't forget to catch Sexagisma. You'll love them!

221 See footnote 169.

Hammersmith, London W6
Sunday 27 April 1986

Dear David

New house, new job, new arrival... Sorry I've not written for a while, but as you can imagine it's been hectic. I suppose the biggest news is, Syl's pregnant – the eagle lands in mid-September and, to be honest, I'm petrified by the whole affair. Pleased, but petrified. We're not going to cheat and find out whether it's a boy or a girl, partly because it doesn't seem natural, but also because it's kind of fun referring to it as, indeed, an 'it'. Plus, it keeps the happy grandmothers from filling the house with the appropriately coloured knitted booties.

Anyway, as soon as we found out, we figured we needed a bigger house, so we started looking and this one pretty much fell into our lap. We're off Hammersmith Broadway, close to the tube and the shops – no doubt Mothercare will be seeing a lot of us in a few months' time. The move was probably the most painless one I've ever had. For the first time, we called in a professional removal company, who came in, put everything into crates, drove over and then unpacked. Twenty-four hours later, it was like we'd never even moved. And, for the first time, I have a room that is completely dedicated to my record collection.

It's the perfect hidey-hole – the rest of the house is tastefully furnished and tidy, with a place for everything and everything in its place, as my old granny used to say before they cut her tongue out. Then you come upstairs, ignore our room and the nursery, just follow the sound of Sigue Sigue Sputnik (the most glorious noise of the year so far), and there it is, wall-to-wall LPs and CDs, boxes full of singles, 13 years' worth of collected posters... I felt quite nostalgic putting them up, remembering the days of hanging around outside concert halls, carefully tearing down a souvenir. I found some great ones – Hunter-Ronson, 10cc, your Bournemouth Winter Gardens show... It'd be nice to have them properly framed, but the posters are so tatty that it'd hardly be worth it.

Anyway, having moved, and already being in shock up to our eyeballs, what better time to throw all caution to the wind and start up my own company? Syl and I had been talking about it for a while now and when I broached it with Jan (the boss), she said she was thinking of getting out of the business for a while and offered to sell me the firm. So I bought her out and relocated it here. It's just Syl and I for the moment, although as she gets – how do you put this delicately? – bigger, we'll probably hire someone else. We've rented a little office up the road, and so far (four weeks in) it's going well.

We had one major stroke of luck on the very first day we opened – a bunch of guys trying to get over to Mexico for the World Cup, who'd been laughed out of every other agency around for leaving it so late to make their travel arrangements. Not only did we get them sorted out, but they told all their friends about us and we've been dealing with them for everything from tube passes to Christmas holidays! Hopefully they'll stick around. It's nice to know we have a concrete customer base this early on.

Sounds like you've been busy as well. I heard somewhere or other that you're making a new album with Iggy – it's about time he had something new out, it's been four years since *Zombie Birdhouse*, and I don't think I've played that one more than twice since it came out. So, a new *Lust For Life*? Here's hoping.[222]

Meantime, we went to see *Absolute Beginners* at the local fleapit yesterday – a little nervously, I must confess, because the reviews weren't exactly the politest you've ever had. But all I can say is, who believes the reviews? I loved it! Was it better than the book? No, it was completely different. OK, so some of the music was a bit dodgy, and I couldn't help notice that one of Patsy Kensit's routines started out as a dead ringer for Screaming Lord Byron in the 'Blue Jean' video. But the story told itself brilliantly and, the beginning, where the Colin

222 The ensuing album, 1987's *Blah-Blah-Blah*, spun off Iggy's first ever UK chart hit, 'Real Wild Child'.

character is trying to summarise what was so special about that particular summer, was bang on target, not only for 1958 but for every year that falls at the beginning of what subsequently developed into a tangible musical/cultural movement. Everything he said about the birth of teenagers could as easily be applied to the birth of glam, the only real difference being that the 1950s gave kids mobility and confidence, and glam gave them sexuality and the individuality to express it. There's probably a thesis in there somewhere!

I hope you don't take this the wrong way, but the biggest surprise about the movie was...the theme music! What is it about you and classic movie themes? First 'Cat People', then 'Forbidden Colours' (I know you had nothing to do with it, but it was your film, so it fits the theory), and now 'Absolute Beginners'. The first time I heard it, I wasn't too sure. Did you know they sent the video out as the support film for *Company Of Wolves*? It looked phenomenal, really stylish and classy, and the Strand cigarettes spoof was perfect. But the song seemed a little...'dreary' was how Syl put it, but I picked up the 12" that weekend and, the first time I played it, it clicked into place. Too bad Diana Ross kept you off No.1[223] – but, at least it was her, and not Cliff and 'The Young Ones'!

If I wanted to step back from the film, I can see why some of the reviews were less than adulatory. For whatever reason, *Absolute Beginners* is one of those books that means everything to the people who read it (you hear stories of Paul Weller walking around with a copy permanently jammed inside his pocket), and their enthusiasm then carries over to all the people who haven't read it, but say they're going to...or say they have, which is often the same thing. So it gets built up into this almighty oracle, almost mythological and certainly untouchable – which means that anyone who does try to touch it is on to a hiding for nothing from the start. Either they stick with the story line then get nailed for leaving the best bits out, or they go off on a tangent and get hammered for that.

223 'Absolute Beginners' reached No.2 in the chart published on 18 March, the last of 'Chain Reaction's three weeks at the top.

Quite brilliantly, the film did both things at once. It's almost as though Temple[224] knew he was going to get panned, so he threw in everything he could, all those little period touches that set the scene so beautifully, and probably weren't even noticed by a lot of people. My favourites were the intro to *Hancock's Half Hour* (sounding a lot like 'Hang Onto Yourself' – I'd never noticed that before!), the R Whites lemonade rubbish bin and another passing Strand reference. Spot the nostalgic former under-age smoker – it's funny, isn't it, how every generation has its own ciggy of juvenile choice? When I was 13 or 14, Player's No.6 were the behind-the-bike-sheds furtive puff of choice, graduating to Embassy Reds when you hit 15. I also remember getting very excited when they relaunched Black Cats, and I went through a phase of buying a packet every week before I finally decided that I didn't really like them too much. They just looked good.

A question! Watching the credits, I saw Peter Frampton's name pass by – not in the actual movie, but about halfway down the crew list, where it gets into the dolly grips and animal trainers. Not *the* Peter Frampton, surely?[225] Hmm, they certainly showed him the way to go!

Have you been keeping up with all the books about you that are suddenly flooding out? I've been trying to, but every time I turn around there's another one grinning out of the bookshelves and I'm probably horribly behind the times on them already. But I did read Jerry Hopkins', and I really wasn't impressed. Apart from a few passages where he labours painfully to show us that he *can* relate to your music, the whole book is little more than a glorified diary, barely linked by random quotes and half-arsed anecdotes. And the mistakes are hilarious! Did you know Ray Davies wrote 'It Ain't Easy'?[226] Or that Lou Reed had a hit with 'Wild Is The Wind'?[227]

According to *Melody Maker*, there are at least three more 'major' biogs coming out over the next few months, including

224 Director Julien Temple.
225 No, it wasn't.
226 It was Ron Davies.
227 No, he didn't.

the Gilmans' spiteful-sounding little tome[228] (I assume you saw the newspaper pieces...and used them as toilet paper?) and Tony Zanetta's Mainman memories that I am looking forward to. I wish you'd sit down and tell the story yourself. It must drive you mad having all this stuff written about you, usually by people who don't know you from Adam but have an address book filled with people who have an axe to grind.

OK, so we all know it's impossible to get into your kind of position without pissing a few people off, whether you do it deliberately or not. But it's a shame that those are the only people who ever get interviewed for these sort of books – because the people who *are* still your friends, and who *do* have good things to say, won't get involved with an author because they know you won't approve. There's a bit of a Catch-22 going on there, isn't there? I read somewhere that that's why you're not working with Tony Visconti[229] any more, because he was a little too free with the inside information? But at least he was on your side – one supportive voice amid a sea of malcontents.

Personally, I don't see the point of the hatchet-job-type books. Criticism is fine, but the author should also remember who'll be buying the book. If I wanted a hatchet job, I'd get a job at Smithfield Market.

And, talking of jobs, I'd better get on... I'm meant to be figuring how to get a minibus full of librarians from Turnham Green to Liechtenstein for a weekend of... Who knows what librarians do in such places. I felt it was polite not to ask.

All the best

Gary

---

228 Journalists Peter and Leni were authors of *Alias David Bowie*, a controversial biography tracing what they perceived to be threads of madness running through Bowie's work.
229 Bowie's producer through the mid- to late 1970s.

Hammersmith, London W6
Friday 19 September 1986

Dear David

I'll apologise in advance. This letter's going to be fractured. Syl went into labour seven hours ago, nearly a week earlier than we were expecting, and the doctors have said it could be another seven before anything happens. So, I'm sitting in the corner of the room and, right now, they have Syl so drugged up that the only thing she'd be good for is a remake of *Cracked Actor*. Hey, Syl, there's a waxworks in the middle of the desert.

Later...
Patricia Elizabeth was born at 2:21 this morning – mother and daughter are doing fine, and father finally understands what 'Kooks'[230] is really all about. I notice you never wrote a follow-up about nappies and sleepless nights, though! Apparently, I'll be getting very accustomed to both in a few days.

Hope all's well

Gary

---

230 Bowie's song to his own newborn son, included on the *Hunky Dory* LP.

```
Hammersmith, London W6
Thursday 30 April 1987
```

Dear David

Sorry for not writing sooner – 'Day In, Day Out' has already all but come and gone,[231] and *Never Let Me Down*, if you believe the reviews, has managed to let everyone down (even the people who liked *Tonight*). Proving that *Absolute Beginners* was no fluke, however, I'm really enjoying it – lop off the first and last tracks (*another* ghastly Iggy cover; his bank manager will be thrilled!) and you've come up with a winner…or, at least, your best album since *Scary Monsters*. It's like you finally got the hang of writing mindless pop songs, and I mean that as a compliment.

There's as much of a knack to writing radio hits as there is to creating 'meaningful' slabs of art – maybe even more so. Art doesn't have to be liked by anybody; its very creation justifies its existence, and success is (or ought to be) a marginal afterthought. Pure pop, on the other hand, has to be just that – pure and popular – and, having played the album a couple of times now, I'm surprised that you picked 'Day In, Day Out' as the lead single. It's probably the worst track on the record. It's certainly the most jarring.

'Time Will Crawl', 'Too Dizzy' and 'Never Let Me Down', on the other hand, scream out for radio play-listing, while 'Zeroes' sounds like it was put together around at least half a dozen classic oldies to begin with. There's definitely a chunk of 'Paper Sun' in there, certainly a bit of 'Eight Days A Week', and the lyric says more about your work than anything you've written in a long time. Back on trial again? Forgive and forget? I guess you were nervous about the reviews as well!

I liked the way you sneaked in a reference to Prince.[232] You were right when you called him a sort of a 1980s version of yourself, in the same way as people used to call you a 1970s version of Mick Jagger. Certainly he's one of the few artists

231 Bowie's latest single spent just a month in the Top 30, peaking at No.17.
232 'Zeroes' namechecks Prince's 'Little Red Corvette'.

around these days who seems to be driven by the need to create, as opposed to simply wanting to sell records, and a lot of the decisions he's made over the last few years echo ones that you yourself could have taken in the 1970s. The difference is, whereas you simply talked about all the side-projects you wanted to involve yourself in – things like *Octobriana* (I bet you'd forgotten that one, hadn't you!), the Scott Richardson album, the Lulu revival and so on – he's been able to go out and do them. Whether that comes down to him having more control over his own destiny than you did, or simply more time on his hands, is a question that you alone can answer.

The only problem I foresee for Prince – and again, you're the role model for it – is what's he going to do when the outrage runs out? No, that's not fair. He is what he is, and if people feel outraged or threatened by what he does, then that's their concern not his. Musical history is littered with characters whose work was always a step or two ahead of the pack, yourself included. But society in general has a remarkable ability to catch up with even the most distant star if he intrigues them enough, and it'll be interesting to see how Prince copes when that happens.

You tripped over the same dilemma a couple of times in the 1970s, which is one of the factors that kept you both interested and interesting the whole decade through. When you created Ziggy, he was unique and his message was a virtual revolution. Eighteen months later, when there were little Zigs everywhere, you killed him off and started again. Then you did it again and again and again, but every time the lag between conception and acceptance grew shorter, until by the time of *Scary Monsters* you found yourself *re*acting to events, as opposed to creating them in the first place. So you took the biggest leap of all and headed off in the one direction where originality and innovation were the last thing on people's minds, and the only point that mattered was the strength of the song. Let's see the buggers catch up with you there!

Prince is in a weird place, because he's already being judged in those terms to a degree, and he might even have tried to get away from it as well, judging by a couple of his recent records. But what was rock 'n' roll suicide for you might not work the same way for him. It's like Room 101 in reverse – instead of everyone's darkest fear, everyone's ideal escape route is in there. And every one is different.

You hated your new-found fame so much that you made a record you hoped would destroy it – and pretty much succeeded at the first time of asking. But other people might spend for ever searching for a similar way out, which is an intriguing thought, isn't it? Imagine, an artist spending his entire career trying to find the one song that will send his entire audience packing, only for each one to turn out even more popular than the last. Indeed, it'd probably create a cult of its own, a sort of unspoken sensory assault course with hordes of anxious fans queuing excitedly for every new record, just to see how fucked up it's going to be. But Lou Reed survived *Metal Machine Music*, Iggy survived *Zombie Birdhouse* and I have a sneaky feeling that you've survived *Tonight* – maybe not with the *Let's Dance* mob, and certainly not with the critics. But there are half a dozen songs on the new album that should restore the most despairing old fan's faith in you, and that's seven more than most people were expecting.

Strangely, one thing that's really helped me with this album is…headphones. I gave up playing things on the cans, man, about ten years ago, around the same time that I realised Pink Floyd are a blues band with an alarm clock, no matter how often the aeroplane flies around your skull. But with Patty – seven months old and saving up for her first tooth – sleeping in the next room (or screaming – I'm seriously thinking about confiscating her Napalm Death CDs), I've had to reacquaint myself with the headphones and, to be honest, I'm rather enjoying the experience.

'Zeroes' is especially good. I love the little snatches of backing vocal that pop out unexpectedly, and Frampton's guitar is as good as he's ever sounded. (You should have made him dig out his old talk box, though.) Whatever made you think of hooking up with him? After all the other guitar heroes you've worked with, an old school friend is probably the last one I was expecting to hear. No complaints at all, though, and I'd imagine spending time with him was probably kind of educational. We all sit around discussing how big *Let's Dance* was, and how terrible *Tonight* turned out to be, but imagine what it must have been like for him, going from the do-no-wrong insanity of *Frampton Comes Alive* to the why-d'ya-even-bother of *I'm In You*! And then there was that *Sergeant Pepper* movie… I remember you saying that *Just A Gigolo* was all your bad Elvis films rolled into one. It was a mercy killing by comparison.

The tour, meanwhile, sounds like it's going to be amazing. Six months on the road with a 60-foot-tall glass spider. Good job you're not scared of insects. I've tickets for the two Wembley shows, of course. I was going to try for Maine Road as well, but not on a Tuesday and Wednesday. The firm's doing well, but not *that* well.

I told you we were going to take on an assistant once Syl decided she couldn't work any more? Well, she never did and the oddest aspect is, having Patty in the office a few days a week has been really good for business. I'm not quite sure how it works, but people come in to pick up a few brochures, get gurgled at for a couple of minutes and end up booking their holiday on the spot. It's happened three times already this week – hell, the kid's barely crawling and we've already sold her into prostitution. In the meantime, if you have any awkward friends or family members staying that you want to get rid of, send them round to buy a bus pass. Patty'll have them poolside on the Algarve before they know what's hit them.

The only downside (am I allowed to call it that? it sounds somehow disloyal) to having a kid is that it's curtailed a few of the more irresponsible urges Syl and I used to have, particularly where money and going out are concerned. Syl's parents are pretty good about coming over once in a while, 'to give the kids a break' as they put it, and my mum comes over when she can (sensibly, she leaves the Rat Bastard at home), but strangely we're not that bothered about going out without her. In fact, the one time we did this week, I had 'Glass Spider' stuck in my head the whole time: 'Mummy, come back cos the water's all gone.' Hey thanks, David. That's a really reassuring line.

Hey, have you heard The Banshees' version of 'The Passenger' yet? It's excellent, totally recapturing the excitement of the original and maybe even surpassing it – they've got the rhythm down so tight it really feels like you're on a train. The whole album's[233] a goodie – in case you've missed it, they've done a *Pin-Ups*, and it's probably the most successful one since *Pin-Ups*, at least in terms of taking songs you know (or should know), restating their original values and then adding something of the band as well.

Aside from the Iggy track, you're not on it, but there's a terrific version of 'This Town Ain't Big Enough For Both Of Us', to remind us what an unstated influence on so many people Sparks were. It's funny, between Sparks and 10cc you can see huge swaths of the 1980s being mapped out, but does any bugger admit it? Of course not. Then there's Roxy's 'Sea Breezes', Kraftwerk's 'Hall Of Mirrors' (that's a weirdie), and the most amazing 'Wheel's On Fire', which makes you wonder what Julie Driscoll would have turned into if she'd stayed in the pop game longer than she did. Or maybe you don't need to wonder, as Siouxsie illustrates it perfectly. And, on that happy note, I'm off to bed. So, I hope all is well – good luck with the tour and see you on 19 June.

All the best

Gary

---

233 *Through The Looking Glass.*

Hammersmith, London W6
Sunday 21 June 1987

Dear David

Oh, the joys of parenthood. We arrived home from the first Wembley show to find Patty was – well, not deathly ill, but I'm sure you remember how earth-shatteringly serious it seems every time a baby sneezes. Better safe than sorry, so we decided to stay home with her, and blew out last night's show – and I promise you that's not intended as a pun.

Could you believe the wind on Friday? There were moments when it looked like the entire stage – never mind the spider – was going to just take off. You must have been petrified up there, watching that monster rocking from side to side; I don't know how much a 60-foot-high fibreglass arachnid weighs, but it probably wouldn't be a pretty sight having it crash down on your head.

The sound was pretty hellish as well. Add a few hearty gusts of wind to the mix and it's amazing how much 'Up The Hill Backwards' sounds like 'Jack And Diane'![234] Everything I'd heard about the European leg of the tour made it sound incredible. Someone I was talking to saw you in Hamburg last week and compared the show to watching a movie, the sound was so good and the dancers were so tight. Wembley, on the other hand, was a bit like watching a school play that found out ten minutes before the curtain went up that they were going to be doing the whole show on ice. The band was great, the set list was amazing and the actual show looked like it ought to be fabulous. But Boreas obviously isn't a Bowie fan – particularly a theatrical Bowie. Everyone says it's one of the show highlights when you turn up on top of the spider, but we knew halfway through that there was no way you'd be going up there. I do hope you'll be bringing out a video of the complete show. I'm dying to see it in its own element – as opposed to suffering it in the grip of others.

234 A John Cougar Mellencamp hit.

I really did enjoy the *Never Let Me Down* material. Like the last tour, the new songs really take on a life of their own once they've been played live a few times. 'Time Will Crawl' was even better than the LP version, so I can't believe the single is already on its way down the chart. You really should have put it out first, and saved 'Day In, Day Out' for the now apparently inevitable follow-up flop. 'Bang Bang' worked really well as well, and that's despite me wishing you'd left it alone on record. Live it takes on a whole new dimension – really punchy, really powerful...and almost as good as Iggy's! I wish I'd been able to see what was going on with the girl in the crowd during that one. From where we were sitting, it rather resembled a cross between Springsteen's 'Dancing In The Dark' video and Meatloaf doing 'Paradise' on *Whistle Test*. It even took me a moment to figure out that she was part of the dance troupe. At first I assumed she really was a fan, and I couldn't figure out why nobody threw her off the stage![235]

'Absolute Beginners' was terrific as well, even if I didn't catch a word of the dialogue around it. I'm assuming (from other reports) that the spoken-word interludes were intended to link the songs together, rather than being asides and greetings to the crowd? Something else to hate the wind for... We caught one word in five, and that was a disconnected mumble in between the crackles and pops. Again, you just have to get this show out on video!

Another highlight that was sorely missed... Why have you stopped playing 'All The Madmen'? I couldn't believe it when I heard you were doing the song, although it did make sense. Was it, perhaps, a special gift to the Gilmans? And, if so, I hope they appreciated it. I didn't really intend reading their book, but there was so much palaver surrounding its 'revelations' that I finally caved in during the summer. There were some interesting interpretations thrown in – they *really* have it in for 'The Bewlay Brothers', don't they? But the idea that pretty much every major song you've written is somehow haunted by your

235 With dancer and current Bowie beaux Melissa Hurley playing the role of the fan, this was indeed intended as a parody of the Springsteen video.

fears of the family history of insanity is too simple-minded for words – (a) because you'd surely have exorcised it by now, and (b) because no single subject on earth is interesting enough to inspire 20-plus years' worth of generally excellent songs!

The other point that they seem to miss is that true insanity is nothing more than rampant creativity – in which case, you shouldn't even worry about going mad because you already have. It only becomes a problem if the 'sufferer' doesn't have a means of channelling the mental overactivity.

If you'd been a regular Man On The Street, a plumber or an estate agent, walking round in brightly coloured clothes and calling yourself Ziggy Stardust, chattering on about aliens and dictators, you'd have been locked up years ago. But you funnelled all that into a career that not only allowed you to work through whichever crazy ideas and delusions you may have been suffering, but also encouraged you towards even wilder ones. When you first came up with the concept of Ziggy, and started telling your friends and family about it, did you even pause for a moment to think about the sheer lunacy of the whole idea? Probably not. But did anybody else? I bet there was at least one person who looked you in the eyes and asked, 'Are you feeling alright?' And not only Ziggy. So much of what you've said and done over the years has been completely beyond the parameters of what society calls 'normal' that the very idea of accusing you of being afraid of madness is, itself, insane. The only thing you have to beware of is the day they find a cure for it.

In the meantime, what you really ought to do is write your own biography, parodying all the books which have been written about you in the last few years. But, instead of interviewing past musicians, producers, long-lost family members and so on, you'd have quotes from each of your own past identities, all slagging one another off and offering the 'real' stories behind the songs.

Back to 'The Bewlay Brothers', if you don't mind. I've seen it described as everything from a twisted examination of gay sex, to a paean to hard drugs and even a presentiment of incipient madness. What the fuck? I always saw it simply as a memory of boyhood, and that period – which we've all been through – where two friends (they don't have to be brothers) create a fantasy world from whatever they have to hand, be it books, television, radio. And wasn't it also the name of your local tobacconist's? But you could lead it off on another trail entirely and say it was about going to a Pink Fairies gig. *Kings Of Oblivion* was one of their album titles, Mick Wayne (from the *Space Oddity* days) played guitar for them for a while, and I'm sure there's more.

How about 'Aladdin Sane'? Everyone makes such a big deal about its apocalyptic subtitle: 1913 – the year before World War I broke out; 1938 – the eve of World War II; and 197? – at that time, who knew? But it could just as easily be a tribute to your own genealogy: 1913 – the year after your father was born; 1938 – the year after your half-brother came along; and 197? – at that time, perhaps, the hope of a little sibling for Zowie. And who will love Aladdin Sane himself? All of them, of course.

See, it's easy and, because you're telling the stories, who would say you're wrong? Even better, though, would be the bits where the characters themselves all start backstabbing one another. You think you have a hard time when you walk into the studio to tell the band, 'I've just written a fabulous song – it's called "87 And Cry"?' Imagine having to sit down with half a dozen past aliases, and trying to convey its merits to them! Ziggy – 'Well, I'm not playing guitar on that.' Halloween Jack – 'Forget rock 'n' roll, this isn't even genocide!' The Thin White Duke – 'Maybe it *is* the side effects of cocaine, after all.'

Seriously, though, I've often wondered whether you do ever fall into the trap of measuring your past accomplishments against your current activities. Wandering dangerously close to the quicksands that I've spent half a page complaining about, 'Zeroes' kind of touches on that with its reference to the toothless past 'asking you how it feels' (or maybe that's a dig at Bob Dylan – quick, write that one down as well!).

But that's an academic response, which you formulate in the cold light of day to chase the demons away. What do you do at three in the morning, when you wake up in a cold sweat with a little devil in your shoulder asking whether 'New York's In Love' really is a fitting successor to 'Panic In Detroit'? Or walking round the supermarket, while the Muzak's playing 'Aladdin Sainsbury?' and wondering, in the words of Richard Harris, whether you'll ever have that recipe again? Do you ever look back on the days when you seemed to have a purpose beyond pop, and wonder where all the good times have gone?

Or – and this must be the answer, because otherwise you really would have gone round the bend – do you keep on doing what you feel like doing, knowing that it's only fans and critics who spend their lives playing comparisons? To coin an utterly preposterous cliché, Hindsight United are a great football team. But if you don't like football, would you ever want to play for them? (Do you know what? I don't think I've ever heard you even mention the game.)

The point is, if you're in a position to do as you please, you have to be enjoying it, and if you're not then you have no business doing it. You can argue (and I've read a lot of people doing that) that playing music is a job, like any other. But it isn't. It's a privilege, not in some highfalutin 'music is the gift of the Gods' kind of way, but simply in as much as, if you're achieving an ambition you've nursed all your life, then you've succeeded in doing something that a lot of people never get the chance to do but continue to dream about regardless.

For them, playing rock 'n' roll (or writing novels, or painting pictures) will never be anything more than a hobby – something they do because they love it. And that is something a professional musician, author, artist, *whatever*, should never lose sight of. You do it because you love it. And the moment you stop loving it, you should stop doing it. You can fake sincerity, but you cannot fake joy. And you know that – you might even have tried it.

Never Let Me Down and the Glass Spider tour are the sound of you rediscovering the passion that used to keep you going, and the continued grumbling of the discontented hordes is just that. Think of it like a curious background noise, an unexplained knocking in the plumbing or something. If you focus on it, it'll keep you awake all night and you'll tear the house down trying to find its cause. But if you turn up the stereo and blank it out, it might as well not be there. I don't know what your plans for the future are, but that's what I'd recommend. Turn up the stereo!

All the best, and have a wonderful rest of the tour. You're doing OK for a 40-year-old!

Gary

To Major Tom

Hammersmith, London W6
Friday 15 July 1988

Dear David

I just bought a bootleg video of your Intruders At The Palace appearance[236] from a stall at Camden Market, and I don't think I've seen you that animated in years. Gone were the vast theatrics of last year's tour, gone was all the uncertainty and struggle of the albums before that. It's almost as if you've physically transported yourself back to the very early 1980s, the period between *Scary Monsters* and *Baal*, before all the nonsense of the last few years (yours and everybody else's), and you're preparing to relaunch the decade all over.

Was it just a one-off? Or are we seeing the seeds for your next move? If so, keep that band – the new guitarist[237] is terrific, scything that instrument to death. Dump the drum machine for a bit of flesh and blood and you could be back to basics big time.

It's been an odd year, music-wise, a lot going on but nothing happening. I do like Gene Loves Jezebel – good, trashy rock in a sleazy glam vein, plus their guitarist[238] was obviously raised on Ronson, and raised well. With so many new bands coming through these days, and most of them painfully indebted to the punk-and-thereafter style of thrashing, it's easy to forget sometimes that, for an entire generation growing up in the early to mid-1970s, Ronno really was the only 'guitar hero' worth his salt. Beck had gone jazz, Clapton was into that laidback JJ Cale stuff, Page and Blackmore were doodling away in their little metal universes, and the rest were a bunch of cults. But Ronson was so versatile, so stylish, he looked as good as he played, and the only reason that he's not talked about in the same way as those others is because punk came along and demolished that whole hero-worship mentality. Otherwise, he'd be a god.

236 Bowie performed one song, Lodger's 'Look Back In Anger', at the Intruders At The Palace ICA benefit on 1 July.
237 Reeves Gabrels.
238 The mercurial James Stevenson.

Morrissey looks promising, as well. I was never much of a Smiths fan, but what I've heard of his solo stuff sounds a lot more interesting. I see a bit of you in some of his stuff, but of course he's of an age – he probably grew up with exactly the same influences and reference points as I did, which means the glam stuff is inevitably going to permeate his subconscious. Good songwriter as well.

But I can't help feeling that when history looks back on the 1980s the whole decade is going to seem like such a gaping void, poor from the point of rising new talent and a nightmare for anyone surviving from earlier decades. It's as though the entire music industry has lost its way, at least from a creative point of view. Even the Stones, always a reliable source of entertainment, haven't made a worthwhile sound since 1979, and everyone else is simply wandering around looking hopelessly lost.

Part of it has to be down to the nature of the industry these days, and the way it's become so image- and product-driven. We always used to joke in the 1970s that so and so was only popular because of the way they looked, but compared with what's going on today they might as well have been dressed and behaving like dustmen. I'd like to blame MTV for pushing style so far ahead of substance, and it's pretty unfair that we don't get the channel over here, because we certainly have to suffer the consequences of its existence. But that's only part of the problem.

Anyone can make a flashy feel-good video these days and, besides, it's not as though most bands have any input into their videos in the first place. The malaise lies deeper, in the way bands are physically projected. You look at some of the truly massive names of the last few years – Mr Sting, Dire Straits, Bruce Springsteen, Phil Collins, that whole stratum of absolute mega-monsters – and I can't imagine any of them breaking through on the strength of their personal appearance or even, really, on the power of their music. It's down to demographics, a term that we never even knew existed a few years ago, but that is now all over the place.

Remember in the late 1970s, once punk had come and gone, how people used to complain about the UK music press isolating little pockets of bands and proclaiming them the vanguard of the Next Big Thing? There was power-pop, 2-tone, mod, the new wave of British heavy metal, positive punk, goth…and probably a whole load more that I don't even remember any more. None of them took off, because the label was created before the audience and none of the bands lived up to their billing.

Well, it works the other way around now. Record companies or whoever look out at the population, isolate a slice of it – say, late 20s/early 30s married couples with kids, a mortgage and a good paying job – and then tailor bands to fit that crowd's 'requirements', knowing that in the general scheme of things music is fairly low down on that audience's list of priorities.

It's a brilliant strategy, because when you think about it these are people who grew up on rock and pop music, who are still young enough to feel some kind of affinity with it and who aren't quite ready to turn into their parents just yet. But they're not 18 and angry any more. They have work in the morning, the kids need new trainers and they have to take the car in for its MOT on Saturday. They're not running round clubs, catching new bands, then heading down to Rough Trade for the latest hip indie. They want music they can play over cocktails, or when they're cuddled up by the fire after the kids have gone to bed, and a stadium gig every two or three years to make them feel part of some special 'event'.

So, nothing too challenging and nothing too brutal, but just enough substance – warm sentimentality, easily digestible politics, caring ecology, whatever – to make the listener feel some sort of common ground: 'Ah, Mr Sting feels bad about the rainforest. So do I.' Add some expert musicianship and pristine production, and a tiny hint of nostalgia to make the connection with the listeners' lost youth… Hey, put on your red shoes and dance the blues! Once again, you were ahead of your time.

Society has always survived by filing everything into categories, and rock 'n' roll is no exception, be it the beat boom, psychedelia, glam, punk, house or whatever. The difference was, the categories that rock itself created were always in direct opposition to those that comprised 'normal' society – counterculture by name and nature. Today, they are an extension of them. A million identical megastores sell a million identical baubles, and a million identical people dutifully go and buy them. Step out of that million, however, and you're fucked. Try finding a turntable with four speed settings. Or a high-street record shop that still carries vinyl. Or a kitchen knife that *won't* cut through metal pipes. They're out there, of course, but they're scarce and growing scarcer, because everything's geared to the common denominator and, if you're not part of that, then you're a freak – and who wants a country full of freaks? Certainly not the music industry. The freaks don't fit the marketing profile – or rather they do, but you have to really manipulate it first.

Punk scared people. It truly did. It also surprised them. How can anyone say they run the music business if they didn't see something that huge bearing down on them? What do you do if your safe, secure job suddenly depends upon visiting a stinking cellar to catch a band called Blind Wank Pig? 'Anarchy – isn't she the girl who unlocks my office every morning?' 'No, you're thinking of Nihilism. She studies Egyptian rivers, you know.'

The barricades went up after that. There will never be another movement like it, because the system won't allow it. Sometimes it's terrifying to imagine what it's going to be like as Patty gets older and starts listening to her own music. What's it going to sound like? Today's kids are the first in history who are growing up on the same kind of music as their parents. Think about it – the 1920s had Big Bands, the 1930s had swing, the 1940s had Hitler, and from thereon in it's been solid rock 'n' roll. Say you were 17 again. Would you seriously want to listen to the same music as your mum and dad? Would you really enjoy bringing the new Jesus And Mary Chain album home and have Dad say, 'It's not as good as their first one'?

But how can you avoid it? Today's parents are trendy! They are hip to the jive. They think it's groovy. They lived through The Beatles, they lived through Pink Floyd and now they're living through Dire Straits and Axl Rose, and they're lapping the stuff up because they want eternal youth as well. And if it's bad now, imagine what it'll be like in another five years, when the first post-punk babies start coming of age? How can rock shock a parent who watched the Pistols on the *Today* show? They've already seen it, they've already done it, they've already bought the ripped-up T-shirt. And, unless they're really stupid, they'll know exactly what Junior's doing before he even knows he's done it. 'Ah, cut the teenaged rebellion crap, cos I saw Sham 69, I'll have you know. And don't run with scissors because you'll put somebody's eye out.'

There is still outrage out there and, God willing, there always will be. But, for every kid stretching sinew in the mirror and sneering 'Gimme danger, little stranger', there's another hundred arranging their baseball caps sideways and simpering along with 'Tougher Than The Rest' – and that's even more dangerous, because it gives the impression of subversion, but it'll never follow through. And that, to finally cut this whole rant short, is why I was so excited by your Intruders show. Because it proved that if we strip away all the excess and disappointment of the last five years (and, yes, Glass Spider was excessive, no matter how much I loved it), deep inside in your soul you still understand that rock 'n' roll is meant to be out on the edge and played from the heart, no matter how far from the commercial arena that heart may lie.

Look back in anger, David – and keep on looking for as long as it takes.

All the best

Gary

Hammersmith, London W6
Friday 30 June 1989

Dear David

The critics hated it, the audience hated it and my eardrums hated it. I cannot believe I'd ever complain that a band was too loud on stage (I once fell asleep at a Motörhead gig), but my head was still ringing this morning. Forget Tin Machine – that was Tinnitus Machine.

If you like a good laugh, you really should have been standing in the queue outside the London shows, listening to some of the conversations going on. Of course you saw all the expected faces in the crowd, the Ziggys and Aladdins, and a surprising number of *Let's Dance*-era Italian waiters – there were even a couple of Screaming Lord Byrons. And all they were saying was, 'I know David said there'll be no old songs, but I've heard they play…' and the Ziggy ones would rattle off the rockers from *Ziggy Stardust*, the Aladdins would go through the *Aladdin Sane* rockers, all the way through your career to 'Modern Love' and 'Bang Bang'.

Then, if you sought out the same people at the end of the show, they'd completely changed their tune. Now they were saying that they knew all along there'd be no oldies in the set, 'not even as an encore to thank us for being there', and 'Of course, you can't really count this as a David Bowie concert, it's more like when he was playing back-up for Iggy.' And that's a seriously twisted compliment if ever I heard one. In fact, that's how I ended up with a ticket for the Kilburn show. The venue was already sold out when I went to buy one, but immediately after the first gig there were so many heartbroken little Ziggys trying to offload their tickets for the next one that I picked one up for face value. And I didn't even have to pay a booking fee! I'll spend what I saved on cotton-wool balls – to stuff in my ears the next time you play.

I really enjoyed the shows. You looked a damned sight more relaxed than I've seen you in years – yeah, you seemed to be enjoying yourself on the Serious Moonlight shows, and the 'Glass Spider' video looks pretty cheery as well. (Thanks for putting that out, by the way. I wish you'd chosen an earlier show – I really wanted to see 'All The Madmen'.) But this time, you were so…is 'casual' the right word? Jeans and jacket, a skinny beardy chain-smoking ciggies, it was like watching a garage band rehearse. But when their mum was out, so they could turn up really loud.

I love what you've done to 'Working Class Hero' – after Marianne Faithfull's version, it'd be hard for anyone to revive that song (and I never really rated Lennon's original), but you did it. Great to hear 'Shaking All Over', too – it's up there with Cliff Richard's 'Move It', the most important home-grown rocker in the pre-Beatles history of music. The twin guitars worked as well. The feel of the album and of the show itself was real garageland, but adding an instrument really twisted the knife and elevated it above the tinny punk rock buzz it could have been and that damages a lot of the other bands working in that area.

That said, have you seen T V Smith's Cheap? 'Under The God' really reminds me of their 'Luxury In Exile' (they played it on a Peel session a while back) – I mean, *really* reminds me. T V is the guy from The Adverts (they opened for Iggy on the second 1977 tour, remember?), and for a long time he was doing a fairly high-sheen, poppy sound that may or may not have worked. Yeah, you can probably identify with that. Then he bounced back a couple of years ago with what really could be called the blueprint for everything you're doing now – and, apparently, for much the same reason. He'd given up trying to figure out what the 1980s wanted, so he decided to go back to basics and do what he wanted. The result is probably the only British band that could give Tin Machine a run for its money in the loud and aggressive intelligence stakes. The only real difference is, the music press doesn't seem to hate them. They don't even write about them.

Oh for the same blissful luxury, you're thinking. A hard-rock album with The Cult's old producer – did you deliberately go out of your way to give the music press such a field day, or was it purely coincidence? Some of the reviews I've read were so hostile, it's almost as if the writers had a personal grudge against you: 'Damn him, I'd never have known I'm a repressed transvestite if he hadn't planted all those ideas in my head. Well, I'll show him...' But really I don't see *Tin Machine* as being much of a departure from a whole slew of things you were doing 'back when you was good'.

Maybe it's a little more one-dimensional; even *The Man Who Sold The World* included a few moments of sonic relief. But it wouldn't be too hard to come up with a compilation album's worth of golden oldies that is just as heavy as this lot, from 'She Shook Me Cold' and 'Running Gun Blues' to 'Watch That Man', 'Cracked Actor', 'Diamond Dogs', 'Suffragette City' and 'Hang Onto Yourself' – oh yes, all the peerless classics that everyone's complaining you don't think about any more. Hell, 'Heaven's In Here' even lifts a piece of 'The Jean Genie' to show off its lineage, but does anyone even notice? Of course not, because they're too busy moaning about what an obsolete old codger you've become, then running off to praise The Pixies, Sonic Youth and the rest for having the anti-commercial balls to make a grungy racket.

Your mistake was even to admit that you were in this band. You should have launched it with zero information, a bunch of kids from a lumberjack backwater in some godforsaken corner of the good ol' USA, who believe feedback is the Lord's way of telling them the drums aren't loud enough. Then, the moment you had *Melody Maker* drooling that you're the next best thing to Mudhoney and Tad, you'd rip off the juvenile face mask and reveal yourself as the grizzled old fart they never dreamed you could be. The backlash would be immediate, but by then it'd be too late. Tin Machine would rule the world.

Two questions come to mind, one of which kind of feeds out of the other. What prompted you to do this, and how long do you intend it to last? The idea that, after nearly 35 years as a functioning solo artist, you'd want to submerge yourself back into a 'democratic' band is, itself, so alien to everything that you've ever done that one can't help but feel it's another 'mask' – the presence of the Sales brothers, whose time with Iggy surely prepared them for your way of working, only amplifies that possibility.

At the same time, though, Tin Machine is such a dramatic departure from everything else you've done that there must be a lot more to it than simply trying on a new disposable suit. It's probably safe to say that, whatever EMI thought they were getting when they signed you, you've gone out of your way to ensure they haven't received it. Maybe if you'd followed up *Let's Dance* with *Never Let Me Down*, things would have worked out differently. But, not only did you not do that, you also made it pretty clear around the middle of the decade that your interest in maintaining a high rock-idol profile was at an all-time low.

So, is Tin Machine the sound of you regaining that enthusiasm? And, if so, is the noise integral to the excitement? Or a by-product of it? It reminds me of sitting on the tube, playing *Metal Machine Music* on a Walkman. Everyone's sitting around you, waiting for the tinny ti-ti-ti-ti-ti sounds of Phil and Bruce and Sting and co, and instead they get an unrelenting wall of gggggggggrrrrrrrrrrrnnnnnnnnnnnngggggggggggggggg... I know, because I've done it. On several occasions. And, when the journey's over and you switch off the tape, Christ, you feel as though you could take on the world. It's like a head-cleaner for the head and that's what you're doing now. Even better, I don't think you give a damn whether anybody else likes it or not and, in that, you're probably not going to be disappointed.

In the meantime, you can take solace from the knowledge that you have at least one completely impartial fan. I was sitting around playing records – oops, showing my age yet again; I meant CDs – the other night, when Patty waddled in – hard to believe, but she's almost three years old – listened for a moment and then demanded I put on Timmy Sheen. Who? 'I'm sorry, but Daddy doesn't have that record,' thinking it must be some hideous alter ego of Timmy Mallett or some such. 'Yes, you do.' 'No I don't.' 'Yes, you do...' And then she started singing it. 'Timmy Sheen, Timmy Sheen...'

OK, you probably figured that one out a lot quicker than I did, but I'll tell you this. I am *so* glad CD players have that 'repeat' button. We heard the song five times before I handed her the headphones and left her to it. Of course, I could hear her singing along in every room in the house and I do now find myself wishing you'd thought of a somewhat less catchy name for the band. But, hey, Timmy Sheen's a big hit in my house and if Patty grows up to be a rock critic I'm sure she'll treat you kindly. She loves the video of *Labyrinth* as well, by the way.

Finally, wonderful news about your back catalogue finally coming out again. I was wondering why the old RCA CDs were becoming so difficult to find, not even imagining that they'd lost the rights to them and were simply using up old stock. I'm glad I bought them all when I did, although now it looks like I'll be buying them all over again. Still, you must be dead chuffed to have found a label that cares about what its output looks like, and spends some time and effort on packaging and marketing, rather than another monolithic major who'll simply stick them in the stores when nobody's looking – if you're lucky. I've picked up a few Rykodisc CDs, and I don't think I've been disappointed by any of them.

I've heard that there's going to be a bit of a lag between the US releases and the British issues, which is a shame. There's even talk that there might be a ban on American copies coming into the country, until the UK issues are sorted out. I do hope not, although you know as well as I do that it'll be completely unenforceable. Not unless customs open every CD-shaped package addressed to every Bowie fan in the country. And even you're not that paranoid, are you?

All the best

Gary

Hammersmith, London W6
Thursday 1 February 1990

Dear David

Well, bugger me! There we all were, cowering in our bunkers awaiting the second blast of Tin Machine, and instead you're running around announcing that Ziggy's playing guitar once again. For the last time? Yeah, right – shades of Hammersmith 1973, I believe? Except, this time I noticed that you never said outright that you won't ever be playing any of the songs again. Just that you hoped you wouldn't want to. There's a big difference, and I hope people remember that in however many years' time, when they start sneaking out of retirement again. Because you know they will!

Obviously the whole outing is being set up to help push the *Sound And Vision* box set, and the so-slowly-emerging reissues. And presumably, no matter how sincere you are about putting the repertoire to a telephone vote, we can already guess which songs you will be playing, and which ones you won't. So I'll list my ten suggestions for you now, and save my 'official' vote for 'The Laughing Gnome'. It's not often the *NME* has a good idea these days, but I must admit 'Just Say Gnome' is inspired. Do let us know how many people phone in with that one. And, if there are enough, I hope you'll trot it out during one of the London shows! Gotta keep the kiddies satisfied, you know – especially if you're setting yourself up for something as theoretically clichéd and loathsome as this.

The 'greatest hits' tour. The Frank Sinatra 'I Did It My Way' tour. The 'please buy my old albums because no one cares about my new ones any more' tour. Sound And Vision has been called all these things, and you only announced the bloody thing a fortnight ago. Then again, what did you expect? Call up Mick Jagger, Paul McCartney, Dave Gilmour, any of that crew, and ask them what it's like for them – they put out a new record and everyone complains it's not as good as the old ones; they tour all the old songs and everyone says they're washed up and don't have the heart to perform the new stuff. There's no way you can win, so you may as well do what you feel like doing... But I never dreamed it was going to be this. Or do you have a fiendish treat in store, and you'll have Tin Machine behind you to tear the songs to shreds?

OK, my vote, and if you wind up including even a couple of these I'll be your penfriend for life. No particular order, and sticking to the period covered by the box set...

'Queen Bitch'
'We Are The Dead'
'Life On Mars?'
'Prettiest Star'
'Drive-In Saturday'
'Lady Stardust'
'John I'm Only Dancing'
'Panic In Detroit'
'Stay'
'The Bewlay Brothers'
'Cygnet Committee'

Can we include cover versions? Probably not, but an honorary mention for 'Wild Is The Wind', something by Brel, 'Alabama Song' and 'Where Have All The Good Times Gone?'. So now you know my favourites. Let's see what the rest of Bowiedom comes up with![239]

Good luck with the tour – and Happy New Year!

All the best

Gary

---

[239] Five of the 15 were aired at least once during the Sound And Vision tour: 'Queen Bitch', 'Life On Mars?', 'John I'm Only Dancing', 'Panic In Detroit', 'Alabama Song' and Brel's 'Amsterdam'.

Hammersmith, London W6
Friday 14 December 1990

Dear David

It's been a long time! I promise I'll try to write more regularly in the future, but I do wonder where on earth you found the time (or Angie found the energy/patience) to maintain a career while still trying to deal with the infant Zowie. Or is that what nannies are for? Patty's turned 4 and, even without doing anything more than speeding good-naturedly round the house, she's managed to turn everything topsy-turvy.

Hmm, thinking about it, maybe maintaining a full-time career *was* how you managed to deal with it. No disrespect to either Syl or Patty, but every time I send someone else off on one of those once-in-a-lifetime, get-away-from-it-all, worldwide cruises, I have to bite my tongue before I ask whether there's room in their hand luggage for a six-foot stowaway.

Actually, things are going pretty good at the moment. The big event for us this summer was the World Cup in Italy. You might remember back when we opened, our first big sale was getting a bunch of kids over to Mexico for the last one? Since then, we've been really pursuing the football market, and with a lot more success than anyone ever expected. It started out getting people to and from away games – finding ways to get them up to the arse end of Northumberland in time for kickoff, and then home for work the next morning, or figuring out places where they could stay in deepest Devon without adding more than a few quid to the total cost. And all it involved was finding the Yellow Pages for different towns, then calling around the hotels and B&Bs, getting their rates. Someone comes in looking for a cheap weekend in Burnley... Sure, we know just the place.

Started doing the same for England matches before the European Championships; now we're keeping our fingers crossed that UEFA lift the ban on English teams playing in

Europe. I've hotels on file everywhere from Marseille to Minsk. Let us know if *you're* ever looking for something cheap and cheerful in some place of darkest obscurity. You must get sick of five-star service sometime! We won't even charge you for the tickets, either. I'll have you come round to the house and put on a show in the back garden.

This is really hard to write, but...can...you...believe...we...didn't...see...you...play...this...year? I don't know if I waited 30 seconds too long to get my ticket application in, but back came the cheques, uncashed and unwanted. So, down to Docklands every night, trying to find an even halfway reasonable tout, only to find there weren't any touts out there! Is this the first time in history that shabby-looking men in shabbier-looking raincoats *haven't* bought up entire blocks of tickets, to sell on at an enormous profit? Or did the Met put their fiercest-looking plods on the beat that night? Still, at least I finally got to ride on the Docklands Light Railway and I didn't even mind not seeing Mickey and Pluto. A Disney ride through the heart of a building site. It'll be lovely when it's finished.

We missed the Milton Keynes gigs because we were in Scandinavia, and we missed the Scandinavian shows because we were back in England. So, don't you dare raise your eyebrows and tut when I say I've bought every bootleg of the tour I can find. I might not be able to see what the audience is going so crazy about, but at least I can hear it. And I'm taking you at your word on this, but at least there's one consolation – I'll never have to watch you dismember 'China Girl' again.

Something I've not missed out on has been the reissues and, can I raise my hand here and say, 'Oops'? I don't know whether you're making the decisions and selecting the tracks, but having thrown the Sound And Vision tour open to the public, surely you could have made a similar gesture with the CDs, and determined first-hand which rarities and obscurities the fans would most like to see unearthed?

I remember back in the late 1970s, around the time the disco version of 'John I'm Only Dancing' came out. You said you had a lot more stuff in the vault, and that it'd all appear eventually. And the *Sound And Vision* box seemed to back you up. But since then, what *is* going on?

The chronology is completely screwed up. According to the single and the *Bowie Rare* sleevenotes, 'Velvet Goldmine' is a *Hunky Dory* outtake. The reissue sticks it on *Ziggy*. The *Glastonbury Fayre* version of 'The Supermen' was recorded during the *Ziggy* sessions; the reissue puts it on *Hunky Dory*. 'Holy Holy' was recorded around the time of *Aladdin Sane*, and now it turns up on *The Man Who Sold The World*, and the original version of that song, which does date from that period, is nowhere to be found. And *Aladdin Sane* comes along with no bonus tracks at all, which seems absolutely absurd – aside from 'Holy Holy' and the sax version of 'John I'm Only Dancing',[240] there's the instrumental 'Zion', which is on so many bootlegs, and, of course, 'All The Young Dudes', which is now being described by someone at Rykodisc as a radio session with its intro cut off (so a friend who gets the American magazine *Goldmine* told me).

Hang on a moment! The song's been on bootleg for years, and the intro sounds complete enough to me. And besides – Ian Hunter mentions hearing your version of it in *Diary Of A Rock And Roll Star*, and I hardly think he'd have got something like that wrong. And what of the rumoured remakes of 'Conversation Piece' (which I've always thought unlikely, though I'd love to be proved wrong) and 'Waiting For The Man'? And then there's all the stuff that we've not only never heard, but we've never heard *of*. One aspect of the reissues I have enjoyed is the way they've pulled out a couple of songs that nobody even knew existed. On the other hand, the remixes have been utterly worthless, and taken up room that could have been far better employed with other new material.

240 See footnote 34 and postscript to the letter of 1 May 1973 for this version's 'discovery'.

I suppose there's always the possibility that a lot of the missing stuff is being saved up for a new rarities album at some point in the future,[241] and I've heard from a few people now that there's likely to be an entire album made up of *Low*-era outtakes with Eno.[242] That's be great, but why stop there? How about an album of all your collaborations from the early 1970s – Arnold Corns, the extra Lulu songs, the Dana Gillespie recordings, 'Bombers' sung by Peter Noone. And I picked up a bootleg cassette from Mott's *All The Young Dudes* sessions, which includes things like 'Shaking All Over', and an amazing version of 'Sweet Jane' with Lou Reed on vocals. There's so much stuff that you're sitting on. Hand it over now!

I'm not complaining about the reissues, really I'm not. It's nice to have the LPs sounding so good on CD, and when the bonus tracks work they really work. And I'm still looking forward to the rest of the albums. I wish someone could have paid more attention to what was being included, and maybe given some thought as to what they'd want to find on a reissue of one of their all-time favourite albums? Certainly not a couple of pointless remixes!

In the meantime, I hope all the palaver about the reissues hasn't derailed Tin Machine (or whatever you're planning next)? It's probably going to be harder than ever for you to persuade anyone to pay attention to your new music with all the old stuff flying around again, so maybe you'll have to hold off on releasing it for a while. Just make it as powerful as the first album, and as completely and utterly shocking. Whether anybody else likes it or not, you'll at least know that you're still back on course.

All the best – and have a happy Christmas/New Year

Gary

---

241 Unfortunately, it wasn't.
242 This, too, did not materialise.

Hammersmith, London W6
Monday 23 November 1992

Dear David

First off, congratulations on the nuptials.[243] It's been such a long time coming that people were beginning to worry that you'd turned gay. Ha ha.

It's been so long since I last wrote, you're probably thinking I've completely abandoned you! I'm so sorry – time seems to fly past so fast that you turn around for five minutes and six months have gone by. My big news is that Syl's pregnant again, but it's been a weird year all round, hasn't it? It started when Freddie[244] died last November – I remember watching the news and hearing the announcement that he was ill, then 24 hours later he was gone. I was never that huge a Queen fan, but it was really hard to take it in. Apart from Marc, he's the first 'meaningful' figure from the whole glam period to go, and – more long-lost memories – you start remembering little snips that now seem so precious. Queen on *Top Of The Pops* doing 'Killer Queen', or that story about him meeting Sid Vicious and calling him 'Mr Horrid'. Stupid things that he himself had probably long forgotten, and might not mean anything to anyone else on earth. But they're part of your own (well, *my* own) childhood, and now they're gone.

The same day he died, I saw the 'Show Must Go On' video for the first time, and it really did bring a tear to the eye. I'd love to know if they chose that song as the latest single because they knew he probably wasn't going to make it through? Or if the song would seem so powerful if he'd hung on for a few more months? A lot of musicians sit down and write what they like to think of as their own epitaph, the song they'd like played at their funeral, and that will haunt their fans for ever after. Marc had 'Spaceball Ricochet', Buddy Holly had 'It Doesn't Matter Anymore'... I wonder what yours is? But how many of them

243 Bowie married model Iman in Lausanne on 24 April 1992.
244 Queen vocalist Freddie Mercury.

have been able to issue the song at precisely the 'right' time? Good old Freddie – going out with impeccable style as always.

I loved your performance at the memorial gig in April, and I was so happy to see Ronno up there with you. It's so horrifying to think that he might be next that I try not to think about it at all. It's liver cancer, isn't it? A lot of what I'm hearing about his condition is rumour, but at least he's been able to keep working. I can't wait to hear his new solo album, and I know he's producing the new Morrissey. I'm glad – he produced two of my favourite albums of the last decade or so, by Kiss That and Ellen Foley,[245] and he brings such a strong sense of dynamics to everything he touches. Even the Rich Kids album! If I've had one enduring problem with Morrissey, it's that his records never have any guts to them. I can't imagine that being a problem this time around. Anyway, it was reassuring to see Ronno looking so well at the memorial – if you see him, please give him my best regards. He won't remember meeting me, but I won't forget meeting him.

As for the rest of the show – after Live Aid, I swore I'd never again devote an entire day to watching something like that, even across a pile of videotapes. But of course I did. A lot of it I really could have lived without (Metallica, Extreme, Guns N' Roses, Lisa Stansfield…), and I can't say Annie Lennox made an even halfway acceptable Freddie substitute for 'Under Pressure'. But 'Dudes' was sensational – you, Ronno and Ian Hunter rolling back the years. It's funny, not so long ago I heard you doing the song with Mott on the 1972 American tour – Cleveland, I think? For a radio broadcast? And it was pretty dreadful. The Wembley version was magnificent, though, and seeing you and Ronno together made suffering the rest of the show seem worthwhile.

Loved 'Heroes' as well. Being as 'Dudes' is pretty much always going to be associated with Mott, I guess that song's the nearest you have to a comparable anthem in the public eye, isn't it?

And then there was the Lord's Prayer.

OK, let's not even mention the way the press nailed you for that. It doesn't matter whether falling to your knees and praying

245 Respectively, *Kiss And Tell* and *Night Out*.

was appropriate behaviour or not, although I think it was. Given the nature of the event, somebody needed to say something a little more profound than 'This one's for you, Freddie. *Wooooooo!!!*' What was most impressive was the way the entire place went so quiet. You caught glimpses of the audience and they were looking around, like 'What is he doing?' Some were shocked, some were embarrassed, a few looked as wrapped up in it as you did. But you caught everybody off guard – absolutely everyone – and in a strange way it was probably the most quintessential 'rock 'n' roll' moment of the day, precisely because of that. It made being a David Bowie fan 'dangerous' again, in that it conveyed membership of a very specialised club that understood what you were doing and wasn't afraid to be ridiculed because of it.

You made the same kind of statement 20 years ago – that first time on *Top Of The Pops* – with 'Starman'. The moment your arm went round Ronno's shoulders, people were either repulsed or enthralled. That's what happened at Wembley, the moment you fell to your knees... There was no middle ground, and *that* is what rock 'n' roll should be about – polarisation. Either people love you for taking a stand or they hate you for being...a queer, a freak, a Bible-basher. And I don't know whether you intended it to be taken as a serious statement on your own life and beliefs, or if it was a purely spontaneous way of saying goodbye to an old friend, but it had a third effect that could never have been premeditated. It proved you can still surprise people.

Now, of course, we have to wait and see whether it was indeed the first act in some monstrous new masterplan. Syl missed the whole thing, but I was telling her about it afterwards and what we've decided is: either you'll never mention it (or do anything like it) again *or* you're going to be back next year while the fuss is still fresh, with a Juju Demon Preacher, caught somewhere between The Crazy World Of Arthur Brown and the Born Again Bob Dylan. I've often thought somebody needs to do a decent rocking cover of 'Gotta Serve Somebody', and that somebody could be you. Go for it!

On to less weighty themes. I did enjoy *The Linguini Incident*,[246] although I was surprised to see you re-creating your old *Let's Dance* persona for the occasion. Maybe there's life in the old Italian waiter yet! And what's going on with Tin Machine? The second album, I hate to say, really was a disappointment, and the shows hardly attracted the most rabid audiences you've ever played for, did they? To make up for missing Sound And Vision, I caught you at Cambridge and both the Brixton shows. I've not been to the Corn Exchange since I used to hang out with Nick and Mandy (that couple from Bishop's Stortford) in the late 1970s, and the place hadn't changed a bit.

It was a great show. Brixton was fun, too, although not as loud as last time and, of course, you had a fuller set list. But I do wish you hadn't filled most of it with 'Stateside'. Much as I admire the sheer democracy of the group, that was taking it too far, and for too damned long. Drummers drum. They do not write songs, they do not sing. Have you learned nothing from the Phil Collins story? On the album the song was endless, but at least you could skip it. Live, I bet if I wandered back into the Academy tomorrow, it'd still be droning on…and on and on and on… I remember reading something about Mott's time with Mainman, when someone said Tony DeFries hated having to deal with drummers. Now I understand why. If ever there was a more convincing excuse not to 'go Stateside', that was it.

Is there going to be a third Tin Machine album? (You'll notice I am very diplomatically not even acknowledging the existence of the live record.)[247] I'm kind of hoping there won't – *Tin Machine II* suggested that, as a creative force, the project has already lost its drive – and *Oy Vey Baby* insists it's lost a lot of its teeth as well. Keep the group together for live work by all means, and you have to hang on to Reeves Gabrels – the best lieutenant you've had since Ronno. But

---

246 A 1992 movie, co-starring Rosanna Arquette as Bowie's accomplice in an attempted jewel heist.
247 *Oy Vey Baby*, recorded on the 1991–92 tour.

perhaps you should use them to back up David Bowie projects, rather than let them muscle in on the songwriting and arranging as well. Everyone should have a garage band for a hobby, if they want. They should also have a full-time job, though, and yours is to make a worthwhile new record.

What are you waiting for?

All the best to you and Iman

Gary

PS What's all the fuss about Madonna's book of dirty pictures? I've always said she's nothing more than a bleached Cherry Vanilla clone, but at least the photos in *Pop Tart* were intriguing. *Sex* could be a lingerie catalogue.

Hammersmith, London W6
Wednesday 28 April 1993

Dear David

What a weird week this is turning out to be. The new baby is three days late and, though we've tried to keep up a normal life, it's impossible. Syl's mother has virtually moved in with us, and every time the phone rang in the office I was expecting it to be one of them announcing it was time we left for the hospital. Finally I closed up and came home for the day, so here I am.

The hospital ballsed up a little and let slip that it was another girl – we wanted to be surprised again – but it probably worked out for the better. Patty (who's 7 this year) was convinced she was going to be saddled with a 'stupid brother', whose only purpose in life would be to break all her dolls, tear up her clothes and play rap loudly while she was trying to watch TV. One of her friends has a brother who's just like that and she'd convinced herself that all boys are rotten. So, the first thing she did when we told her the news was call us into her room to watch her unpack the suitcase she'd hidden under her bed, full of all her 'running-away' supplies – one change of clothes and more dolly accessories than I even knew she owned. Good to see she was planning it seriously. Now all she wants to know is which of the names she's chosen for the baby we think is best. We have a choice of Whitney, Gabrielle or Little Patty. Looks like we have a hard decision ahead of us.

How's married life going at your end? Well enough to get the creative juices flowing again, it seems. I won't claim to be the biggest fan of *Black Tie White Noise* you're ever going to meet, but I do at least admire your intentions. 'The Wedding' is an intriguing opener, and I was impressed by 'Pallas Athene', even if it might have been better to drop the lyric. It's interesting to see you approaching that modern club sound on your own terms, especially when you compare it to the somewhat slavishly hip efforts other 'veterans' are making buffoons of themselves with.

'I Feel Free' worked pretty well, although I wish you'd pushed Ronno further up in the mix. The first time you work together on record in 20 years, and the poor sod is barely audible!

The only things that fell completely flat were the Morrissey and Scott Walker covers.[248] The original versions were so clearly written and performed in your style that there was no way you could improve upon either of them, nor any real point in trying. 'Nite Flights', in particular, collapsed because you do cover it so straightforwardly. You had the same problem with 'Bang Bang' on *Never Let Me Down* – the original version sounds fresh and improvised, with the lyrics and intonations simply rattling out apparently ad lib. A cover retaining the same words and expressions simply loses the immediacy that made the original performance so powerful.

The track I really like is 'Miracle Goodnight', with that wonderfully quirky little rhythm and the little honks peeping out from behind all the corners. I still can't decide what it most reminds me of – an old ska number or a recent Paula Abdul single, but no one can mistake that very obvious nod to the Velvets' 'Heroin' in the first spoken passage. An intriguing little concoction.

Love the 'Jump They Say' video as well – more than I like the song, in fact. As for what it's about, your relationship with your late half-brother is well known enough today that the only question anyone can ask is why it took you so long to address it. Think what it'd have done to all the 'scared of being a loony' stories if you'd put it out in 1986!

What surprised me most was that you went back to Nile Rodgers to produce, yet ended up with an album that has more in common with current club occurrences than anything *Let's Dance* even pretended to portend – all the more so since you are so obviously keeping at least one eye on Suede's emergence.[249] Of all the bands to have been saddled with the 'new Bowie' tag

---

248 Walker's 'Nite Flight' and Morrissey's 'I Know It's Gonna Happen Someday'.
249 Bowie and Suede's Brett Anderson conversed for the benefit of the *NME* shortly before the release of their respective albums in early 1993.

over the years, they're certainly the most enjoyable, and probably the most convincing as well.

I had hopes for Pulp a few years ago – their *Freaks* and *Separations* albums, if you heard them, had a few very nice little twists to them that I'm sure you'd recognise. But I'm not sure how much further they can take the worm's-eye view of the class divide. Suede, on other hand, are saying and doing all the right things but (more importantly) they're also looking right as well. The singer has enough of the Bryan Ferry about him to stop him from being labelled a simple Bowie clone, but they definitely have that subversive 'Rebel Rebel' feeling pumping in their veins, and I only hope they don't start taking it all too seriously.

That was the one point that Brett Anderson made very well in the *NME* piece – and that you completely missed the significance of – when he said he never wanted the band to appear like a media fabrication, and you (somewhat sniffily, I thought) responded that you were never anything *but* a fabrication, so that's where the two of you differ. Actually, it's where you converge the closest. Being a fabrication is not a problem; it's *appearing* to be one that is most bands' downfall and, no matter how artificial Ziggy may really have been, you played it so well that the fakery wasn't apparent. People believed you, they believed *in* you and, so far, Suede are maintaining that same illusion. Behind closed doors, they may be transformed into the most uninteresting dullards on earth, a whole group of David Jones from Beckenhams. But nobody knows and, so far, nobody cares.

Anyway, it's so encouraging to see a new band coming through that cares about what its audience sees in them. Can you imagine anything duller than watching a band who not only look like their audience, but sound like them as well? – 'This is a song about trying to decide what colour shirt to wear in the morning.' And then they turn up in the *Melody Maker* saying how much they were influenced by The Velvet Underground – 'I'm waiting for my bus...'

I'm all for bands trying to break down the wall between performer and audience, but do they all have to look so fucking dull? There's this curious belief going around right now that if a band looks 'normal' and talks about everyday stuff, they're suddenly somehow more 'real' – like, they're not going to take us for a ride because they buy their Marmite from the same shops as us. What bollocks! Who would you rather put your faith in on Christmas morning: the fat, jovial Santa Claus whose knee you sat on in the department store two weeks ago, or the dirty old man with the fake beard and stained vest who hangs up the costume at the end of every day and spends the rest of the year in rehab? Bands can sing about reality as much as they like, but there's more to the human condition than grumbling about having a dicky tum. If I want to be hit on the head with the misery of the modern world, I'll switch on the evening news. And if I want to hear another song about the rigours of being in a rock 'n' roll band... 'What a super idea, I think I'll sing a song about my job.' I got dem old man-who-goes-down-sewers-in-big-wellies blues again, momma.

God, I sound like one of those little East End entrepreneurs who pop up in 1950s rock 'n' roll movies: 'You gotta give the people a show, Lenny!' But it's true. Great chefs don't hand you their shopping list when you go out for dinner; great movies don't tell you how many yards of film stock they used up in filming; and great authors don't write novels about their typewriter ribbons. So why do bands seem to think it's OK for them? And, more pertinently, why do people let them get away with it?

Five hours later...
Hi. And weighing in at a crib-busting 9lb 8oz, Bernadette Constance Weightman arrived at 3:46am, Thursday 29 April 1993. Mother and baby are completely shagged out.

All the best

Gary

Hammersmith, London W6
Monday 3 May 1993

Dear David

What's happening to us? First Freddie, now Ronno. We all knew he was ill, we all knew it was only a matter of time, and after watching him on the Freddie Mercury memorial last year it did occur to me that this might be the last time we'd ever see him play. But it still seemed so sudden, and so utterly pointless. You watch the news and you hear all these new and inventive ways they've found of killing people. So why don't they take that money and spend it on finding ways to stop people dying? It's ridiculous that one part of the body gets diseased and the whole system shuts down because of it. It's like slinging out a turntable because the needle's gone blunt.

I've been reading the obituaries, of course, but none of them seems to capture what I need to hear, what will make some kind of sense out of it. There's nothing like death to bring the clichés rolling out, and the bigger the name who died, the bigger the clichés they're buried in. It's an awful waste. Obituaries, appreciations – call them what you will – offer perhaps the one occasion in a journalist's career when it's OK to get personal, when the dreaded mask of 'detached objectivity' can slip and people won't call them out on it.

Instead, the formula book is dusted off and once again we have to read that 'rock has lost one of its best-loved sons' and 'the world of pop is mourning'. And, for every writer who does allow a genuine tear to stain his story, there's a bucketload more wondering whether you spell 'He will be sorely missed' with one onion or two.

The power of musicians to touch the hearts of their followers, and to keep touching them long after the hits have dried up, is something that only a true fan can understand. And true fans are, by their very nature, completely inarticulate on the subject. Why waste time explaining what so-and-so means to them when it's a lot easier and more effective to show it. The kid who had a Ziggy tattoo back in 1972 made a commitment then that will remain with him for ever. Why ask him to tell you why he got it? The fact that he did it all answers that question, and more.

I could never put into words why I kept on listening to everything Ronno did in the years after the Spiders broke up. I'd never extend the same courtesy to Earl Slick or Carlos Alomar, and they made a lot more records with you than he did. Ronno produced the *Visible Targets* EP, and I sent away for an import. Slick made a solo album, and who cares? Did you hear the Kiss That album that Ronno produced a few years ago (around the same time as the Sandy Dillon gigs)? It was excellent, but I'd never have even noticed it without his name attached. Or Morrissey's *Your Arsenal* last year? What a masterpiece – 1980s Indie Mopster In Rockabilly Alien Abduction Shocker. Morrissey's best record, Ronno's best production, but you can't help wondering, even while you're playing it, how he could even have found the energy to get up and do it, knowing he had this stupid, stupid disease and that he might not live to see the thing released. Don't you reach a point where you say 'Fuck it' and let go? Or, at least, *try* to?

He was lucky, I suppose. He saw that album come out, he saw your new one, and even if 'I Feel Free' isn't exactly the best performance either you or he has ever put their name to, it doesn't matter. (You're aware, of course, that the opening chords are a dead ringer for the disco version of the *Star Wars* theme, aren't you?)

I'm curious to hear the other songs you recorded with him. I heard that you did 'Like A Rolling Stone' and the Furs' 'Pretty In Pink'. There's talk that the solo album he was working on is going to come out in some form sometime. Is there any chance you could donate them to it? Or even put together a tribute of your own? Regardless of how little contact the pair of you had or didn't have over the last 20 years, your names are inextricably linked. I'm not going to say you owe him anything, but you should at least acknowledge that many people think that you do.

I'd loved to have seen the sessions themselves, two old rockers on the wrong side of 45, remembering the days when they were still young together. Replaying the old records is all well and good, but it can't compete with the emotions you must have been experiencing in the studio – innocence recaptured, exuberance reborn, and all about to be snatched away by the knowledge that science can put a man on the Moon but can't even remove a bit of dust from a man. We've lost a good man and a phenomenal musician, but we've also lost a little piece of our past, and Ziggy will never play guitar the same again.

Take care of yourself – we're losing so much of our childhood furniture that the bits we have left are precious beyond words.

Gary

PS I don't know if you noticed, but Bernadette was born the same day he died. I toyed with the idea of adding 'Michelle' to her name, but decided not to in the end. I don't need the permanent reminder.

```
Hammersmith, London W6
Thursday 2 June 1994
```

Dear David

By now, I'm sure you've heard what's being said following your no-show at the Ronson memorial concert? But quite honestly I'm on your side in this one. Forget the quality of the show itself – Hunter apart, I don't think any of it even began to do justice to Ronno's memory. And forget the fact that if you had turned up Ronno himself would have been shoved into the shadows and it'd have been the Marc Bolan funeral circus all over again.

The fact is, loss is a private affair and one pays tribute in the way that means the most to oneself. Trotting dutifully out to dab an eye in public might be good for the 'image', but the response to your performance at the Freddie Mercury gig proved that, even on these occasions, the critical knives are still out. You do what you feel and they rip you to shreds; you don't turn up and they do it anyway. The only middle ground is the respectfully grim-looking Professional Mourner and, quite honestly, there were enough of them already at the show.

Besides, I'm not 100 per cent convinced that you weren't there, and I know from the whispering and pointing that a few other people thought they saw you as well. Of course, there are probably a hundred people who fit the description – raincoat, shades and cloth cap, smoking like a chimney, talking to a tall black woman wearing pretty much the same kind of gear, and it could have been any of them. But you never know.

Is it disrespectful to say that it was a miserable apology for a memorial? I don't know what I was expecting to see, but something in keeping with the sheer versatility of his career would have been nice. It seemed very slung-together-at-the-last-minute... Either that, or it was being organised along the lines of a school amateur dramatics night: 'Let's do the show right here!

Nigel's brought a Party Seven.' I'm sure everyone who performed had their own reasons for being there, and their own relationship with Ronno to celebrate – Dana Gillespie was entertaining, Peter Noone and Steve Harley were fun. And the sort-of-Spiders turned in a competent set, even if they might have been better off picking songs that weren't so reliant on the guitar. No one can replace him, so why even try?

You weren't the only no-show by a long chalk, though; just the only one anyone remarked upon. Where were Michael Chapman, Bob Dylan, Sandy Dillon, the rest of Mott, Kiss That, Roger McGuinn, Morrissey, any of the dozens of other people whose music he beautified and whose immortality he helped assure? Maybe some weren't invited, maybe some sent their apologies, and maybe some had changed their phone number. Whatever, there was a real undercurrent of bizarre politics swirling around the entire affair. It was almost as if it was being set up in a way that ensured you wouldn't want to turn up, so they could get extra publicity from the ensuing 'controversy'. Or am I being overly suspicious?

But when Roger Daltrey is the belle of the ball, you're better off cancelling the whole event – not out of disrespect to Daltrey, who turned in a pretty good performance, but out of respect for a life that meant an awful lot more than a rousing rendition of 'Summertime Blues'. If you did go incognito, good for you. If you didn't, your reasons for not being there were probably a lot more honourable than many other people's reasons for going.

On to possibly cheerier subjects (at least from a fan's point of view)... I see Mainman appear to be back in business. I just picked up the official reissue of *Santa Monica 72* and, while I can't say it's much better quality than the bootlegs, they've done a great job with the packaging and it's nice not to feel like you're breaking the law when you recommend that someone goes out and finds a copy.

Are you involved in any way with the reissues? I know there are more on the way – a Dana Gillespie compilation and the

Astronettes album look the most exciting, although I'm curious to see the Iggy And The Stooges collection. So much rubbish has come out over the years from the *Raw Power*-era sessions that it'll be very interesting to see what the 'official' archive contains.

All the best

Gary

Hammersmith, London W6
Sunday 20 November 1994

Dear David

It's funny. You go months without any musical excitement whatsoever (unless Generation X reunions and your 1972 live album count?) and then something happens and you don't know how you could ever have become so pissed off with everything. I went to see Sparks at the Empire last night and all I can say is – bugger me! I've kept tabs on them ever since the days of 'This Town', but have to admit they've tried my patience even more than Certain Other People we could mention. But the new album's[250] pretty good, tickets were only a tenner and, let's face it, Shepherd's Bush is so close to home it was practically in my back garden.

The place was packed, which only half surprised me – when bands have been away this long (first London show in 17 years), you figure people have either completely forgotten them or have saved up all the enthusiasm they ever felt, waiting for a moment to let it all out. This was definitely a let-it-all-out night. Even with my sharpest elbows and boniest hips, I could only push halfway through the crowd and, by the time they came on it was like being back at the Marquee for Eddie And The Hot Rods, when they crammed 1,000 people into a room for 700.

But what a show! I haven't felt like that at a gig in years. In fact, I've probably never felt like that at a show, because I've never been old enough to want to. I really was feeling like a kid again. They started with 'The Number One Song In Heaven', just a tape playing the intro and an empty stage, and it really was lump-in-the-throat time. I can't even explain why – something about seeing a band that meant something to me way back when, who themselves remember what that something was. Out of 'Number One', straight into 'Never Turn Your Back On Mother Earth' and, quite honestly, they could have left the stage

250 1994's *Gratuitous Sax And Senseless Violins*.

there and then, I'd have been happy. As it was, from there it was a pretty predictable set – loads of old songs, chunks of the new album, plus one or two they could have left at home. But they'd already done the emotional damage by then and they couldn't put a foot wrong. The equivalent would be you opening a show with 'Quicksand', then banging into 'Dudes' or 'The Jean Genie'. It'll never happen (you'd probably think it crass!), but in terms of audience manipulation it'd be a killer.

How are things going with your new album? I can't wait to hear it. But, of course, you knew that anyway, didn't you?

All the best. If I don't write again beforehand, Happy Christmas!

Gary

To Major Tom

Hammersmith, London W6
Friday 30 June 1995

Dear David

'Not tomorrow,' you announce at the outset of *Outside*,
'it happens today.' And, would it be churlish to emerge
80 minutes later to admit that 'surprisingly it does', with
'surprising' being the operative word? I think it's fair to say that
any response to a new Bowie album depends largely upon how
the listener has dealt with the previous decade's worth of... I saw
one review that summed up your last ten years as 'creative
tomfoolery', and that may be the best way of putting it. The false
dawn of Tin Machine notwithstanding, the general consensus is
that you cashed in your iconographical chips the moment *Let's
Dance* went stellar, and that everything you've done since then
has been less a reflection of your personal prides and prejudices
than a callous conceit aimed at alternately retaining and
destroying a fame which you'd once only been able to conjecture.
When Ziggy reached his peak, he died. When you got there, you
didn't know what to do.

Maybe it's the knowledge that, in a lot of people's opinions,
you no longer have anything left to live up to that powers *Outside*
to heights that you personally haven't reached since *Scary
Monsters*. That, and a reunion with Eno, the last outside musician
to truly inspire you to new creative heights. As far as I'm
concerned, your last pairing produced two of the decade's most
important records, swiftly followed by one of its most
disappointing.[251] You'd already said what you needed to by then.
In terms of innovation, *Lodger* had nothing to add until it was
almost a decade old, and the Intruders At The Palace gig at least
proved you still had some of your old experimental teeth left in.
Would it be damnation with faint praise, then, to say that *Outside*
picks up where that album left off? Maybe. But I'll do it anyway.
Besides, now at least it's travelling in the right direction again.

251 The trilogy of *Low, Heroes* and *Lodger*.

For a concept album, it's surprisingly relaxed – it sounds like you set out to conspire rather than perspire, creating a record that successfully avoids traditional concept album traps (Tommy, can you hear me?) by upping the musical stakes whenever the narrative slips. Neither is the story too obtrusive. Occasionally, I was left wondering precisely what was going on but, otherwise, *Outside* exists exquisitely both within and without the strictures of its premise.

The best tracks, of course, have to include 'Hearts Filthy Lesson', 'I Have Not Been To Oxford Town' and 'No Control', because they highlight you as a songwriter rather than the groove-mood merchant of too many recent efforts. It also helps that you've finally rediscovered your heritage sufficiently to lace *Outside* with musical in-jokes. The vari-speed tricks allow everyone from the Laughing Gnome to the Thin White Duke to take a fleeting vocal bow; Mike Garson's piano is spectacularly *Aladdin Sane*-y; and 'Hallo Spaceboy' is, quite simply, the best David Bowie song you've written since I don't know when – all the more so since we never find out who the Spaceboy is. Ziggy Reborn? Major Tom Rediscovered? I'm plumping for the latter. Does he want to be free? Yes, he wants to be free. And tell my wife, bye bye. Brilliant.

With all that going on, it would have been so easy for the whole thing to vanish up its own backside. What's amazing, then, is how unselfconscious it all is, as though you're referencing the past as much for your own sake as the listeners', planting friendly little landmarks in some increasingly unfamiliar territory.

Is *Outside* the 'return to form' that we'd almost given up hope of hearing? Instinctively, the answer is no, but what is 'form' for you anyway? *Ziggy* was not *Low*, *Low* was not *Young Americans*, and *Outside* is none of them. The fact that it can be mentioned in the same breath as those albums, though, should count for something, as should the fact that for the first time in too long you're sounding like you mean what you're singing and aren't simply making an album because it's less mess than washing the dog.

I know some people have said you might have been better off if you'd linked with someone a little more contemporary than safe old Eno – himself irreversibly contaminated by all those years making U2 sound palatable – but that will come when you tour with Nine Inch Nails. For now, we should be grateful that you have Chic and Frampers out of your system! Besides, Eno is still one of those minds that time and technology will never pass by, and elements of *Outside* are no less thrilling than the best of *Low*. It's just that our sense of surprise has been deadened by progress. In the old days, people would be trying to work out how you created certain sounds for years to come. Today, they simply dub the effects straight on to their own record, and it doesn't matter how it was made in the first place. By the time you hit side two of one album, it's already been sampled for side one of another.

You do still lapse into that awful overtheatrical voice that you adopted around the same time as you stopped relying on your own natural theatricality, but there are more textures at work here than on any album in 15 years. You haven't sounded this musical since *Scary Monsters*, nor quite so obsessed in even longer. Hey, maybe now you've started designing wallpaper, you've realised you can stop recording it!

Good on ya, spaceboy. Now make the live show as exhilarating!

Gary

Seattle, WA, USA
Sunday 15 October 1995

Dear David

And what, you may ask, am I doing in Seattle, USA? Bathing in the warm glow of having seen you play last night, of course... What else?

Actually, that's not strictly true. I'm on a 'fact-finding mission', as my American hosts might say – and the fact that you were playing here at the same time was simply an added bonus. What happened was, having spent much of 1993–94 dealing with American companies for the World Cup, once the tournament was over I figured that I really needed to use some of the better-placed contacts for something a bit more lasting than a one-off football tournament.

That's when I hatched the idea of Rock Tours, linking with different tour operatives in various cities around the country, then packing a minibus full of music fans over for a week of driving around local shrines, going to gigs, hitting the record shops, the lot. We started out with LA, San Francisco and New York last autumn, picked up New Orleans and Chicago this spring, and now we're adding Seattle. I think it's going to work, as well. If someone's into this particular scene, the tour's going to blow their heads off (ha ha!). It starts out at Kurt Cobain's birthplace, in this ghastly little logging town at the arse end of nowhere, winds up at his death house and hits every significant venue in between... All the ones that the city isn't in the process of tearing down and turning into ugly modern apartment blocks, that is.

Personally, I found the whole place a little one-dimensional and parochial – the American equivalent of Southampton, only without the interesting bits. The moment that summed the whole place up for me, oddly enough, came at your show last night, when you started 'The Man Who Sold The World' and a girl sitting behind me announced, 'Hey, he's doing a Kurt Cobain song.' I know you probably wouldn't even have been doing it if it hadn't been included in their *Unplugged* show, but I still thought that was taking things a bit far.

What was your take on that whole Cobain affair? Aside from the fact that the whole thing was almost impossibly sordid. Nirvana were a good band, Cobain was a convincing frontman, and *Nevermind*... Well, it wasn't quite my cup of tea, but I can see why so many people liked it. But how did the fame thing spin so completely out of control? We didn't get much of a sense of what was happening in Britain, but whenever I was in the States the press – and that's the tabloid press, not the music mags – was treating him like he was Sinatra or Cher or someone. They placed him on that level of absolute superstardom that completely transcends an artist's actual work, then used that as a stick to beat him down with.

It was quite horrific to see – even people like Jagger and yourself were around for 10, maybe 15 years before you'd broken through to that level, by which time you'd also earned enough respect to protect you from some of the harsher bullshit. Like, what do you care if the *National Enquirer* suggests you've had a face-lift?

Cobain, though, had no preparation and no warning, because how could anyone (even music industry veterans) have predicted that it would become that enormous, and that quickly? One minute he's a pop star who's just sold a few million records (big deal – it happens every day); the next, he's up there with Elton, Minnelli and the cast of *90210*, and there's paparazzi camped out on his front lawn, waiting for him to shoot some smack into his eyeball. And when he didn't, they said he did anyway. The whole business about whether Courtney Love was doing drugs while she was pregnant was obscene – they wouldn't treat a welfare mother like that. But, because she'd married the most famous man in the world (or so you'd think, from the coverage he got), the most horrendous stories were headline news – and, for possibly the first time in the history of gutter-press journalism, people actually believed what they read.

Of course Cobain couldn't deal with fame of that magnitude. Who could? I think that's what he meant when he started saying that he never wanted to be a rock 'n' roll star. A lot of people heard that, then shrugged and asked, 'So why did you join a band?' What he meant was, he didn't want to be *that* sort of rock 'n' roll star. Up there with Sonic Youth? Fine. As big as Nine Inch Nails? Great. U2 and REM? Let's give it a go. But from nowhere to Michael Jackson in 25 seconds? Forget it.

The problem is, suicide really doesn't answer the question, 'If you weren't God's Gift to the Scurrilous Tabloid, what would you rather be?' Stone cold and stiff isn't a career option, if only because you're really not going to feel the benefit. If you don't like your job, you should change it, and you can't even argue that it wouldn't have been that easy, because of who he was. He was only Kurt Cobain for as long as he said he was. Clothes on the beach, note in the wallet and off into the sunset we go, ho ho. Goodbye Kurt Cobain…Jim Morrison… Tom Major, see you at the burger bar with Elvis.

Anyway, I'm in Seattle and last night was an excellent show, by an excellent band. OK, I'll confess that the Duchess of Dorsey[252] is an even worse Freddie substitute than Annie Lennox was, but she is a superb bassist. Well-chosen selection of material as well – 'Scary Monsters', 'Joe The Lion', 'Andy Warhol'… I really never expected to hear any of those songs performed live again, although after the Sound And Vision tour pretty much banned you from your 'greatest hits' repertoire, there's probably no end to the obscurities you can dig out now. I found myself calling out for 'Running Gun Blues' at one point.

I know why you did it, but I'm not sure that Nine Inch Nails was the wisest pairing you could have selected. Mutual admiration societies are all very nice, but just because the artists love one another, their audiences are not necessarily going to follow suit – particularly when they're as partisan as yours and

252 Bassist Gail An.

theirs are. Of course it was smart to align yourself with someone who's as popular in America as he is at the moment – the Suede connection was never going to pay off in the US. The difference is, Suede's debt to you is as stylistic/cultural as it is musical, in much the same way as your debt to Lou Reed was in 1972.

The only NIN stuff I've heard has been the hit singles, but as far as I can tell they have no common ground with your music, no matter how much Trent Reznor raves on about listening to *Low* while recording. Suede fans can slip from *Dog Man Star* to *Diamond Dogs* and the smile will never leave their faces. But it's a hell of a long way from 'March Of The Pigs' to 'Subterraneans', and I really can't see the body-pierced hordes of Reznor finding it an easy transition. And the traffic goes both ways. I admit it, I hated NIN's set, couldn't see a single redeeming feature to any of it, and I only hung around because I knew that at some point you'd be coming on stage to join them and I didn't want to be trapped in a corridor when it happened. But one of the people I went with wandered outside during their set and said the concourses were packed with your fans. I also noticed a lot of people walking out while you were on, but you can bet they were NIN fans who'd hung around to see what the fuss was, then departed, darkly mumbling that Reznor should have been headlining. Ho hum. It's their loss...

Talking of oldies but goldies, have you been keeping up with the Mainman reissues? The *Rarestonebowie* comp was a bit of a con – the track listing was amazing, but the recordings themselves seem to be taken from exactly the same bootlegs that we've been listening to all these years anyway... Or not listening to, in some instances, because the sound quality was so dreadful. I was also intrigued by the inclusion of a couple of songs from Earl's Court in 1978 – what were *they* doing in the Mainman vault?

The Astronettes' album, meanwhile, was an almost frightening prospect. When you think about it, it's been a legend for the past 20 years, with an entire mythology growing up around it. Early versions of later songs, dry runs for future covers – without anyone hearing a note of the actual music, its reputation alone was ginormous. And we all know what that means. The first time I heard the Beach Boys' *Smile*, that doyen of Missing Mythological Masterpieces, my only question was how anyone thought it was worth releasing in the first place. Well, you'll be pleased to know I didn't have the same response to The Astronettes. It was fascinating – probably more historically than musically – but I was amazed to hear it essentially rewriting your own musical history.

Cut back to that period as you released *Young Americans*, with the world screaming betrayal as David goes disco without a word of warning. And you sat there smug as a bug in a rug, listening to the two-year-old tapes of The Astronettes and chuckling, 'Fat lot you all know. I went disco years ago.' You're probably still smug as well, imagining a bookshop full of learned biographers rushing to re-evaluate your career in the light of The Astronettes' revelations. Brilliant!

Well, I'd better wrap up for now, and try to get some sleep. The trouble with these flying visits (I left London three days ago, and I'll be back again the day after tomorrow) is that you really never get to grips with the time difference, and end up burning the candle at ends you didn't even realise existed. Painful!

All the best

Gary

Hammersmith, London W6
Sunday 10 December 1995

Dear David

Great show at Wembley, and I was going to congratulate you on a considerably more astute choice for support than Nine Inch Nasties... I loved Morrissey's set, love his new material and think he's got one of the best live bands around right now. But, from where I was sitting, it sounded like I was in the minority and, whatever the real reasons for him quitting the tour might have been, the lack of a machine gun to take out those idiots in the front row might well have been part of it. It's kind of twisted, isn't it? I read a load of reports from the American tour, saying NIN's fans didn't want to give you a chance when you toured together, and now it's your fans proving just as boorish.

In terms of actual musical courage, Morrissey is probably the closest we have to a 'new you' – that new album[253] might be a difficult one to get into, but it's a brave move anyway and does repay a few listens. You'd have thought the Ronno connection might have brought a few extra cheerleaders out as well, although maybe it's only my generation that now cares about such things. I was talking to this bloke sitting next to me during the interval and he was saying he'd been a fan of yours for 12 years, seen every show, bought all the records, blah blah blah – and it took me a while before I did the maths. Twelve years takes us all the way back to...*Let's Dance*.

It really doesn't seem possible, does it? Twelve years from *Hunky Dory* to *Let's Dance*, and it hangs there like an eternity, so much happening, so much changing and so much to absorb that it's still very easy to get completely lost in it all. Twelve years from then until now, and it vanished in one very uneventful wink of an eye. In the 1970s, we had regular albums, occasional tours, nonstop rumours and a battalion of your friends and relations to

253 The unjustly maligned *Southpaw Grammar*.

occupy our time with. If *you* weren't doing anything, there was always Mott or Lou or Ronno, or whoever.

There was no way the 1980s could compete with that, but they could at least have tried. There's this whole generation grown up for whom 'old Bowie' is remembering hearing 'Let's Dance' on the radio on the way to school, or going to see *Labyrinth* a dozen times during the holidays. I grew up remembering you as the Leper Messiah. They got the Goblin King. My God, no wonder they booed off Morrissey. They'd probably have booed at Ziggy as well. 'Play "Tumble And Twirl", you bastard! "Magic Dance"!'

Anyway, so Morrissey's off the tour and Echobelly are on instead. Fair enough – they're not a bad band as second-generation Britpop goes... It's a shame Suede weren't available, though! When history looks back on the 1990s, *Dog Man Star* is probably going to come out among the best albums of the entire decade, with Morrissey's *Your Arsenal* coming in a close second and something by Pulp running in third.

Which is very sad from the point of view of pushing musical boundaries forward... All three of them could easily have been conceived in the 1970s. *Dog Man Star* even has its own 'Lady Grinning Soul'. But it's a merciful relief, as well, to know that some people are still able to make worthwhile, intelligent rock records without first switching on a bank of machines, then releasing the computer printout. Just think – in a few years' time, 'Do Re Mi' is going to be utterly meaningless and sheet music will be published in binary code.

As for your live set, it's good to see you sticking by your earlier convictions and still avoiding the 'obvious' songs. It brought you a bit more stick than I was expecting, but that's the UK press for you. If you'd revisited *Sound And Vision*, they'd never have forgiven you for that, either. Let the buggers shift restlessly in their seats and wonder if they'll ever get to tap their toes. *Outside* should have warned them that you have no interest in sitting back in a comfy rocking chair just yet, and if they can't accept that you're still progressing as an artist then maybe they shouldn't call themselves fans. There are enough other bands out there who give their audiences the smash hit singles every time they go out, so let the moaners go and worship them.

So, what's next for you? I read that *Outside* is simply the first of five albums you're planning with Eno. How unlike you to be thinking so far ahead! Of course, it remains to be seen if you make them, but I'll wish you luck anyway. And, of course, have a lovely Christmas and a wonderful birthday. You're 49 and, goodness me, you don't look a day over 50.

Thanks for a memorable year!

Gary

```
Picture Postcard - Helsinki, Finland
Saturday 24 February 1996
```

Ground to Major...

Heard the Pet Shops' 'Spaceboy' mix[254] in the car on the way to the airport... *Spot on!*

Bye bye, Tom!

Gary

---

254 The duo remixed 'Hallo Spaceboy' for Bowie's latest single release.

Hammersmith, London W6
Wednesday 12 March 1997

Dear David

Have you ever wished you could erase your history? I don't mean in the Orwellian way of pretending it didn't happen, and I don't mean tearing up your life and starting again, Major Tom style. I'm thinking more along the lines of... Maybe 'erase' is the wrong word, so how about 'manipulate'?

You've released a new album.[255] It's the best that you can do, and one of your best in a long time. But, even as the review copies go out, you know it's going to be crucified because there's a dozen more albums that came out before it, and it's going to be lined up alongside every single one. And it doesn't matter that some were recorded when you were young and insane, some came along when you were coked up and crazy, some were made in the pits of depression, others in a fit of Howard Hughes isolationist fervour. This new one has to stand proud alongside each of them, because otherwise it's shite. And, of course, it's not going to, because it's not only competing with the others on musical merit, but there's all the other baggage that goes along with it. Your own, and the listeners'.

It's a problem you've had for a long time, and occasionally you've been able to get round it. The Berlin albums[256] are viewed as a single entity, if only because you said they were, and *Outside* falls in alongside them, simply through association. The Tin Machine albums are a law unto themselves, and the rest of your 1980s and 1990s output is so neatly book-ended by Nile Rodgers productions that they exist in an odd twilight world of their own as well.

Rather than encapsulating separate phases of your career, though, maybe you need to remind people that they represent separate personas as well. This is what you meant back in 1973 when you said, 'I can't afford to be one thing all the time. For

255 The *Earthling* CD.
256 *Low, Heroes* and *Lodger*.

the sake of getting away from the straitjacket of an image, I shall contradict myself.' You warned us then what you intended to do, and you followed through. The Ziggy-period records really were made by this chap named Ziggy Stardust; the Halloween Jack albums were by Jack himself. (Vic from the 'Blue Jean' video obviously recorded the 1980s stuff.) In which case, *Earthling* is so clearly the return of the Thin White Duke that it's ridiculous to read reviews complaining that it's not as good as *Pin-Ups*, or whatever. Of course it's not. What does 'I Can't Explain' have to do with jungle?

Actually, I'm not convinced that this whole Bowie Goes Jungle hype isn't a rather large scarlet fish. I know you've had a few late nights in dark clubs with Goldie, and obviously you've incorporated some modern dance textures and techniques into the music. But if *Earthling* is anything, it's the sound of the well-oiled and shit-hot live band that Tin Machine never became, working with each other in the studio as effortlessly as they've spent the last two years working on stage. Hey, you even started playing the songs in concert before taking them into the studio (well, some of them, anyway[257]), and that also shows.

You may think you've made a jungle record, and your record company certainly seems to believe it. But I listen to *Earthling* and I hear echoes of *Station To Station* shot through with ghosts of *Scary Monsters* and the better lessons learned from *The Buddha Of Suburbia*.[258] In other words, it's further proof that your best records tend to be made when you're not trying too hard to be you.

If there are any drawbacks, it's that you sometimes let the sonics get the better of the songs. 'Battle Of Britain' could probably have benefited from a bit more of a tune, and 'I'm Afraid Of Americans' strikes me as something that would have worked a lot better on *Outside* – or at least on the Outside tour.[259] No surprise that Trent Reznor's doing the remix – with Americans like him around, no wonder you're afraid of them.

257 'Telling Lies', 'Little Wonder' and 'Seven Years In Tibet' all appeared in Bowie's live set during 1996. More of the album was previewed at his 50th birthday concert in January 1997.
258 The all-but-overlooked 1993 soundtrack to the Hanif Kureishi teleplay of the same name.
259 Bowie later revealed that the song was reworked from an *Outside* outtake.

Then again, you certainly had a lot of them running around your birthday bash! I hope you received the card I sent – you've been zipping around so much lately, I ended up addressing it c/o Madison Square Garden, figuring that was the one place where you'd have to be at some point.

A friend mailed a video of the show over to me. Unfortunately, I ended up forwarding through more of it than I was expecting – but, hey, we can't all be Frank Black/Foo Fighters/Sonic Youth fans, can we? Robert Smith was excellent, though. Did he really give you a fossilised chameleon as a birthday present? What fun. Lou Reed was entertaining as well (as always). The look on his face when you kicked off 'Queen Bitch' really was one of the highlights of the show.

One thing did strike me, though, and it's pretty much the same complaint I had about the Mick Ronson tribute a few years back. No one can complain about the number of special guests on display, but one could wonder what, precisely, they were doing there? OK, given the surroundings and the Pay-Per-View TV[260] aspect, they probably made sound, economic sense. But really, Robert Smith and Lou Reed were the only ones who belonged there. Morrissey, Brett Anderson, Richard Butler, Iggy – that would have been far more your style. Or (the greatest in-joke of all) if you'd re-created the 1971 *John Peel Sunday Show* broadcast – George Underwood! Dana Gillespie! Arnold Corns!

At least they'd have known all the words.

Anyway, 50 years down. Here's to 50 more...

All the best

Gary

---

260 The birthday concert was broadcast on US PPV during March.

Hammersmith, London W6
Friday 15 August 1997

Dear David

And so the most unexpected (not to mention generally uninvited) resurrection of the decade continues apace, with a performance that both defied and defiled every pop obituary you've received this decade. Right from the start, you were rolling back the years. You might have been playing a club – 300 fans instead of 3,000 – and, if you didn't make eye contact with every soul in the room, those giant eyeballs certainly did.

I'm pleased to say I never bought into the Ziggy revival whispers surrounding the Phoenix show, lovely rumour though it was. What would have been the point of you doing that? Just another over-loud festival gig and who knows if it'd even work in the outdoors? If you're going to resurrect Ziggy, with all the potential pitfalls that entails, you're going to do it somewhere a little more permanent, and with a little more style, than that. What would have happened if it had rained? Nobody thought of that. Wham bam, I'm glad I brought my brolly.

The only shows I saw in the end, then, were the Shepherd's Bush ones. I'd intended trying for some of the others, but it didn't work out. Besides, as Syl rather kindly pointed out, 37-year-old businessmen probably aren't the kind of audience you want to attract any longer. So I'll save my pennies for the next Sound And Vision tour, and stay home and listen to some nice Dire Straits albums.

Just for a moment at the Empire, though… Fuck 37, I didn't even feel 17! There were songs I never expected to hear, and feelings I never expected to feel: the goose pimples down the back of the neck when you kicked into 'Queen Bitch', the rush of adrenalin for 'Stay' and, though I'd never have dared hope for it, the most magnificent 'Dudes' I've ever heard. Or was it just old raindrops and a panic attack as I made one last grab at my youth before it slipped into bones and shadows?

Musically, the live show continues *Earthling*'s unstated insistence that the 1980s (or, at least, your approximation of them) never happened. For the first time in your post-Ziggy live career, you appeared to enjoy playing with the oldies. Interesting to see a couple of the Never Again songs sneaking back into your repertoire, as well. First 'Heroes', then 'The Jean Genie', 'China Girl' and 'Let's Dance'. I loved the new arrangement you played at the Bridge School gig last year, by the way. (I bought the bootleg.)

I know, even at the time, you never swore you'd *never* play those songs again; just insisted that you hoped you wouldn't want to. I get the feeling, though, that you're not quite as uptight – and certainly nowhere near as confused – as you were back then, and you've finally realised it wasn't the songs you needed to kill off, but the baggage that came with them.

Live, you've done it. The new and old songs really do work together these days, and that's the first time I've ever been able to say that about one of your shows. In the past, there was always a kind of unspoken 'Here's another one that I want to fuck up' vibe to the oldies, but they blend so beautifully now. Another consequence of having a long-term settled band, perhaps? Put a group of musicians together for a tour and they're gonna play what they're told. Actually piece together a functioning, living band and, so long as you don't let them get out of control, they're going to take on a life of their own and that can only be to the benefit of the music. I may still cringe every time Gail Ann opens her mouth to sing, but at least she's not doing 'Stateside' and, besides, it's only once or twice per show. The rest of the time, she's flawless.

So, how about capturing this lot on a live album? And a good one this time, none of those arty-farty remix-and-remodel things you've thrown at us in the past – just one good, long, straightforward blast, old and new side by side. For the first time since the Spiders, you have a live band that's worth preserving. For the first time in history, let us hear them while they're hot.

I loved all the musical in-jokes as well: the hint of 'Time' that Mike Garson dropped into the ending of one song; the Ian Hunter ad lib at the end of 'Dudes' ('Hey you there, with the glasses, I want you at the front'). Well, you there with the goatee, we want you there as well. And the fact that you pulled it off without either Ronno and Hunter simply reminded me how much I missed seeing them up there.

There's something about that song – it was always an anthem, but now it's a hymn. The question is, to what? A rallying cry, a requiem, a love song, a death march, it's probably been battered about by more well-meaning cover artists than any other song you've written, and that includes all the bashings that you've dealt out to it. But it's only this time around that you've come to understand how resilient the song really is.

It doesn't matter what is done to it, cos it still comes out smelling of roses. You only have to hear that riff, and a quarter of a century rolls back like sweetie wrappers, until 25 years are 25 minutes, and the kids still have hope and youth on their side, the old really are back at home with their Beatles and their Stones, and T Rex and TV are truly all that matters. But now the dudes are into their 40s or worse and, though the song remains affecting, it is heartbreaking as well. Play it, and remember how it felt to be young. Play it, and relive the dreams that the years have crushed. Play it, and wonder how long it'll be before we're too old to remember any of that. And, if it makes the people who bought it feel like that, what on earth must it do to the people who made it?

From the look of things at the Empire, the answer to that question is…nothing! You have finally shaken off your past. I just wish you'd show me how it's done.

All the best

Gary

Hammersmith, London W6
Monday 2 March 1998

Dear David

The kids were asleep, Syl was watching *Friends*...so I slapped Pulp's *This Is Hardcore* on the headphones (can you spell 'g-e-n-i-u-s' – it's the midlife-crisis album of the decade!) and took a 'tour' of Bowienet the other night. I've not written for a while, so I thought maybe I could find an email address, and just drop you a line and say 'Hi'. Unfortunately, Bowienet doesn't really encourage that sort of contact, does it? In fact, it doesn't seem to encourage any human approach whatsoever and, somehow, somewhere, I fear you've got it all wrong.

Bowienet is a wonderful source of information and knowledge, but there's not really anything there you can't find elsewhere, is there? Indeed, there's probably a lot less. I'd like to see you sit down with all your old bootlegs and tell us what, if anything, you intend doing with them. Will we ever see the 1980 Floor Show on DVD? Nassau Coliseum on CD? The BBC sessions or *Christiane F*?[261] Give us the inside scoop on all the unreleased songs that have made it out on the underground, and publish a cyber-biography. That way, Bowienet would be offering something spectacular.

Right now, it's more like some dusty, crusty drinking club, with you as the dustiest, crustiest old man of them all, holding forth with your memoirs of the Relief of Mafeking. 'I losht my teeth in the Boer War,' you say, and the minions dutifully applaud, grateful for the tiniest scrap from your bountiful table. It reminds me of the Rykodisc reissues when they first came out – people were so grateful for what you were giving them that they completely overlooked everything that was withheld, and I'm not even complaining that we didn't get every song from every session. A bit more accuracy alone would have kept me happy.

---

261 After several years as bootleg-only releases, great swathes of the BBC archive were finally released during 2000. The *Christiane F* soundtrack followed in 2001.

After all that – and to paraphrase 'Law' – I'm not even looking for knowledge any more. I'm looking for certainty, that what I believe to be true really is true and that the truths I believe in are certain. And there, I fear, the World-Wide Web, Bowienet and beyond is no more enlightening than an evening spent drawing Neanderthal eyebrows on to pictures of Oasis. It's vaguely amusing for a while, but where do you go from there?

The mistake we all make is in thinking that because you've made a difference to our lives, then we've made a difference to yours. And it's not true, is it? Apparently, you occasionally visit the chatrooms yourself and interact with the users. But I was wondering, precisely which 'you' is it really? David Bowie the arch-ironic prankster, creator of Nat Tate[262] and Ziggy Stardust? David Bowie, the *Zeitgeist*-zapping iconoclast who gave us 'Dudes' and 'Art Decade'? Or David Bowie, the remarkably perceptive young man who looked into a crystal ball in 1972 and warned us, 'The artist doesn't exist. He's strictly a figment of the public's imagination'? That's the one my money's on, because the only David Bowie you're going to find on the computer is a computer image himself, a flickering 3-D graphic that has no time for the past and no vision of the future. It lives exclusively for today because, according to its own life's directive, that's the only reality that matters.

'Dear David. In 1990, you said you'd never play "The Jean Genie" again, but I saw you in concert last week and you were still playing it. Am I right to feel cheated?'

'Dear Cheated. Welcome to the world.'

Ah, reality. When will people understand that logic and reality aren't simply incompatible but are polar opposites? Reality is not logical and never will be. History happens and that is a fact. But it's only when the historians get hold of it, to warp and misshape it, that it appears as though we are travelling through time in some kind of linear fashion – cause/effect, action/reaction. Of course that's not really how it works, but that's what we're taught, because the alternative (chaos follows accident follows unforeseen

262 A wholly imaginary artist created by Bowie for a supposedly serious biography, which was greeted not only with laudatory reviews but also a host of 'Ah, I remember Nate'-type reminiscences from critics who really should have known better.

happenstance) is too awful for 'society' to contemplate. We are brought up to believe that civilisation is the result of centuries of social and intellectual evolution. In fact, it's the barely functioning consequence of a series of acts of random vandalism.

You understood this, and you turned people's need for 'order' to your advantage. Why be trapped into one musical career when you can skip around as you see fit and let everyone else try to fit them together...because they always do, even if they have to construct the most elaborate fantasy world in which to make it workable. Today, anybody who wants to know who 'David Bowie' is can pick up any one of 30-plus 'biographies' and digest your development in bite-sized morsels.

But it's a joke, isn't it? Even the concept of 'development' is a fraud. Technology develops, capabilities develop, ideas develop. But does music ever really change? The Beatles wrote 'Please Please Me' in 1962 and released 'One After 909' in 1970. But which is the oldest song? It's not the oldest record. According to Tony Visconti you wrote 'It's No Game' when you were 16, and called it 'Tired Of My Life'. But if you hadn't changed the title, would the song have sounded at all old-fashioned when it turned up on *Scary Monsters*? Songs are as old as the memories that store them. Intellectually, I know that The Shangri-Las' 'Leader Of The Pack' was first released in 1965, but in my heart it is as integral a part of autumn 1972 as 'Mouldy Old Dough' and 'Wig-Wam Bam'. I was 5 in 1965, and I'm sure I heard it back then – I remember 'Like A Rolling Stone' and 'I Got You Babe' vividly. But I was 12 in 1972, when I bought the reissue, and that's where it sticks in my mind.

Orwell was wrong. The past is so malleable that it's barely worth recording any more. I recently saw the reissue of *Never Let Me Down* and noticed you'd removed 'Too Dizzy' from the album. And, in years to come, when the last vinyl record is in a locked museum archive, and the original CDs have all rotted away, old men will look at it and murmur, 'I'm sure there was one other track on there.' But they will be hooted down as senile decrepit fools. We are at war with Eurasia. We have always been at war with Eurasia.

And we will remain at war with Eurasia until the day the missing song is magically restored, at which point we will be at war with Eastasia. We have always been at war with Eastasia.

Bowienet is the telescreen through which that truth will be perpetuated. You feed the fans what you want them to be fed, and they accept the food because they believe the alternative is slow starvation. But is it really? Next time you're passing the vault, play 'Cygnet Committee' again. For the longest time, I'd marvelled at that song, the prediction of punk was spot-on – you could even cast Malcolm McLaren in the role of the 'thinker', growing older and so bolder. Now I marvel at it even more. It's about you and us and, if you juggle the pronouns (*we* gave *you* life, *we* gave *you* all, *you* drained *our* very souls dry…), you'll understand. I don't think you've ever written another song that honest, that intense, that committed – and so utterly and diametrically opposed to everything you have become.

I often wonder what happened to the boy who wrote that song? Do you miss him? So young, so idealistic, knowing he's been betrayed, but still convinced that there's a way round the obstacle and it'll all come right in the end. Is he still around, peeping out from behind your latest mask, wondering if it's finally time to launch the next revolution? Or did you simply blast him off into space with an endless supply of needles and the promise that you'd visit occasionally?

As I grow more accustomed to reading about you in the financial pages than in the music press, I also find myself thinking increasingly about Major Tom. You really did a number on him, didn't you, labelling him a junkie and reducing him to a bogeyman. But you know what? He was probably the smartest character you've ever created…which means that he's probably the smartest person you've ever been. He escaped while he could.

Ashes to ashes?

Gary

Hammersmith, London W6
Saturday 31 October 1998

Dear David

OK, I admit it. I'm back on Bowienet and, I have to admit, I'm rather enjoying myself. Funny thing about the Internet – you spend years denouncing it, then one day you get sucked in and, before you know it, you're surfing and trawling and mousing like a veteran, and you've completely forgotten that there was ever a time when the whole thing was as appealing as a package trip to hell.

I'm not even going to get into any discussion of what my favourite features on the site are. There are a few places I habitually check out, and a lot that I've clicked on once. The songwriting idea is definitely intriguing, though – it'll be interesting to see what comes out of it,[263] although rather than the winning entry (which is sure to be of a reasonable standard), I'd love to hear some of the losers. The very idea of co-writing a song with David Bowie is bound to bring some absolute basket cases out of the woodwork, and I'm sure I'm not the only person who considered crossing out everything you'd already put into the song and sending it back as an instrumental.

The other idea I had was for a conclusion to the Major Tom story – one is somewhat overdue, after all. It's called 'Major Tom's In Rehab', but the only lyric I've come up with so far is 'Major Tom went into space, flying around, he's off his face'. Don't worry, though, cos I have absolutely no intention of completing it.

I've really got into e-bay as well, and have spent a fortune filling in the odd gaps in the collection – your records and others. Old T Rex things I never dreamed I'd find, a Rollers bootleg (can you imagine?), a couple of early (pre-Chinnichap) Mud singles... Oh, and a US promo of 'All The Madmen', which I was starting to suspect didn't even exist. Tons of fantastic video

263 Bowie published an incomplete version of the song 'What's Really Happening' on the site, then invited members to complete it, the winning version to be included on his next album. The contest was won by Alex Grant.

stuff as well, but let's not get into those realms. You probably wouldn't approve.

Really enjoyed *Everybody Loves Sunshine* on telly the other week, although I can see why it went straight to TV. Can I say you made a very convincing gay gangster? It's funny, you can take the boy out of the homosexual role-playing, but you can't take the homosexual role-playing out of the boy. Goldie was great in it as well. So, after that, my brother-in-law Pete and I decided to spend a weekend watching every movie you've ever made – or, at least, all the ones that are on video. (So, no *The Image*. Damn, and we had 15 minutes that we were desperate to kill, as well.)

The kids loved *Labyrinth*, and *Absolute Beginners* is still a masterpiece. But please don't be offended when I admit I forwarded through huge chunks of *The Man Who Fell To Bits* – mid-1970s sci-fi looks so old-fashioned these days! And some of your more recent efforts, I hate to say, really didn't do much for us, either. Loved your Andy Warhol in *Basquiat*, but hated the film itself. *The Hunger* still works, though, but my favourite has to be *Cat People*, which I consider yours by default. The theme song is as big a star as either Malcolm McDowell or Nastassja Kinski! As for future projects, I'm curious about *Exhuming Mr Rice*, if and when it ever comes out. Sounds like a twist on a modern-day *Hunger*…for kids?[264]

Will you be doing the soundtrack as well? It's funny how important movies have become for breaking new music these days. I know there's still a Top 40 chart, but things are in and out faster than a sparrow's fart these days, and there are so many different formats that they're not even that much fun any more. There was a time when a new single might offer valuable clues to an artist's new direction. Now it's one more song off the same old album, with a couple of live tracks and a remix or seven.

If you want to know what's really going on with an artist, film soundtracks seem to have picked up the slack. I first noticed that when you did 'Real Cool World', and let us know you were

264 Retitled *Mr Rice's Secret*, the film finally appeared during 2000.

back with Nile Rodgers.[265] Now there's *The Rugrats Movie* to look forward to, and the long-awaited reunion with Tony Visconti.[266] But again it's telling that the song's scheduled for a soundtrack rather than a one-off single. Is that the nature of the music industry itself talking? Or is it a financial thing? All facetiousness aside, I'd be interested. Or maybe I want to reassure myself that it's not my perception of things that is changing, just society's ability to resist whatever is foisted upon it by whichever nebulous Big Brotherly Business is top dog today.

Do you remember when big macs were simply oversized raincoats?

Gary

---

265 In 1992, prior to the full-fledged reunion for *Black Tie White Noise*.
266 The song, 'Skyway', was dropped when the relevant scene was cut from the movie.

Hammersmith, London W6
Thursday 18 March 1999

Dear David

I wanted to hate it, I swore I would loathe it and, even before I sat down in my seat, I was asking Syl whether she'd seen enough. But 90 minutes later, I was prepared to stand stark naked in the middle of the street and proclaim *Velvet Goldmine* to be one of the greatest rock movies ever made. And, basically, anyone who can't understand that needs to stop taking themselves so damned seriously.

I read all about your objections to the film, how you pulled all your songs from it and, yes, I can even understand why you might get a little miffed about seeing huge chunks of your life (or, at least, Ziggy's) stirred into the plot. But if you could distance yourself from being an artist, and look at it from the point of view of a fan (which is what Todd Haynes[267] so obviously is), then you'd see that he hit the right button every time.

Besides, it wasn't only you who was under the microscope. Everybody who was around at the time made an appearance in one way or another, and usually for a good reason. Lou's remark about it being fashionable to say everyone's bisexual was as priceless in the film as it was at the time, and everyone who damns *Velvet Goldmine* as gay porn in glam clothing is completely missing one of the film's most valid points.

You were 'inside the storm', as it were, and fully aware of how calculated and stage-managed the whole thing was. But to those of us who were lapping it up, the audience you were selling it to, that's exactly what you were giving us – gay porn. Who was it who mimed giving his guitarist a blow job every night on stage? Who was it whose hips went into hypergrind overdrive during 'Let's Spend The Night Together'? Other rock stars wanted to lay all the chicks, you once said. You wanted to lay *everyone*. Now put yourself in the mind of a 12-, 13-, 14-year-

267 The movie's director.

old boy, and bombard yourself with all that imagery. That wasn't simply gay porn, that was the hardcore nasties, and if *Velvet Goldmine* takes the message and uses it as its medium, well that's what fantasy is all about. I watched that film and, I swear, there was barely a moment in it that didn't ring a bell of some sort or other.

Now, I hate Michael Stipe[268] as much as the next man, and I did ponder the irony of Steve Harley, who's spent the last 25 years denying Cockney Rebel was ever a glam band, surrendering one of his best ever songs to a movie devoted to the age. And, like I said, I wanted so much to hate that film. But I couldn't. And why? Because I lived half of it, and I daydreamed the rest. If Todd Haynes got it wrong, then so did all of us who were around back then… In which case, can I have the last 26 years of my music-loving life back, please?

In the meantime, I am curious as to what you'll be countering *Velvet Goldmine* with. Rumour insists that you're planning to revisit the Ziggy story for a film of your own. If so, it's going to be interesting to see what you have to work with, being as you've already rejected your own self as a suitable role model!

See you at the drive-in!

Gary

---

268 One of the film's backers.

Hammersmith, London W6
Tuesday 6 June 1999

Dear David

Tell me something. All this interest you're suddenly paying to your back catalogue – it wouldn't have anything to do with that Bowiebonds business, would it? One minute you're sitting on the archive and barely even giving us a glimpse at it, and the next you're pumping out the reissues and threatening to compile a box set of rarities.

Not that I have any complaints whatsoever – after 20 years of picking this stuff up on bootleg, it'll be great to finally hear it without the flaws and dropouts attached. And no, I don't begrudge you making money from your catalogue – every other bugger seems to have, and if you've got it you might as well flaunt it.

I'm a little surprised at how *obvious* you're being. OK, so full disclosure and all that, and no one will ever accuse you of sneaking around behind your fan club's back, getting rich off their devotion. Why would they? Big companies have been sponsoring bands for years now and, again, someone has to make money off the music. So who better to do it than the artist?

But there's still something faintly distasteful about knowing that every move you make now is going to be calculated against however many million Prudential Securities[269] paid out, with your back catalogue essentially reduced from a work of art to a mere commodity, to be shifted around and rented out according to how much you think it'll bring in. 'Oh, we're running short this quarter – better stick out a BBC album' or 'I need a few bob, let's get "Fame" into a car commercial.'

I want to trust you to treat your heritage gently, and remember that it's our heritage as well. I read on the Net that they're reissuing *The Linguini Incident* as *Shag-O-Rama*, in the hope that the *Austin Powers* crew will pick up on it. That's fine

---

269 The sole purchaser of the entire bond issue paid $55 million for the catalogue.

– it was a fun film, but it's hardly hallowed ground. And it's nice that you're reissuing all your albums again, this time in their original form. The Ryko deal's expired, the extra material wasn't always done well, and sometimes it's nice to hear an album as its maker intended, without having a ton of bonus extras cluttering up the finale. But how the hell are you expecting to sell these things? 'New and improved, with 20 per cent less than before!'

Is it true there are going to be lyric sheets this time? That's going to be interesting. I've kind of grown attached to the 'fumpy pumps' in 'Sweet Thing', and I love 'Forgiven! Fuckin' A!' in 'Zeroes'. At last, comprehension will dawn – and, right now, we need it. Half the stuff you're on about these days, I don't even begin to understand. You're running Websites for American football teams? How peculiar – in 30 years, I've never heard you mention sport once. But stick a dollar at the end of the sentence and you're mousing your way to a million. Do you realise you're in the *Financial Times* as often as you're in the music papers these days and, yes, how very nice that you should be proving so successful in fields (how did they put it?) 'unrelated to what business strategists might call your core competencies'.

But why are you ramming it down our throats like this? Paul McCartney has money and I'm sure he invests it wisely. Ditto Elton, ditto Jagger, ditto a hundred others you could name. But you're the only one who attaches his own name to everything, trading upon brand loyalty like a supermarket launching its own peanut butter. And of course I'm aware that no one – not even the most blinkered, devoted fan – is being physically forced to buy into any of these thrusting new adventures. But you hope they will and you know they're going to; otherwise you wouldn't attach your name in the first place.

What starry-eyed, middle-aged space invader can resist a Bowiebanc cheque book? Or an Internet address at *davidbowie.com*? And what's a David Bowie credit card, if not the grown-up equivalent of the old T-shirts we used to wear so proudly? Except this time we'll never get too fat for it. Plus, there's something extraordinarily appropriate about having your face on a flexible friend – they used to say that you bent both ways as well, remember?!

It's a tricky one, though. I remember when you were championed as one of the few viable challengers to the orthodoxy of modern society and, perhaps, you still are. In terms of name and image alone, Bowiebanc has got to be trendier than Nat West or Barclays and, who knows, maybe your interest rates will be competitive as well. But for me, rock 'n' roll has always been an escape from the realities of life and work and finance, no matter how fleeting the illusion may be. You've slammed everything into such close proximity that even that satisfaction is swirling down the plughole.

I don't know. You will do what you feel you need to, and what's a fan base anyway if not a bunch of sheep who bleat a little if you don't feed them right but will roll over for a tummy rub every time you snap your fingers? Always have been, always will be. Me, I'm just grateful you're still putting out records that we can buy in the shops and haven't decided to supply them only to customers opening a new bank account. Damn, I shouldn't have said anything. You'll probably do it now.

All the best (really!)

Gary

PS Maybe you should do your next world tour by hot-air balloon. Let's see Richard Branson top that!

Hammersmith, London W6
Sunday 10 October 1999

Dear David

You've said in a little over 40 minutes of music what I have been trying to say in almost 40 years of life. The first time I listened to ...*hours*, I realised you understood me. The next time, I couldn't shake the feeling that it was *about* me. A dialogue, you say, between a middle-aged man and his younger self – a ruthless examination of the dreams and ambitions that were once at his fingertips and the multitude of ways in which they can all be flicked aside. You only got one piece wrong – I haven't been dreaming my life away, I've been living my dreams away.

I stopped keeping a diary long ago, but I have kept my letters to you and, when I look back at the years when I first left school, I don't even recognise the boy who wrote them. Would he recognise the man he became? I took the first job that was offered to me, and it was just a job, something to pay the bills and kill the time between gigs and girls and new Buzzcocks singles. More than 20 years later, I'm still in it, but where are the gigs and girls today? I've been to 15 concerts in the last 10 years, and most of them have been yours, while the only girls I spend time with are 6 and 14 years old respectively. The last book I read was about a boy wizard named Harry Potter (to Bernadette), and the last magazine I looked at was this month's *Mojo*. It has The Beatles on the cover. That probably says it all.

I'm happily married, in that Syl and I only fight over the same things that everybody else fights about. The business is doing brilliantly and our closest friends are the dearest people in the world. All of whom we've met through the kids. You once said you never wanted to be a rock 'n' roll star. Well, neither did I, and boy did I succeed! I'm just not sure I needed your new album to remind me of the fact.

You're everywhere these days, aren't you? I switch on the telly, I open a paper, I turn on the radio, I go to the shop, I fire up the computer. I asked you once how you deal with your past, how you are able to section it off and stop it from stepping out while you're asleep and haunting you with its might-have-beens. ...*hours* has answered that question. You don't, because you don't need to. You have people like me to do it for you.

Left to your own devices, you'd simply march resolutely on, eyes straight ahead, and never even glance back for an encore. 'Here's an old song,' you'd announce, and it'd be your last B-side. It's the fans that keep reminding you of what you once were and who you could have been – not because they want you to return to those personae, but because they want to return there themselves. I was talking to someone the other day, and they asked me what I'd do if I could travel into the future. I told them I'd hijack a time machine and go back to my childhood, but it was only later that I realised that's not what I meant at all. I'd go back to the feelings I remember from my childhood, and that's a very different thing. What is childhood anyway but the interminable years you spend waiting to be old enough to not do any of the things you thought you were going to?

I look back on the 1970s and it's impossible to believe they were anything but a happy land of absurd loon-pant adverts and the Next Week Box in the *NME*, doing the Footsie to an eternally joyful soundtrack of songs drawn in equal portions from *Top Of The Pops*, television jingles and the TV themes with the most wankworthy stars. The girls all looked like Katy Manning and Cherry Vanilla, the boys all dressed like Patrick Mower and Jason King, and every football match was a nine-goal thriller.

I look back over the things I wrote as a child – letters to you included – and the day-to-day grind of reality simply didn't intrude. If television was so wonderful, how come I never watch the repeats of *Love Thy Neighbour*? If the music was *still* wonderful, why don't I own a single Status Quo album? And

I don't think the price of a handful of Black Jacks ever crossed my mind. (Four for 1p, if I remember correctly.)

And that's the point. It's the things you take for granted that you miss most when you're older. Familiarity breeds contempt. But it also breeds heartbreaking nostalgia. The smell of a dusty valve record player, plugged into the light fixture. The theme to the Tony Blackburn show. Chrissie in *Man About The House*. You don't even notice things like that when they're there – they're a part of the furniture and life goes on. Then you turn around and they're gone. The most descriptive writer in the world probably couldn't perfectly recapture the sensation of emptying an entire box of Imps on to your tongue at once, five minutes after finishing the last swig of cherryade. We just keep on hoping that one day someone will.

A lot of Britpop's appeal these last few years, at least to my generation, has been its invocation of an earlier, more pleasant (no, make that 'simpler') time. (Do you realise how many 30-somethings actively enjoy Blur, Pulp and Suede records?) The moment itself was very short-lived. As soon as the bands realised what people wanted, most of them came over all self-conscious and lost the original alchemy. But the very success of things like 'Disco 2000', *Parklife* and pretty much anything by Saint Etienne proves they got it right to begin with. And it's sad that, for many of us, that's the only connection we still have with our childhood – other people's memories of the things that were the most important to us.

That's what ...*hours* says to me, and it's ironic that the music that means the most to me (ie yours) should be the music that finally makes me see it really doesn't matter. You said something – back in 1972, I think – about how not one artist, nor one song, has ever changed the world. I disagreed with that at the time, and have continued to do so for the last 27 years. No, one artist cannot change *the* world. But if he changes my world, and the next person's, and the next person's, and so on for countless millions of people, then surely that is just as good?

Or is it? Because does anything really change? If David Bowie hadn't come along, somebody else would have filled in instead, and I might be writing to Bryan Ferry now, asking if it's true that Roxy are reforming. Or maybe I wouldn't be writing to anyone, and just burning CDs of my favourite glam rock records, in chronological order as they entered the Top 30 chart, to convince myself that somehow I still feel the way I used to. But I don't, because music... It can do a lot of things, more than any other art form on earth, but it can't turn the clock back. And, even if it could, would we really want it to? There's a nice line in 'Something In The Air' – 'I've danced with you too long.'

How much easier it'd be to believe that, underneath the façade of modern life, people remain the same as they always were, with the same dreams and ambitions and standards and beliefs that they've always had, and that 'progress' and 'change' are simply industry's way of making us buy something we've already got. In a perfect world, people would still eat chips out of newspaper, suck on Olde Englishe Spangles and have sex with the lights out, lying down and no tongues. In an imperfect one, they get Styrofoam cones, peanut butter Snickers and aerobically balanced, low-cholesterol bondage. And, because sales of chips, sweets and gas masks never went down, these magnificent innovations are proclaimed a success. Business insists that because people buy something it proves they like it. Common sense dictates that sometimes they buy it because they don't have a choice.

But, of course, you know that this theory is flawed and, if you don't believe that, dig out some childhood toys. I found an early 1970s Plasticraft set the other day and couldn't wait to try it out. Big mistake. It was sticky and messy, it stank to high heaven, and it wasn't nearly as fascinating as I remembered it... Which brings me back to where I started.

Travel back to the days you recall the most fondly and all you'll discover is a load of old cack. It's not the specifics of day-to-day life that mean so much, but the overall aura of an era that's gone – an aura that never existed in the first place. I don't know why you've done it or what you hope to achieve, but ...*hours* is your way of communicating that knowledge and, if the slower songs don't make the point hard enough, 'The Pretty Things Are Going To Hell' is the brat-beating baseball bat that pounds the message home. As you yourself say in the song, yes we wore it well. And, yes, it wore us out.

But we wore it anyway, didn't we?

Gary

Hammersmith, London W6
Tuesday 8 August 2000[270]

Hammersmith, London W6
Thursday 6 June 2002

Dear David

Belated congratulations on the birth of baby Alexandria. It's been a while, hasn't it? I meant to write when the happy day arrived, but time slips by so quickly now... Or is it just the mind? As middle age grows more comfortable, sometimes I find myself wondering.

Do you realise it's 30 years since I first started writing to you (give or take a month)? I was 12 and you were 25, but really we were both just children. Now we have children of our own, and they're older than we were then. Looking back, could either of us have imagined that all these years later...?

But no, let's not get into that again. I guess, all I really wanted to do was wish Ziggy a happy birthday. At least *he's* still the same.

All the best

Gary